Waterstone's guide to
London Writing

'London: a nation, not a city.'
Benjamin Disraeli

WATERSTONE'S

A comprehensive
guide to writing
about London –
from Pepys, Evelyn
and Dickens to
Martin Amis,
Peter Ackroyd and
Iain Sinclair.

Waterstone's guide to

London Writing

**More than 150 writers on London reviewed and discussed.
Original articles by Iain Sinclair, Michael Moorcock,
Neil Bartlett and many more.
Compiled and written by Waterstone's booksellers.
All for just £3.99 Available 5th February 1999**

Also available

Waterstone's Guide to Scottish Books
Waterstone's Guide to Irish Books
Waterstone's Guide to Children's Books
Waterstone's Guide to Science Fiction,
   Fantasy and Horror

Waterstone's Guide to Poetry Books
Waterstone's Guide to History Books
Waterstone's Guide to Crime Fiction

GRANTA

GRANTA 65, SPRING 1999

EDITOR Ian Jack
DEPUTY EDITOR Liz Jobey
MANAGING EDITOR Karen Whitfield
EDITORIAL ASSISTANT Sophie Harrison

CONTRIBUTING EDITORS Neil Belton, Pete de Bolla, Frances Coady,
Ursula Doyle, Will Hobson, Blake Morrison, Andrew O'Hagan

FINANCE Geoffrey Gordon, John Moreira
ASSOCIATE PUBLISHER Sally Lewis
SALES David Hooper
PUBLICITY Gail Lynch
SUBSCRIPTIONS John Kirkby, Darryl Wilks
PUBLISHING ASSISTANT Mark Williams
TO ADVERTISE CONTACT Jenny Shramenko 0171 274 0600

PUBLISHER Rea S. Hederman

Granta, 2-3 Hanover Yard, Noel Road, London N1 8BE
Tel 0171 704 9776 Fax 0171 704 0474
e-mail for editorial: editorial@grantamag.co.uk

Granta US, 1755 Broadway, 5th Floor, New York, NY 10019-3780, USA
Website: www.granta.com

TO SUBSCRIBE call 0171 704 0470 or e-mail subs@grantamag.co.uk
A one-year subscription (four issues) costs £24.95 (UK), £32.95 (rest of Europe) and £39.95 (rest of the world).

Granta is printed in the United States of America. The paper used in this publication meets the minimum requirements of American National Standard for Information Sciences—Permanence of Paper for Printed Library Materials, ANSI Z39.48-1984. ∞

Granta is published by Granta Publications and distributed in the United Kingdom by Bloomsbury, 38 Soho Square, London W1V 5DF, and in the United States by Penguin Books USA Inc, 375 Hudson Street, New York, NY 10014, USA. This selection copyright © 1999 Granta Publications.

Design: The Senate
Front cover photograph: Peter Fleissig; back cover: Peter Marlow

ISBN 0 903141 26 4

COLD NEW WORLD
GROWING UP IN A HARDER COUNTRY

WILLIAM FINNEGAN

'This is a timely, deeply compassionate book that begins to break an American taboo. William Finnegan is an American Dickens who reports brilliantly from behind that society's façades of wealth and promise'

JOHN PILGER

A Paperback Original, £8.99
on sale in bookshops from 19 February

AS SEEN IN
GRANTA

We wish to inform you that tomorrow we will be killed with our families
STORIES FROM RWANDA

Philip Gourevitch

'I know few books, fiction or non-fiction, as compelling as Philip Gourevitch's account of the Rwandan genocide. He has taken one of the most staggering horrors of the twentieth century and explained it in a way that not only could I understand but I found impossible to put down. It is a tremendous feat of reporting. As a journalist he has raised the bar on us all' SEBASTIAN JUNGER, author of *The Perfect Storm*

on sale in bookshops from 26 March, £16.99 hardback

PICADOR

'Among the most emotionally wrenching,
subtle works of the century'
amazon.com

'A stunning novel in which a meticulous grasp of historical
and natural detail, insight into character and pulse-pounding
action are integrated into a dramatic adventure story'
Publishers Weekly

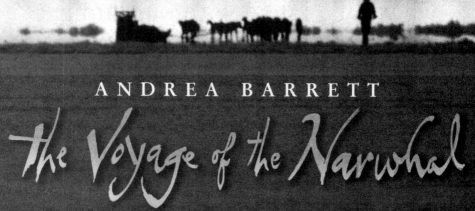

ANDREA BARRETT

The Voyage of the Narwhal

exploration, endeavour and evolution in the frozen north
Available from 1 March 1999

GRANTA 65

London: the lives of the city

LONDON VIEWS

FISHING, WRITING AND TED

INTRODUCTION

Some cities in the world have no legend outside their immediate hinterland. A few, of which London is certainly one, have many. People who come to London also bring it with them in their minds. They have a feeling of how the city should be before they meet it.

The expectation has often been historic, and today is sometimes met (beefeaters, the Queen, the Tower) and sometimes disappointed (fogs, bowler hats, gracious manners). But history hasn't always been the main attraction. The visitors drawn by the Great Exhibition of 1851—as in the Cruikshank cartoon on page 116—came to see modernity in a grand display of the machines, ideas and artefacts that were shaping the Victorian world. The exhibition marked, as it turned out, the peak of Britain's eminence in technology. Within a few decades, other nations had matched and then overtaken British expertise, and London never again had quite the same pull on the technical and scientific imagination. It remained one of the world's foremost cities, its civilization still held a powerful appeal (Henry James said that for him the city offered 'the most possible form of life'); but it was no longer a herald of the future, and when it grabbed more than its usual share of world attention it did so because of wars (the Blitz) or pageantry (coronations, abdications, royal marriages). Not until the 1960s did London again to the world at large symbolize newness and invention—'Swinging London' in the coinage of an American news magazine—when, rather to its own astonishment, it briefly outshone American cities as the world's leading influence on the tastes and behaviour of the young.

Then, in the mid 1990s, began the period we are still living through: 'Cool Britannia', another piece of American magazine era-labelling. There are reasons to be sceptical. British culture has become addicted to branding and marketing, and the eagerness with which British politicians seized and touted a phrase coined on a newsdesk in New York did not inspire trust. And what, exactly, did it describe? A few conceptual artists, a young prime minister, a rock musician or two, some nightclubs, shoals of restaurants: is that what it amounted to? London is a city of unreliable tube trains and impoverished schools. Charles Saatchi's art collection and Terence Conran's restaurants can easily seem irrelevant.

Still, the slogan isn't completely empty. London has changed and promises to change further. Large stretches of the inner city have been colonized by the young, abandoned warehouses and factories have been knocked into flats, anything without a job (an old brewery, a disused power station) gets one as an art gallery, the streets are fuller for longer into the night, there is a lively, enterprising sense about the place (even if people do seem to drink too much). Some of this optimism may not last; the money which fuels it may run out; the economy may plunge into recession. But something more permanent has been discovered, or so I like to think. London has a fresher, more assertive identity. Partly, this has political causes; the prospect of a re-established city-wide government. Partly, it has to do with race; London, with a quarter of its population non-white, is the most successfully multicultural city in Europe. Finally, it may spring from the growing realization, among the people who live in it, that the great strength of London is its almost limitless variety, history overlaid on history, messy, unplanned, and never, no matter how long you live here, completely charted. A place of strange and often unprofitable profusions: which other city in the world contains thirteen different railway terminals, some small region of the hinterland served by each, or ten different daily newspapers?

No, nowhere else will really do.

Writing about London has often been inspired by this jumble and complexity, or what Samuel Johnson described as the city's 'wonderful immensity'. Dickens, of course, and Gissing in the nineteenth century, Patrick Hamilton in the 1930s, Martin Amis, Peter Ackroyd, Iain Sinclair and Will Self more recently. One effect has been a swollen, imaginary London, larger in the mind than in reality. How, in 1998, does London figure in the league table of great cities? Reckoned by its population, hardly at all. Mexico City comes first with more than fifteen million people, then your finger has to move quite a way down, past Manila, Calcutta, Bombay and São Paulo, past even Moscow and Paris (though nine million people in Paris suggests the boundary has been drawn too freely), until, twenty places from the top, you reach London. Slightly smaller than New York, about the same size as Tehran; only slighter larger than Lima, Peru.

Almost seven million people live here, about twelve per cent of the total population of the United Kingdom; a disproportionate city, too dominant for the small island it governs, though no longer able to boast, as it could throughout the nineteenth and much of this century, that it was the largest city in Europe and, for some of that time, in the world. Between 1700 and 1800 it almost doubled in size to a million people. In the next hundred years, in what the historian Stephen Inwood describes as London's 'explosive century', its population went up by a fifth in every decade. By 1900 it equalled the populations of continental Europe's four greatest cities—Paris, Berlin, Vienna and St Petersburg—combined. In Britain, you could heap together the people of Manchester, Birmingham and Glasgow and still not reach half the London total. Today that imbalance is even greater: London has shrunk since the Second World War, but northern cities have shrunk more.

But numbers no longer explain its importance to the rest of the world; the fact that London is still among the quartet of 'global cities' with Paris, New York and Tokyo. The answer here is money and the financial institutions and companies which deal with its flows. Such skills could easily have left London with the industry and imperial trade they once supported; they could have died like the Thames. Instead—an achievement of Thatcherism—they were encouraged and expanded. London became one of the three zonal capitals of capitalism. It processes about $300 billion in foreign exchange every day, as much as New York and Tokyo together. It does half the world's shipbroking, half the world's company mergers and acquisitions. No other European city yet comes close to it as a source of bank lending and fund management. It makes more international phone calls than anywhere else in the world. It speaks English.

None of this, apart from the last, is secure. Europe's single currency could damage its advantage. Frankfurt, the financial centre of Europe's greatest economy, might one day overtake it. If it does, the present may turn out to be London's last great age, with the Millennium Dome as the equivalent of the Great Exhibition of 1851, this time symbolizing not so much a pinnacle of achievement as a bump of misplaced optimism. Whatever the future, this issue of *Granta* reflects the present and immediate past of a great cosmopolitan city which is forging a new personality—in England, but not quite of it—as a new city state.   **IJ**

GRANTA

TRAFFIC
Ian Parker

1.

When London motorists see the state of the traffic in old black-and-white photographs of Holloway Road or High Holborn—a cart, a dog, two or three motor cars sailing through empty space like boats on the Thames—they catch a glimpse of something deep inside them: an image of their own delusion, a map of their madness. For this is the traffic we imagine we deserve. This is the traffic that we would have got this morning, when we headed off so cheerfully for Camden Town—if only things had not turned out so horribly, as they always do. Despite being the rule, bad traffic is somehow also the perpetual exception, like bad weather in winter. If only it hadn't rained, we wouldn't have got wet. If only we had set out eighty years ago, we would have been there by now.

In Cairo or Bangkok, we would live without hope. In central London—where traffic moves at an average of about ten miles per hour throughout the day, and in which a typical vehicle spends about a third of its time stationary—there is just enough slack to let us dream. There is a memory, or a false memory, of the Embankment on an autumn evening, when nothing stood in our way, or a Sunday in the City. We have driven over Tower Bridge at three in the morning. And our hopes for a rush-hour clear run—for a turn-of-the-century Pall Mall—are never quite dashed. And this guarantees constant, gnawing disappointment. Londoners arrive at each other's homes shaking their heads, surprised and aggrieved. Their cars promised them power, autonomy and control, and London traffic takes all these away—which is why people suddenly accelerate to sixty miles per hour, if they can, even on the approach to a red light at Knightsbridge.

London is not like other cities. American cities have grids and freeways. European cities have congested centres, but their centres are smaller than London's. And in the cities of the developing world, there may be traffic turmoil, but this will not be inner turmoil. The rules are more lax. People will be driving as it makes sense to them, sounding their horns. They will be in general agreement about fairly basic driving etiquette. In London, drivers are in continuous, stressful argument with a well-mannered alter ego. There is a decent, safe, thing to do—but then there will be a BMW that needs immediate

11

chastising; or, say, an amber light that will get you on to a green round the corner, and give you a chance of a clear run on to Vauxhall Bridge. In an interview shortly before his arrest in London last October, General Augusto Pinochet praised Britain for its impeccable driving habits; his countrymen were 'rude' in comparison. But he had perhaps not experienced the anguish of driving virtue unrewarded, nor seen what happens when two conflicting London motoring philosophies decide to settle the point with baseball bats.

London's congestion and fury has a possible compensation—and this is the chance to swagger, to take credit for technique and local expertise. Because the roads are complicated and full, because 140,000 people come into the centre of London by car every morning, because accident rates are way above the national average, a journey well executed can be paraded as a kind of athletic success. London drivers prize exquisite rat-runs behind Harrods, as they do a magical Covent Garden parking space, or a neat, anticipatory lane change in the Wandsworth one-way system. If you are driving into the West End on the Westway, there comes a point where you must decide whether to stay with the flyover, or swoop down through Paddington. If you leave the road unnecessarily, you have tossed away a rare minute or two of romantic, Americanized motoring. But if you stay and hit a jam, you will be unhappy, because escape is impossible. (The police who run the traffic lights on Marylebone Road use this stretch to 'store' traffic safely when things turn ugly further on, as they also store traffic on the southbound carriageway of Park Lane. These are places where a queue will not cause other queues.) Driving in at speed, you must choose Paddington or not-Paddington. But you cannot see if there is a queue ahead until you are almost upon the slip road. You have a second, or maybe less, to react; and—if things go well—the rest of the day to feel shamefully victorious.

British culture has been slow to mythologize London traffic, to make a fuss of it in fiction. French films have lingered over congestion (*Traffic*, *Weekend*), and we are accustomed to New York traffic filmed from every angle—speeded up and slowed down and forming hypnotic patterns at night: red lights ebbing and flowing like the display on a graphic equalizer. But London hides its traffic away, partly because London is a less giving place in which to shoot films (you have to steal locations; you have to organize illegal rolling roadblocks, three cars abreast with hazard lights flashing); but partly, perhaps, because London is in a kind of denial, and hopes to keep alive the fantasy that the Golden Age of London motoring is still within reach, and that our next journey will rescue us from disappointment.

Of course, like all Golden Ages, this motoring Golden Age—Mr Toad dashing up Whitehall—is a half-truth wrapped in disenchantment. While British car ownership has risen from 8,000 in 1903 to one million in 1930 and over twenty million today, average traffic speeds in the centre of London have barely changed in a hundred years, and have only dropped by about two miles per hour since the late 1960s. Long before 'jams' entered the English language from America, London was already quite familiar with 'blocks'. Gustave Doré's print *Ludgate Hill—A Block in the Street* (1872), is probably the first visual representation of London gridlock: a hearse, barrows and sheep in packed, motionless frustration below St Paul's Cathedral. In Evelyn Waugh's *Scoop* (1938), Julia Stitch's miniature black car becomes embedded in a block between Hyde Park Corner and Piccadilly Circus ('...the line of traffic was continuous and motionless, still as a photograph...'). And there are photographs that dare to argue with the photographs we remember. A set commissioned by London Transport in 1923 does include the kind of images that feed our fantasies: a single car on Fleet Street; a man dashing along a pavement, showing a flash of white sock. But this same set has a photograph of the junction of the Strand and Wellington Street. Here, in 1923, two policemen are doing their best, but horse-drawn and motor vehicles are nose-to-tail and stationary under advertisements for Oxo and government surplus underwear. A great queue stretches out on to Waterloo Bridge, and it disappears into fog halfway across the river.

2.

'He asked me the way to Bolsover street. I told him Bolsover street was in the middle of an intricate one-way system. It was a one-way system easy enough to get into. The only trouble was that, once in, you couldn't get out. I told him his best bet, if he really wanted to get to Bolsover street, was to take the first left, first right, second right, third on the left, keep his eye open for a hardware shop, go right round the square, keeping to the inside lane, take the second Mews on the right and then stop. He will find himself facing a very tall office block, with a crescent courtyard. He can take advantage of this office block. He can go round the crescent, come out the other way, follow the arrows, go past two sets of traffic lights and take the next left indicated by the first green filter he comes across. He's got the Post Office Tower in his vision the whole time. All he's got to do is to reverse into the underground car park, change gear, go straight on, and he'll find himself in Bolsover street with no trouble at all. I did warn him, though, that he'll still be faced with the problem, having found Bolsover street, of losing it. I told him I knew one or two people who'd been wandering up and down Bolsover street for years. They'd wasted their bloody youth there.'

From *No Man's Land* (1975), by Harold Pinter, Act II.

3.

In the world of London's traffic lights, seven seconds is a long time. In seven seconds, you can start a traffic jam. Or you can get about four cars past a green light—or sixteen cars, if there are four lanes. So if, at a crucial, congested junction, you find a spare seven seconds in the traffic lights sequence—seven seconds doing nothing, lying about—then you have made a discovery that can change people's lives.

Stuart Beniston is a leading traffic signal engineer. He works for a civil engineering consultancy in Derbyshire, having previously worked in the public sector. His job is to broker subtle compromises between movement and non-movement. He strives to keep our faith in a repeated little drama of responsible citizenship: After you. No, after you. And, in 1997, it was Beniston who found seven spare seconds at the Hanger Lane gyratory system. When we met there recently, on a bitterly cold afternoon at the start of the evening rush hour, he told me how it had happened. But first we went for a tour. He showed me markings in the road, and shouted over the traffic about offset timing and modelling software. As we talked, it became dark, and his fluorescent jacket began to shine in the headlights.

The Hanger Lane gyratory system—a London joke gone stale—

is six miles west of Marble Arch, and is where the A40, running out of London towards Oxford, meets the A406 North Circular. To use the language of the traffic professionals, this is where a major London orbital meets a major London radial—which is a rare and significant event, because most roads in London are radial; they go in and out. Before the M25 orbital motorway was built a few miles further out, the North Circular was the only real exception to the rule that all roads in England lead to London, and in London they lead to the centre.

This used to be a humble crossroads, controlled by traffic lights. Then in 1980, concrete was poured, and 'gyratory' found an unexpected place in London's day-to-day vocabulary. You have to imagine a very large roundabout, like Marble Arch or Hyde Park Corner, but rectangular rather than round. Traffic joins at the four corners of the rectangle, where there are traffic lights, and it moves round the system in a maximum of eight lanes, stopping now and then at other lights. In the middle of the roundabout, sunk below car level, there is room for a fairly large boating lake, or Brighton's Royal Pavilion; but instead, we find the kind of pinched scrubby parkland that calls out for body parts in bin liners. Here, in the middle of the roundabout, there is also an overground Tube station, Hanger Lane. And underneath everything runs the A40, whose slip roads come up to join the gyratory system at two of its corners.

Stuart Beniston took me to the roof of the Amoco office building, which stands high above the north-west corner of the gyratory. From here, we could see the lights of central London. Below us, there was thick thundering traffic, and more traffic queuing to join it from the north: we could see three-quarters of a mile of slow-moving headlights. For most of the day, Beniston said, and for seven days a week, about 8,000 vehicles an hour use the gyratory, which is the kind of flow you get on a busy section of the M4 (both directions combined), where no one has to stop for traffic lights or think about bus stops and vicars on bicycles. The truth is, too many people want to use Hanger Lane—and traffic, somewhere, will have to slow down and back up. The trick, said Beniston, is to keep the slow-moving traffic off the gyratory itself, where it will block up an entrance or an exit, and cause a jam that could take hours to clear. As far as possible, you want to synchronize lights to form 'platoons' of vehicles that will pass through the roundabout in convoy, and then off, uninterrupted, to the Home Counties and Heathrow.

In 1996, when the gyratory had long since earned a kind of macho-comic reputation for delay and grief—and when creative London drivers were making elaborate back-street diversions to avoid it—the Highways Agency asked Beniston to suggest improvements that would not involve building new roads: the improvements would have to derive from new signalling, and new lane markings. (In a country that has decided to stop building roads, it is Beniston and his colleagues—the people fine-tuning an existing network—who suddenly find themselves key players in their industry.) Beniston came down to London, he watched the traffic, he gathered data, he noted the existing traffic-light times, and—with the help of a computer modelling system called TRANSYT—he began to consider his options.

At the top of the Amoco block, in the cold, we were watching the traffic lights below. There are about 11,000 sets of lights in the country; there are 3,500 in London, and of those, about 2,000 can be influenced remotely by the Metropolitan Police: their usual sequences, which perhaps favour one direction in the morning, another at night, can be overruled by the police in response to accidents, or other oddities in traffic flow. The police choose from a number of existing sequence programmes—or 'plans', as they are known. The lights cannot be asked to flash randomly, say, or remain permanently green in one direction. Three computers survey the whole London network, and raise the possibility of *Italian Job* sabotage.

Beniston produced his digital watch. He said that a usual traffic-light cycle (that is, the time from the start of the green to the start of the next green at the same place) will be somewhere between twenty-four and 120 seconds. The London average is about 100 seconds. These seconds are divided up with enormous care: pedestrians may get a few seconds, traffic in every direction has to get a green phase, and between each green phase, there must be a 'clear time'—which is the interval between the lights in one direction turning red and the lights in the other direction turning green. But, as every driver knows, not every leg of a junction gets an equal share.

Traffic signal engineers are in the business of redistributing time, for the greater good of society. The shortest green times in London are about ten seconds (these are the nervy, scampering green phases where cars dash across Oxford Street, or out into Piccadilly—with the last, guilty car trying to merge with the group in front, like a fare-dodger shuffling behind you through an automatic Underground ticket barrier). The longest, the most leisurely green times are about eighty seconds in a 120-second sequence, for cars sailing up the Finchley Road on a sunny day, listening to Patsy Cline.

When he looked at the Hanger Lane figures, Beniston could think of ways of improving the painted lane markings (and he devised a kind of spiral arrangement that flings drivers into their exits as if by centrifugal force); and he was sure the existing, pre-programmed plans could be made more efficient. And then Beniston made a great discovery: there, in the eastern side of the gyratory, was a set of lights throwing away time. Traffic coming south, and wanting to turn west towards Oxford, had a crazily extravagant clear time. A previous programmer had needlessly linked this traffic to the movement of traffic alongside it, heading south. A stage in the sequence had been given ten seconds, when it needed just three.

Beniston pointed out the junction he meant: 'I thought, hang on. Just because *they* need the time, it doesn't mean that *they* need the time. It was a breakthrough. A bit of luck, really. A nugget of green time. Now, I had seven seconds available for the three critical movements—there, there and there. And it meant that it was a much more comfortable junction generally, and we could keep the whole side of the gyratory clear.' It would clear the south side, and free up the whole system.

Incorporating the extra seconds, Beniston devised a set of new timing plans for different parts of the day: for peak and off-peak, for clearing the gyratory after an accident, for getting rid of Wembley Stadium traffic, and so on. And one morning, in March 1997, he had a chance to test his theories. He met up with a technician at Hanger Lane, and the technician opened a roadside controller cabinet and plugged in his laptop computer and set the lights to Beniston's plan. It was eleven o'clock. 'The traffic had been a bit messy and congested when we did it. And then the plan went on. And suddenly everything started going really nicely. Straight away.' His plan left an immediate clockwise trail of clearer traffic. 'If I'd got it wrong,' he said, 'it would have suddenly snarled up worse than normal. I'd have felt terrible. But I was looking at it, thinking yes, this is looking really good.' The technician had gone back to his office. Beniston had to celebrate on his own. He walked round Hanger Lane, very pleased.

4.

'When I got on to the main road, I couldn't believe it. It was amazing. It was quite eerie. You know those films, when it's the end of the world, and there is nobody about, and the grass is growing up through the pavements? There were so few cars that whenever I saw one I became quite indignant that they weren't watching the funeral. I didn't want anything to do with it myself, but I was still looking at them and thinking: how unpatriotic.

'I had a tape in the car: Neil Diamond's *Greatest Hits*, and I was singing along to "September Morn". And I just drove straight through. Straight through Streatham, straight through Balham, Tooting, Wandsworth Bridge Road. Nothing. I only had to stop for traffic lights. Nothing else. You could go as fast as you wanted. And I was thinking, why can't it always be like this? It reminded me of when I was about eleven, and the only person I knew who had a car was my friend's father, who was the manager of the local Boots, and he had a green car, I think it must have been a Ford, and occasionally he used to take us out: her, me, her sister. On Sundays we'd go for a little drive, and the roads would be so clear. I don't think there were yellow lines then. You could just park anywhere. You'd drive into a little town, you'd park, and get out, walk round, have a cup of tea.

'When I got home, I looked at my watch. I thought, the drive of a lifetime. It'll never be repeated. There are no circumstances in which it could happen. I don't think even a coronation. We'll see what happens when the Queen Mother goes.'

A woman driver describing a journey through London on 6 September 1997, during the funeral of Diana, Princess of Wales.

5.

After the First World War, as the fashion for motoring grew, white lines began to appear on Britain's roads. The rule was still to keep to the kerb, but, if the surface would allow it, white centre-lines could now be found at a few sharp bends and on an occasional humpback bridge, and white 'stop' lines were painted on some busy junctions. By 1926, a Ministry of Transport document (Circular No. 238 Roads) was already observing how white lines were able 'not only to reduce the number of accidents, but also to assist materially in the control of traffic by the Police'.

At this time, lines were being drawn as each County Surveyor saw fit—there was no agreement on where, or how, they should be painted. But standardization gradually emerged. Much of the modern motoring landscape took shape in the early 1930s: the first Highway Code, the first driving tests, the first pedestrian crossings; and in an experiment in 1931, a continuous five-and-a-quarter mile centre-line— the first of its kind—was painted on the Great West Road, which runs out of London through Brentford. Four years later, dotted white lines first appeared, two feet long and twenty-four feet apart, painted on seventy miles of the A30 and A38 in Devon.

The width of white lines was agreed in the early 1940s, during a rash of line-painting inspired by wartime blackout restrictions. A Ministry of Transport Committee decided that a line two inches wide was too spindly; and that a six-inch line was, regrettably, too expensive; so a four-inch line was agreed. (The modern European minimum is almost identical: ten centimetres.) In the late 1950s, the first central double white lines—devised by the City of New York twenty years earlier—were painted in Britain. The first yellow lines were painted experimentally in Slough in 1956. And in 1960, white lines were first painted to mark a road's edge.

This is when the boom began in the line-painting industry. When you look at a photograph of Trafalgar Square in 1960, you see white lines at traffic lights—stop lines—but no lane divisions, no arrows, no hatching, no friendly messages to pedestrians. This is London on the brink of the modern traffic age. In 1960, the first section of the M1 had just opened, from St Albans to Rugby; the Hammersmith Flyover was under construction; car ownership would rise, in a decade, from 4.9 million to 9.8 million (it had been just two million in 1950; as late as 1949, there were more vehicle miles done by bicycle than by car). In 1960, the London Traffic Management Unit was set up, and it had soon made daring innovations: box junctions, urban clearways, tidal-flow schemes on Albert and Hammersmith bridges, and London's first major one-way schemes, starting with the Tottenham Court Road and Gower Street scheme. (By 1965, there were forty-nine such schemes, covering fifty-eight miles of London street.) In 1960, a new magazine, *Traffic Engineering and Control,* was first published, which pointed to a free-flowing, ten-lane future. ('Every pedestrian crossing,' ran an impatient feature in the first issue, 'every traffic light, every "no-waiting" sign, is a confession of our failure as a society to solve the problems confronting us.') In 1960, a new discipline, traffic engineering, was emerging in London local government and in the universities and at the Road Research Laboratory—undertaken by home-grown mathematicians and bright young men and women bringing curious new masters' degrees back from American universities. (These are people who, in the years to come, would invent mini-roundabouts, and give thought to the way in which bunched-up cars on a motorway sound an echo of a slow-moving lorry long after the lorry has moved on.)

And in 1960, Colin Halstead started painting lines in the road. He has since tried other jobs, including hotel work, but the money is quite good, and there used to be travel: line-painting in America, Germany and Nigeria. 'A lot of people think it's an idiot job,' he said, 'but I like it. You're left alone, no one bothers you.'

I met Halstead at about half-past ten at night, at the junction of Great Portland Street and Marylebone Road (and near the top of Bolsover Street). He had just started his shift and would stop at about three in the morning, then drive to his home by the sea in Kent and take a purifying shower. He had a 'tailor' machine in front of him—a steel tub about the size of a lavatory, heated by a large calor gas canister fixed on one side. In the tub, there was white plastic paint as thick as melted cheese. Halstead had a stick, and he stirred now and then. 'You don't want to get that on you,' he said. 'Go straight through you.'

Halstead and his colleague were painting the arrows, the hatching, the stop lines, the bits and pieces. 'The worst is the pedestrian Look Left and Look bloody Right,' he said. Later, a sprayer lorry would arrive to do the simpler markings that run in the direction of the traffic. But now Halstead's colleague was dashing fearlessly among the cars with a bucket's worth of paint and a metal mould on a stick. When the lights turned red, he would start pouring, and could finish a lane's width of stop line before the lights turned green. One fastidious driver was nervous she would spoil the effect, and was reluctant to move forward. For her benefit, Halstead kicked at the paint—to show it had dried the moment it touched the cold tarmac.

The traffic was relentless: young couples with a glass of wine inside them, dashing home for *Friends*, annoyed to find a truck with flashing lights pushing them out of a hard-won lane. 'This is a terrible road to work on at any time,' Halstead said, and yet he was very calm. His job involves standing in the road for hours on end, with noise in his ears, breathing fumes. He gets home stinking of exhaust. But he has become used to it. Sometimes, when new men start on the job, they are nervous. 'They get frightened. They say, Oooh, no, we don't want to go out into that. But you do get used to it.' The trick is not to try to direct the traffic. 'You just confuse them. And if they crash they think it's your fault. Just leave them to sort it out.'

6.

'The London panorama under a sky of June feasted [Gammon's] laughing eyes. Now he would wave a hand to a friend on the pavement or borne past on another bus; now he would chuckle at a bit of comedy in real life. Huge hotels and brilliant shops vividly impressed him, though he saw them for the thousandth time; a new device in advertising won his ungrudging admiration. Above all he liked to find himself in the Strand at that hour of the day when east and west show a double current of continuous traffic, tight-wedged in the narrow street, moving at a mere footpace, every horse's nose touching the back of the next vehicle. The sun could not shine too hotly; it made colours brighter, gave a new beauty to the glittering public-houses, where names of cooling drinks seemed to cry aloud. He enjoyed a "block", and was disappointed unless he saw the policeman at Wellington Street holding up his hands whilst the cross traffic from north and south rolled grandly through. It always reminded him of the Bible story—Moses parting the waters of the Red Sea.'

From George Gissing, *The Town Traveller* (1898), Chapter VIII.

7.

There are junctions whose existence is known to every Londoner, but whose place on the map is known to few. Not everyone could point to Savoy Circus, Gillette Corner, The Sun in Sands Roundabout— but everyone with a radio knows the words, because they are repeated day and night, and through repetition they have gained the gravitas and the melancholy glamour of Rockall or South Utsire on the late-night shipping forecasts. These names may mean nothing to you, the traffic reports tell us, but they are dangerous places, where travellers may easily come to grief. Listen, beware.

No one says 'the Talgarth Road section of the A4' with quite the authority of Sally Boazman, who, when we spoke, was the morning traffic reporter on the BBC's Greater London Radio, but who has since joined Radio Two. She is affable and amused on air— you could not fault her DJ banter about flyovers and hangovers— but she has an edge of reporterly seriousness, a commitment to the subject, that is lacking in some of her competitors. They tend either to be younger and dizzier, trying to get a foot in radio's door; or they're giving themselves showbusiness airs. (In Boazman's stern phrase, this is 'putting yourself in front of the information'.)

It is Boazman's great professional happiness to see traffic not moving. I met her one Friday morning in her little studio in Scotland Yard, and as we spoke she was sometimes interrupted by events shown on her monitors. 'Oh!' she would say, seeing confusion at Whitechapel. 'What's going on? Can you see? Have the police got control of that?' A little later, she cried out 'Blimey!' at the sight of a broken-down van on the hard shoulder of the M25, just south of Junction 16. 'You see how my heart jumped there?'

While Capital Radio has an aeroplane, the 'Flying Eye' (which Boazman treats with half-serious disparagement: 'Can it go up in the rain? Can it go in a tunnel?'), GLR has precious access to the Metropolitan Police's network of traffic cameras. To a visitor, this is a magical toy. Three hundred cameras are fixed on posts and high buildings across London, and each has a number. On Boazman's desk was a little grey keypad. Tapping in a number, you can call up a clear, colour image of a London street; tapping in one number after another, you can skip across London at the height of a lamp-post—Bayswater, Old Kent Road, King's Cross—as if editing a rather earnest pop video for a song about urban dislocation. You can turn the camera, and you can zoom in—a fat man in a hat at Hammersmith, someone asleep in the Strand. Boazman has seen road rage on the cameras. She has tried to follow police chases, hopping from one camera to another. And at my suggestion, we tried to peer in an upstairs room in Camden High Street. 'Let's have a look,' she said. 'Hmm.' (I believed her when she said this was not normal practice.)

I watched Boazman preparing for a live broadcast, tapping her way through the camera codes, reading faxes, ringing London Transport to consult about the Circle Line. And then a red light came on, and she launched, unscripted, into: 'Euston Road eastbound... If you're coming up from Isleworth... If you're going out of town on the A3... Nasty accident in Hollybush Hill.' When she finished, she waited a second to see if the disc jockey would need her for a moment's chat, and then she was off-air. I wondered if she ever used the traffic reporter's cliché, 'sheer weight of traffic' (reduced to 'SWT' in some police circles), and she said, 'No! I never use that expression. You'll never hear me say it. Sorry, I'm getting rather heated here. And I never say "an earlier accident". I hate that. I made a decision in life never to say "an earlier accident". I say, "an accident, earlier".'

I asked her, Is London traffic getting worse? 'Yes,' she said. 'It's definitely much worse than when I started doing reports in the early Eighties, and a lot worse in the past four or five years. You feel there's a very fine balance; and one minor thing can start a terrible queue. But the main thing is the rush hours are getting longer. Before, you'd say the evening rush hour starts about four, goes on to about six. Now it starts about half past three and goes on till about eight in the evening. And the same in the morning, really. It used to be the rush hour started about half past seven and went through until nine, but now, if you look at the Blackwall Tunnel—one of my favourite spots—it can be stuck at half past six in the morning.'

It was midday on a Friday, just ahead of a school half-term. 'Look,' she said. 'That's the rush hour starting. That's the Westway, going out of London on the M40. The mass getaway has started. It's going to get worse and worse and worse for the rest of the day.'

It was starting to rain. 'Spray, spray!' she said. 'Good, good.'

8.

On Tuesday 10 December 1996, Robert Thomson, then thirty-five years old, from Hoo, Kent—a man later described by the AA as a 'total prat'—was driving on the southbound carriageway of the A102(M) towards the Blackwall Tunnel, which is one of the crucial links in London's traffic system. He was in a large white Mercedes truck, and the truck was carrying a crane that rose high above the road. Ignoring warning signs of height restrictions ahead—or persuading himself that his load could make it, or forgetting altogether that he had a load—he approached the mouth of the tunnel without apparent anxiety. And at about two-fifteen in the afternoon, at the entrance to the tunnel, the crane on Thomson's truck hit a gantry above. A reinforced steel frame crashed down on to the truck. Thomson stopped, and so, very soon, did everyone else. Mr Thomson had set in motion one of the worst traffic jams ever seen in London.

The lorry had to be prised out of the tunnel; and the tunnel's structure had to be checked for safety. And this was on a day when the eastbound carriageway of the Limehouse Link tunnel was closed for maintenance, and the QE2 bridge at Dartford was also closed southbound. All the major routes in east London quickly filled, and then—as people struck out into the unknown—so did all the minor routes. Junctions became blocked, and queues were soon covering an area sixteen miles square, from Liverpool Street in the west to Leytonstone in the east. It was estimated that 250,000 cars were affected. One-hour journeys became six-hour journeys. People abandoned their cars. In an echo of nineteenth-century practice, fire crews had to walk in front of their vehicles, asking cars ahead to mount the pavement. Drivers stuck in the Rotherhithe Tunnel, the nearest river crossing to the Blackwall Tunnel, had to breathe through handkerchiefs as fumes from stationary cars built up. It took one woman eleven hours to get from the north of the river to the south.

The Blackwall Tunnel was reopened in the early hours of Wednesday morning. In the immediate aftermath, police did not release Mr Thomson's name. 'If we named him,' a spokesman told the London *Evening Standard*, 'half of London would want to lynch him.' But they revealed that he was feeling 'sheepish'.

9.

The traffic police call them 'peds', but they seem to mean it kindly. I met Ben Plowden, director of the Pedestrians' Society, on the steps of the National Gallery, and we went for a walk around Trafalgar Square.

'Brixton High Street,' he said, 'which is my local shopping street, serves two mutually exclusive functions. It's a major shopping centre, where I should think ninety-five per cent of the people visiting are doing so on public transport or on foot, and it's also the A23, which is the major road from London to the South Coast. At any moment on a Saturday, the people on foot probably outweigh the people driving through Brixton by about twenty or thirty to one, and yet the space of Brixton High Street is designed, laid out, managed, timed, almost exclusively for the benefit of people travelling through it. And I think this raises quite interesting philosophical questions: why is that? Why are people travelling through on four wheels, in rather small numbers, the ones who have priority at the junctions? Why is everyone else hemmed in behind a quarter-mile of continuous crash-barriers? There's a really profound implied statement underlying that, about who counts...'

Here, we made a dash across several lanes of traffic to reach the centre of the square. 'Go! Go!' cried Plowden. Under Sir Norman Foster's World Squares for All plans, the road we had crossed will eventually become pavement, filled with cappuccino and laughter. In the meantime, only tourists get across: Londoners resent the inconvenience and danger, and keep to the edges. A bus climbed on to the pavement in front of us.

Plowden is a man who can see transport thinking turning his way. Britain seems to be entering its second age of modern motoring, where it is agreed across a surprisingly wide spectrum that congestion cannot be defeated by road-building, and that some form of levy on driving in London (or, to put it more seductively, some sort of 'congestion charging') is inevitable, and will be a good thing, for it will free up the roads for bus lanes and bicycles, will reduce pollution, and provide revenue for grand public transport projects. (The new mayor of London will have congestion-charging powers; the government is giving other local authorities the right to set up pilot schemes.) In this new motoring age, a key text will be *Traffic Impact of Highway Capacity Reductions* (1998), by Phil Goodwin and others, which Plowden describes as the 'final piece in the jigsaw' for much progressive transport analysis. Goodwin studied one hundred instances of planned or emergency road closure—Oxford Street in 1972, Interstate 10 after the Los Angeles earthquake in 1994, Hammersmith Bridge in 1997—and saw how car drivers adapt their behaviour; they take other routes, they travel at other times, they catch the bus. They are not all so foolish as to sit in queues in the surrounding streets, shouting obscenities at one another. For people claiming extra space for bikes and for peds (and forty per cent of journeys made in inner London are made exclusively on foot), Goodwin's work makes a handsome academic chaperone.

We walked back towards the National Gallery. It was the evening rush hour. Everywhere, pedestrians were overriding the provisions made for them; slipping through gaps, dashing between buses. A mother with a pushchair and bright bleached hair became stuck on the wrong side of a barrier, and a taxi grudgingly agreed not to run her over.

10.

Among the officers in the Central Command Complex of the Metropolitan Police, there is resistance to the word gridlock. 'Don't ever mention that filthy disgusting word in here,' I was told. 'Gridlock is an American word. It's a traffic condition that only occurs in a grid system of roads, which you're only likely to get in America or Canada or—all right, fair enough—Stevenage New Town, but in principle you can't get gridlock in London.' He took out a piece of paper, and drew a grid, and then described the police's preferred language for London traffic. 'Green is light traffic flowing freely, amber is medium traffic flowing freely, blue is heavy traffic flowing freely, red is heavy traffic stationary for less than three minutes, and black is bus driver, feet up on the dash, reading the newspaper. And you don't get black traffic in London very often.'

We were standing in front of monitors in a very long and windowless room in the middle of Scotland Yard. From here, the police can overrule the usual traffic-light 'plans' in central London. As I watched, they were trying to favour Northumberland Avenue at the expense of Victoria Embankment. It was clearly a subtle art: a new plan goes on, but is taken off after a few minutes, then put on again. (A plan applied cack-handedly can create surrounding queues that take hours to disperse.) As they worked, the police seemed serene and upbeat. They were accentuating the positive. They had the air of group leaders in a therapeutic workshop for neurotically impatient London drivers. Where an ordinary driver would see a queue, the police tend to see a moving queue. 'That's running quite well,' they said of traffic crawling along Trafalgar Square.

It was tempting to hope for worse. Gridlock, or something similar, is an oddly seductive fantasy—spectacular and decisive, but safer than an earthquake, at least for those with strong lungs. Looking at the monitors, it was hard not to hope for a lorry to lose its load of ball-bearings at Paddington, or for a fuse to go at Parliament Square, and then a bomb scare at Waterloo and a burst water main at Euston—or any combination of four crises at four key junctions, which is what experts (and Ben Elton's novel, *Gridlock*) think would bring London into a 'superjam' state. (For best results, these crises would occur in the morning, when people would be more impatient to get on their way, and be more likely to make the fatal move of abandoning their vehicles.)

But traffic was moving quite freely. The police made bantering conversation about idiot commuters. There were further thoughts about American grids. And then we caught sight of something on Piccadilly eastbound. A parked van had blocked a side junction, and a lorry unable to turn left had stopped. Nothing could move. A bus conductor had left his bus to investigate. When the camera swung round, we could see that Park Lane was already filling up southbound. And as we watched, it was becoming difficult for traffic on Hyde Park Corner to get past Piccadilly, down towards Victoria. 'That's going to get blocked off completely. Once that happens, I'll lose Park Lane, and then the queue will go back right round, and eventually the whole thing will stop.'

They called for a police motorbike, and we saw it arrive two minutes later. The van was asked to move. The bus conductor got back on his bus. 'See. Moving nicely now.' There would be no gridlock, no breakdown of civil government, and no looting.

11.

In March 1931, Londoners saw something for the last time. Along a stretch of Marylebone Road, in front of Baker Street Underground station, straw was laid on the ground by workmen from a sympathetic borough council. Above, in the mansion flats over the station, the novelist Arnold Bennett lay dying.

He had been in Paris at the beginning of the year. He had taken tea with André Gide; he had dined with Mr and Mrs James Joyce. And he had emphatically drunk from a carafe of water in his hotel, scorning popular suspicions about Parisian hygiene. Back in London, he became ill, and after a wedding reception in the Savoy Hotel in early February, he took to his bed, and never rose again. He was diagnosed with typhoid. He became delirious. His gall bladder was infected. For three weeks he hiccupped.

Outside, the straw was laid for the great novelist, and the noise of heavy traffic—traffic still without rubber tyres—was softened. Visitors to Bennett's deathbed had not seen this old-fashioned courtesy for a long time, and the sight scared them.

Bennett died on 27 March. It was a rainy night, and the straw became wet and slippery. According to Reginald Pound's 1952 biography of Bennett, a passing milk cart skidded and overturned just after midnight. Its churns fell on to the pavement below Bennett's flat with a huge crash.

12.

A few weeks ago, in a building that has the best views of central London, two rather grand, youngish people were sitting opposite each other with a desk and a computer between them. The woman wore a vivid pink suit. The man wore cuff links and red braces. He leaned way back in his chair, hands behind his head, and laughed an Alan Clark laugh: 'Yha yha yha yha!'

Although it would not have been clear to a passer-by, this was a court, of sorts, and the woman in pink, Verity Jones, was a kind of judge. In the decriminalized world of London parking offences, the Parking Appeals Service is the last port of call for a person not happy with a parking ticket. It processes 35,000 appeals a year, which is about one per cent of all London tickets issued. This is an office that knows the difference between a parking space and a parking place, and whether a car park counts as a road and whether a tuna-fish sandwich counts as a load. This office hears the phrase 'It's not the money, it's the principle' more than most. And it has an enviable high-rise home in New Zealand House, on the corner of Haymarket and Pall Mall. It's an oddity of London local government—where people grow old waiting to hear news of their council house repairs— that a charming former champagne dealer, contesting a penalty stuck to an MG parked near his Kensington home, should find himself in this haven of computerized efficiency, where people answer the telephone almost before it has begun ringing.

Stephen Cleeve looked supremely confident, which may be how he always looks. The Royal Borough of Kensington and Chelsea (which was not represented at the adjudication) had accused him of having illegally parked his MG on a pavement—on a 'crossover', which is the place where a car crosses a pavement to reach a front drive. But it was Mr Cleeve's contention that he had parked on a stretch of actual street—street that happened to lead to a set of iron gates, giving it the air, as it were, of a crossover. He suspected the traffic warden of having a vendetta against him: 'Always the same chap,' he said.

Verity Jones, who is a barrister, read the evidence on her computer screen. She then looked at Cleeve's photographs of the crime scene. Some questions were asked and answered—with both appellant and adjudicator using amused inverted commas round phrases like 'vehicular access'. Cleeve laughed a lot, and toyed with a Rumpolian persona. 'Flimsy evidence!' he cried out at one point.

It was over in ten minutes. On this occasion, yellow lines had served as Cleeve's great friend. He had parked on a single yellow line, and where there is a yellow line, there must surely be a street. 'I don't think the council can have their cake and eat it,' said Jones. She would allow his appeal. Cleeve said, 'Oh, very good. Thanks very much, Verity. The best man won.'

In the waiting area outside, while his paperwork was being processed, Cleeve told me about his parking history. He said he gets 'hundreds' of tickets. Half of them he accepts in good grace— 'Sometimes, you've got to park, you just chuck the car down and go'—but he resents the others: 'Yesterday, I was at London Bridge, I put in one hour twenty minutes on the parking meter. That was all the change I had. And someone I went to see was late, so they made me late, and I had a long walk back. I was eight minutes late, and I got a ticket. He said he'd just given it to me. And I asked him if he enjoyed his job. He said, Not really. I said, Give it up then, and smiled and got in the car and drove off.'

We talked about public transport. 'I've been on the Tube twice in my life,' he said. 'I just find it always breaks down. It's just so much aggro.' He recently decided to wait for a bus, but then hailed a taxi instead.

13.

Seen at the wheel of his or her car, a typical American has the air of someone with various projects underway, just one of which happens to be driving a car. He or she will also be involved in the solemn business of, say, sitting comfortably. A London driver—even a London driver on the telephone—always looks more fully consumed by the act of driving, and rarely achieves the state of blissful, armchair disengagement allowed by automatic gears and carefully engineered holders for cans of soft drinks. It does happen: a few years ago, a very relaxed London taxi driver picked up a Japanese visitor at Heathrow, who asked for Knightsbridge. The driver meant no harm, but at some point on the journey into town, the tourist slipped his mind. The driver made a long journey to Herne Hill, parked in a front drive, turned off the engine, and went into his house, closing the door behind him. The Japanese tourist was left in the taxi, wondering.

More often, London drivers are in the grip of fear. And they fear many things: they fear arriving in London, and they fear leaving it. (London hates to let you go: it's not like *Withnail and I*. If you drive out of London towards Brighton, there are seventy-five sets of traffic lights before you reach the motorway, and a dozen false dawns.) London drivers fear the morning peak, and the evening peak, and the school run rush hour, and the West End theatre rush hour. They fear Saturday afternoon traffic and Sunday night traffic. And they fear the prospect of leaving a good London parking spot: when a car fills the space they have left, they feel troubled and adrift, regretting their recklessness. There are Londoners—they are real and many—who will take a taxi from home, rather than risk giving up a resident's parking space, a lovely space, right in front of the house.

London drivers fear routes that are off their private mental map of London, and will go miles to 'get their bearings' by a landmark that is in the wrong place. They fear being a passenger in a car driven by someone with a preposterous mental map of London, but to which it would seem impolite and neurotic to draw attention. They fear violence (sixty-one per cent of London drivers, compared to forty-three per cent nationally, lock their cars from the inside when driving at night). They fear streets that once let them down badly, and can never again be fully trusted; they fear wildly revving Post Office vans; they fear the thousands of streets whose parked cars make it just too narrow for two cars to pass, and where they must play complex, draining games of oscillating generosity and aggression. They fear losing face by slowing down more than absolutely necessary when passing between width-restriction posts. And although they do not exactly fear being late—London drivers are usually in a place beyond that—they have a great fear that they are losing a race. The race is with an imaginary car that set off from the same place at the same time, but then did not get stuck behind the 31 bus, did not miss the lights, did not make that unforgivable lane error on Commercial Road. This car is way ahead. ☐

Royal Festival Hall
Hayward Gallery
on the South Bank

Patrick Caulfield

'... one of the finest painters at work in the world today...'
Andrew Graham -Dixon , Art Critic

4 February – 11 April 1999

Literature on the South Bank

FICTION, POETRY AND TALKS

Presenting all the best writers all year round.
Highlights have included:

Martin Amis	**Umberto Eco**	**Salman Rushdie**
Simon Armitage	**Nadine Gordimer**	**Vikram Seth**
Margaret Atwood	**Seamus Heaney**	**Susan Sontag**
Paul Auster	**Czeslaw Milosz**	**Wole Soyinka**
Julian Barnes	**Toni Morrison**	**Amy Tan**
Richard Dawkins	**Walter Mosley**	**Gore Vidal**
Rita Dove	**Camille Paglia**	**Derek Walcott**
Carol Ann Duffy	**Caryl Phillips**	**Marina Warner**

Join our **free** mailing list for **advance information** about events and **priority booking**.
Either call 0171 921 0971 or write to: Literature Events, Marketing Department,
Royal Festival Hall, Belvedere Road, London, SE1 8XX or email: ddezylva@rfh.org.uk

BOX OFFICE 0171 960 4242

For your FREE Literature and Hayward Bulletins with full details
of all the above and more please call 0171 921 0971. Online: www.sbc.org.uk

Funded by
THE
ARTS
COUNCIL
OF ENGLAND

sbc

GRANTA

ARRIVAL
Albino Ochero-Okello

Albino Ochero-Okello

A s I stood in front of the immigration officer, I was already worrying about my answers to the questions he might ask. What would I say if—when—he asked, 'Why are you coming here?' And what would I do if they didn't let me in? I tried to be calm and to compose myself.

I was asked for my passport which I had ready in my hands. I handed it to the immigration officer. The immigration officer took it and looked in it. He then asked me one of the questions that had been burning in my mind, 'What have you come here to do?'

I answered, 'I am a refugee. I have fled my country to seek political asylum here.' The immigration officer told me, 'Please could you go and wait inside that office over there. Somebody will come and attend to you soon.'

I went to the waiting room that he had pointed out. It was next to the interview rooms. When I went in, I saw two women sitting on the chairs, holding their children on their laps. They too were asylum-seekers, waiting to be interviewed.

In the same room there was also another woman sitting on a chair. She did not have a child. She was sitting by herself at the corner of the waiting room. From the look on her face, I could tell she was not at all happy and was worried about something. She looked very, very depressed. She was probably fearing the consequences of her fate.

In the same waiting room there was a young man sitting by himself on a chair. His face, also, showed no joy at all. The atmosphere was very tense. The young man's face looked familiar to me. I remembered that I had seen somebody looking like him before somewhere. 'Where have I seen this person?' I asked myself. I could not immediately recall. But then I suddenly remembered. It was in the aeroplane. He had been on the same plane that I had flown in on. We never talked to each other in the plane.

So when I saw him in the waiting room I smiled at him and went over. I smiled again and then greeted him. 'My name is Okello. I come from Uganda.' I told him, 'I have come here to seek political asylum.'

'How about you?' I asked him.

The young man introduced himself to me saying, 'My name is Frederick.' He went on, 'I, too, am from Uganda and have come here to seek political asylum.'

From Frederick's accent, I immediately knew that we were both from Northern Uganda where the civil war was raging on like wild bushfire. Frederick is an *Acholi* and I am a *Langi*, the two tribes that were being persecuted since the change of regime in Uganda. Although we were from different tribes, we spoke similar native languages. We could understand one another. Meeting Frederick was a great relief for me.

From the moment that we introduced ourselves and realized that we were in the same boat—fleeing from our country for our lives— we became friends. For me, to find a fellow Ugandan in the same situation as myself gave me a bit of confidence. But the confidence was not strong enough to prepare me for the interview with the immigration officer. I was still feeling very traumatized from the experiences that I had had at home.

After everyone else had been interviewed and cleared by the immigration officer, our turn came. The immigration officer called us to the side interview room. He was a young white gentleman. He was helpful and understanding. He was human in his work. It did not take him very long to realize that I was traumatized and he seemed sympathetic. I was unable to tell the immigration officer much about what had forced me to flee my country. The feelings and the pains of what I'd experienced at home were too much for me to bear.

Another thing that hindered me from telling all my problems to the immigration officer was that I felt he might be the eye of the government. Because of this, I felt withdrawn and insecure, anxious lest I emptied my heart to somebody who would betray me. Such mixed feelings are felt by many refugees when they first arrive abroad seeking political asylum. Not even afterwards, when I was given leave to remain, did I feel comfortable talking about it.

During the interview, the immigration officer asked me for my personal details. I gave them to him. He then asked for the details of my immediate family members, my wife and children. Again I gave them to him. Then he asked for details of my other relatives, my father, mother, brothers and/or sisters or of any other dependants. Again I gave them to him.

When this was done, the immigration officer asked me, 'Why have you come to the UK?' I replied, 'To seek political asylum.' Then

I explained to him in brief why I had fled my country, Uganda.

I told him about the vicious problem of the political situation in Uganda whenever there is a change of regime. I explained, 'In Uganda, when the leader comes from your tribe, it may sound like a good thing. But in reality, you are in serious trouble when he is kicked out of power. It has become customary in Uganda that, when a ruler is kicked out, all the people who belong to his tribe and those of other tribes who were associated with his regime are held liable for the sufferings that other Ugandans are alleged to have experienced during his time in power. The vicious cycle of punishing the tribe-mates of deposed rulers for the sins committed under their ruler's regimes started when Idi Amin burst on to the arena of politics on 25 January 1971. Milton Obote, the president he overthrew in a bloody military coup—his tribe-mates suffered a lot. When Idi Amin's turn came and he too was deposed, his tribe-mates suffered the same fate, and the same happened after Obote's second presidency in May 1985 and General Tito Okello's military junta on 25 January 1986.'

When I told the immigration officer this, he sighed. 'Oh, I see. Is that how politics works in your country?'

'Yes. But I think similar things are probably happening in other parts of Africa too,' I answered.

'It sounds terrifying,' the immigration officer said. He then asked me, 'Can you tell me precisely why your life is in danger? Be more specific.' So I told the immigration officer my role in the politics of Uganda. I told him that I had been branch chairman of the political party of the civilian government that was overthrown by the military junta in May 1985. I told him that being in such a position at that time had put my life under constant threat. As I started to tell the immigration officer my story, tears began to roll from my eyes. The memory of what had happened to me and to my parents at home triggered this. The whole episode of what had happened at home started to come alive in my mind. I felt a big lump come into my throat but I swallowed it.

The worst memory was reliving the way my elderly, partially blind father was stripped naked by the so-called Karamojong cattle-raiders. They stripped my half-sister Maria too, and then shot her dead in front of him, before driving off with his 400 head of cattle.

The thought of the fate of my family, the wife and three children that I had left behind, increased my grief. I thought about my daughter Gloria, who had been very unwell when I left, and whom I did not expect to live for very long.

With all these memories flooding back into my mind during the interview, I found it too much to say anything any more. I just sat there, my face looking down at the table and the tears rolling down my cheeks like a river.

It was impossible to continue with my story. I could not do it because of the lump in my throat. I felt like a dead person.

The interview had taken about twenty minutes. Although I did not tell the immigration officer who interviewed me everything, he seemed sympathetic and understanding.

When the interview had finished, I was asked by the immigration officer to go and wait in the waiting room. Inside the waiting room I saw my friend Frederick sitting on a chair. I asked Frederick if he had been interviewed. Frederick said he had. We stayed in the waiting room for about ten minutes and then the immigration officer came in. He told us to wait there for a few minutes more and he would be back soon.

The time was nine p.m. There were hardly any asylum-seekers left in the waiting room. The two women with their children had been cleared and had left. The third woman, the unhappy one, was still there. Now she did not just look unhappy, but she was crying. I could see the tears rolling continuously down her cheeks. 'What is the matter?' we asked her.

'I have been told that they are going to deport me back home,' the poor woman replied.

'Where do you come from?' Frederick asked.

'I come from Nigeria,' she replied.

'What have you come to do? I mean, why have you come here?' I asked.

'To seek political asylum,' the woman answered.

Before we could find out more from the woman about the circumstances that had led her to flee her country, another immigration officer came in. It was not the one that had interviewed me. This one was a woman. She smiled very broadly at us. Her smile restored some calm and a sense of hope in us. She came over and addressed us by our names, 'Okello' and 'Frederick'. 'Follow me,' she said. We picked up our small bags and followed her. Our bags had hardly anything in them. Mine contained two shirts, two pairs of trousers, and a towel. I had also brought a Bible.

We followed the immigration lady not knowing where we were being led to. My heart started to beat rapidly. I was thinking that this is it. We are being led back to the plane to be deported back to Uganda.

I whispered to Frederick in our own language, 'Hey, Frederick. Where do you think we are being taken to?'

'I don't know. Let us keep on praying to God,' Frederick answered. The immigration lady led us through the maze of the huge immigration building. We went through many doors and eventually ended up outside the building. There was a van waiting with two security guards. The immigration lady handed us over to the two immigration security officers. She told us that they were taking us somewhere to sleep. Then she said goodnight to us before going back into the huge building.

One of the immigration security officers opened the door of the van for us with his keys. The keys were chained to his waist. He told us to get in. We got in and sat down. The immigration security officer locked the door behind us and went and sat in front next to the driver. Then they drove off.

I asked myself, 'Why did they have to lock the door of the van?' I did not understand why. I didn't immediately realize that we were being locked up because we were detainees. The immigration security officer was just doing his job. Maybe he'd had past experiences where people who were being led away had jumped out of the van and escaped. They didn't want to take chances which might engage them in chasing about after runaway asylum-seekers.

After about ten minutes' drive, we arrived at the Beehive, as we later found out it was nicknamed. It was a detention centre. The van stopped in front of the gate. The security officer got out and unlocked the gate, and then came and unlocked the door of the van. He asked us to get out and follow him. We followed him inside and he handed us over to the duty officer.

We saw many people of various nationalities inside the Beehive. We later found out that the majority of them were political asylum-seekers. Some of the detainees were sitting in the living room watching the TV. Others were making telephone calls. Some were relaxing in their rooms with the doors open. Others were walking up and down the corridor.

I could not tell what the exact reasons for the other people being in the Beehive detention centre were. I didn't really want to know about other people's problems. I had my own problems to think about. So I minded my own business and did not bother to ask any of the detainees why they were there.

After a short wait, we were registered by the immigration officer on duty. He showed us to our room. It was a double bedroom, which we were to share. Nothing about the atmosphere of the Beehive made us feel we were being imprisoned or detained. It was quite clean and nice. After we had been shown our room we went and had hot showers. Then I sat on my bed and rested for a while. My bed was well made. I put my bag next to a small chest of drawers. I lay back on my bed for about twenty minutes feeling relaxed after the long, long journey from Uganda. I took out my Bible and read a chapter or two, thanking God for helping me over the first hurdles in my endeavour to gain political asylum. I felt lucky that I hadn't been thrown back on to the plane instantly and deported back to Uganda.

Later we went and ate some dinner. We had tinned fish, beef, potatoes, rice and an assortment of other dishes. I think the woman who served us the food probably guessed that we were new arrivals, exhausted and hungry. The strain showing on our faces was not solely from exhaustion and jet lag, but was also caused by worry about the future. We did not yet know what the future held for us.

Although the food was nice, my appetite had vanished. It had been wiped out by the fear of what would happen to me in the morning. The anxiety kept the adrenaline dripping inside me all the time. I was feeling hungry, but I could not eat.

When we had finished our dinner we went to the living room. We sat down to watch the TV. I watched the TV with my friend Frederick until about eleven p.m. We then decided to go and sleep. The weather seemed very cold that night. The detention centre veterans said it was warm compared with other times of the year, but we found it very cold. I had come from a country which has hot weather almost all year round. When the central heating went off at ten-thirty p.m. the centre seemed freezing to me.

Frederick and I said our prayers and then got into bed. But it took me a long time to fall asleep. Thoughts about my future here and the fate of my family back at home in Uganda kept me awake. I tried to forget all about it, but it was impossible. The thoughts kept on coming back again and again every time I closed my eyes. I struggled to make myself fall asleep. But it was all in vain. It was a long time before I eventually fell asleep.

The following morning we woke up, had a shower, said our morning prayers and then went and had breakfast. A short while later the immigration security men arrived. One of them came inside and asked, 'Where are Okello and Frederick?'

We answered, 'Here we are, Sir.' The immigration security officer greeted us and then said, 'Please take your belongings and then follow me.'

We followed him outside, into the van. He locked the doors and drove us back to Gatwick Airport immigration office.

When we arrived at Gatwick Airport we had another interview. This time I was interviewed by a woman. She was a very kind woman, at once charming and good-looking. She said, 'So you are here to seek political asylum?'

I answered, 'Yes madam.'

'Do you have any family?'

'Yes madam.'

'Where are they?'

'I left them in Uganda.'

'Do you have any children?'

'Yes. I do have some children.'

'Do you have any intention of bringing them here to join you in the future?'

I paused for a moment and looked into her face. She smiled at me. She looked very positive and welcoming. I answered, 'Yes madam. If possible.'

The immigration lady then asked me about my family. I felt a big lump come into my throat and was choked by it. I could hardly speak a word. I immediately started to think about my little daughter Gloria, who had been ill when I left, Henry, Ronnie and their mother. Then I thought of my poor old father and wondered how he was coping with the loss of his daughter.

These thoughts brought tears flooding into my eyes. I wondered what could be happening to my family. Given the volatile security situation in Uganda when I fled, it could be anything. There was a ferocious civil war going on in the East, and in the North, where my family lived. Although the tears flooded into my eyes, my eyes were closed. My mind was far away back in Uganda thinking about the fate of my family.

When I opened my eyes, the immigration officer was looking at me. She asked me if I was all right.

'Yes madam. I think I am all right.'

She paused for a moment to allow me to compose myself. Then she asked me, 'Would you like to bring your family over to the UK?' I felt my hopes rise at her words. I thought that at least then they will not be left to suffer for long by themselves. I answered her, 'Yes madam, if it is possible.'

At that moment, the moment when the immigration lady asked me if I wanted to bring my family, I felt hopeful for the first time since arriving in Britain. 'Would you be able to help me?' I asked.

The immigration lady looked at me sympathetically. She smiled and then she said, 'Well. If you win your case, and after you have settled, if you would like to do it you may get in touch with me and I will give you contacts for some organizations that are set up to help refugees with their cases.' I then asked her, 'But madam. How will I contact you? I don't know your name and I don't have your telephone number.'

'Don't worry,' she said. 'Here.' She wrote her name and her office telephone number down and gave them to me. But unfortunately I later lost the piece of paper when the bed and breakfast hostel where I went to stay was attacked by an arsonist. Because we had to vacate our rooms in a hurry, I left it inside. I will never be able to thank that immigration lady enough, though. I would like to thank her again but

I can't. Whoever she was and wherever she may be working now, all my best wishes for her.

After a brief interview, the immigration lady told me that my case would be passed on to a higher authority who would notify me in due course of the result of my application. But it may be some time before you hear from the Home Office, she told me. 'In the meantime, you have been given temporary admission into the country. This is a letter with some rules and regulations about your stay.

'Take it,' she said. 'Read it well when you reach the bed and breakfast hostel. And remember to keep it in a safe place. You will need to refer to it whenever you wish to contact us.' The immigration lady put the letter in an envelope and gave it to me. I took it and said, 'Thank you. Thank you very much.'

'You're welcome,' the immigration lady replied with a smile. Her smile was not only warm and welcoming, but also reassuring. The letter I had been given was a standard temporary admission pass. The same type of letter is normally given to every political asylum-seeker entering Britain.

After she had given me the letter, the immigration lady made a few telephone calls. She was calling various bed and breakfast landlords, trying to find a free room. After making a few calls, she found one who had spare rooms for us. I listened to her talking on the phone: 'Yes. Yes. That's fine,' she said. 'Yes, two of them. That's OK. I'll send them over right away.'

I could hear the voice of the other person at the end of the line. It was a man with an Asian accent. He asked the immigration lady, 'Do the two lads speak a little English?' The immigration lady reassured him, 'Don't worry about that. That's not a problem. They both speak very good English.'

'Did you say they're coming today?' asked the voice on the phone.

'Yes, they'll be coming today. They should be there in a few hours' time.'

'Good! I'll be waiting for them, then,' the landlord said.

But the few hours that the lady had said it would take us to get to the bed and breakfast hostel turned out to be a rather optimistic estimate.

Smiling at me with that reassuring smile, the immigration lady said to me, 'You will soon be OK. I have found a place for you to live.' 'Oh. That is very kind of you,' I replied wearily. Although it was very difficult for me, I managed to splash out a little smile. But inside I still felt traumatized, and worried about my future.

The immigration lady told me to wait for a few minutes. She then went to another room to interview Frederick. When she came out, she said, 'Okello, please follow me.' She took me to where Frederick was waiting. She said, 'OK. I have found a place for the two of you. It's a bed and breakfast hostel in west London.'

We thanked her and she gave us a photocopied map showing the location of the hostel. We hadn't realized that it would be up to us to navigate our way to the bed and breakfast hostel by ourselves. After giving us the map, she gave us some train tickets. She said, 'And here are your travel tickets for the train. They are one-day Travelcards. If you want to travel for the whole day with them, you can. You can use them up until twelve midnight.'

'Thank you,' we said.

She said we could travel with the tickets up to twelve midnight. But even if we had wanted to use our one-day Travelcards to travel for the whole day, where would we have gone? We were new to the country. We hardly knew anybody. Let alone where the bed and breakfast was that we were booked to go and live in. We did not know where it was or how long it would take us to reach it from Gatwick Airport.

Anyway, at this stage we did not plan to travel anywhere until midnight with our Travelcards. What we felt instead was a feeling of relief. It became apparent that we were not going to be thrown back into the frying pan after all. The lump which had been stuck in my throat since the day before when I arrived in the country slowly began to ease and melt away.

The immigration lady explained to us how to get to the bed and breakfast. 'I will put you on the train from here and you will have to go up to London Victoria station. When you arrive at London Victoria, you may change either to the Victoria underground line, then to the Piccadilly Line, and get off at Hammersmith. Or you may take the District Line from Victoria up to Hammersmith, if you prefer.

'Whichever line you choose to travel on, take it up to Hammersmith station and then get off. When you come out of the station take the number 266 bus. It will take you near to where the bed and breakfast hostel is.

'Alternatively,' she said, 'you may take the Victoria Line and change to the Central Line, then go up to Shepherd's Bush station. When you arrive there, get out and take the number 207 bus. The number 207 bus will also take you up near to the bed and breakfast hostel where you are supposed to go and stay.'

The explanation given by the immigration lady was difficult to master. However, we listened to it all very carefully. Imagine all those details given to be mastered by the newly arrived asylum-seekers. People who haven't been in the country before. People who have not come under any normal circumstances and therefore are far from relaxed, people who may be thinking that they're being followed or who're filled with uncertainty about their future. We decided that the immigration lady must have taken it for granted that, because we were highly educated, we would experience no difficulties in finding our way through the meandering maze of the city to the bed and breakfast hostel in west London. But the maze to the bed and breakfast hostel was too complicated for us to follow. It was a very big challenge for us to undertake.

The immigration lady finished her briefing about the location of the bed and breakfast hostel and took us down to the trains. At the platform there was already a train waiting to leave in a few minutes' time.

The immigration lady saw us on to the train and then she wished us good luck. She waved goodbye to us for a few seconds, smiling, and then she went back to her office. When she left, I asked Frederick, 'Do you think we will make it?'

Frederick answered, 'I don't know. Anyway, we will try.'

We sat in the train for a few minutes waiting for it to leave. I closed my eyes and started to contrast the trains back at home in Uganda to the British train that we were currently sitting in.

When I'd heard the immigration lady talk to us about taking the train, I'd said to myself, 'By the train?' I thought I had said it to myself. But it seemed I'd said it aloud and the immigration lady heard me.

She answered, 'Yes. By the train. You will have to travel by the train.'

I must've looked downcast. But she reassured us that it was OK. She said, 'It is faster by train than by bus. It is the easiest and quickest means of transportation here in the UK.'

'Is it?' I asked.

'Oh yes, it is.'

I exclaimed at the idea of travelling by train because back at home in Uganda people hardly travel that way. I started to think of the hazards, the inconveniences and the difficulties that people who use the train there always face. Travelling by train in Uganda means travelling in the company of an assortment of livestock including cattle, goats, pigs and chickens—just to mention a few—and not forgetting a range of agricultural produce. So I thought that travelling by train here would also be full of such hazards. Fortunately it didn't seem to be the same case here in the British train.

The first impression was marvellous. The seats were smart. There was no overcrowding. There were no domestic livestock nor agricultural produce being ferried inside it alongside the passengers. The condition of the Gatwick Express train did not turn out to be as we had feared.

We quickly realized that we were in a new world, Great Britain. We were in a developed world, much more developed than our country, Uganda, which had been ravaged by brutal civil wars. It was inevitable for us to make such comparisons and contrasts. Without them it would have been difficult for us to understand the full meaning of development when people spoke of it. □

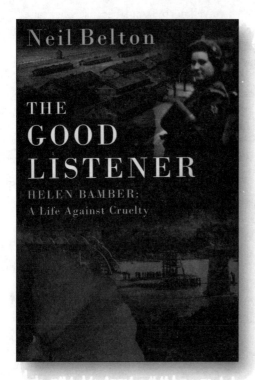

GRANTA

THE LAW OF
DIMINISHING RETURNS
Dale Peck

Someone told me they were more careful in England. He said they were more careful in Europe actually, because of all the wars. He said as a result of centuries of conflict they had less to spare over there, less to waste, and so, dutifully, but not, like the environmentalists in the States, piously, they collected their cans and plastic and paper, their dead batteries, bald tyres, and scrap metal and turned it all in for recycling, they built energy-efficient appliances, took shorter showers, swaddled their children in cloth rather than disposable diapers. On account of the wars? I remember asking. They bombed the *shit* out of that place, my informant told me. Trenches, he said. Mines. Mustard gas. It all had its effect, and they're still feeling it today. Blood, he said. Blood is a poison. On some battlefields it was years before anything would grow. He had said they were more careful in Europe but I had to settle, when I left, for England—the language thing—and I guess I just hoped that the English would follow the European example. I liked the idea of living among a careful people: I liked not just the idea of frugality but of return, of reuse, of, to put it bluntly, second chances, and it seemed at first that England, that London, where I settled, did offer that. Within a week I had a flat in a terrace house, in Bethnal Green admittedly, but it was cheap and clean, two large barren rooms with a view over my downstairs neighbour's vegetable garden, I had an umbrella, a Travelcard, an adaptor cable for my computer, a phone number even, and I had Derek. That's *my* name, I said, when he told me his. It wasn't actually, but I would have used the line no matter what his name had been. I was a new man in a new country and I had decided that a new name—not a new name, but a borrowed name, a recycled one—suited the occasion, if only for a night. Your name's Derek? he said, fancy that, and then he grinned and he said, Fancy a walk in the park, Derek? I thought he was joking, and brought him instead to my place—I'd gone, on a Sunday night, and on the advice of a gay guide I'd bought, to a loud little club just down Mile End Road—and in the morning I woke up with a large bruise on my tailbone, because I had blankets but no bed. No bed and no Derek: he'd slipped out in the middle of the night, leaving only the bruise and a note next to the phone. *I took the liberty of taking your number*, he wrote. *You're a sound sleeper.* He had, in fact, peeled

49

off the tiny piece of paper affixed to the phone which BT had provided me with, and thus he didn't just take my number, he deprived me of the ability to give it to anyone else, because I hadn't yet memorized it. I think that's how he got me. The sex had been great but it had also just been sex; it was the peculiar piracy of peeling off a sticky phone label and pocketing it, so odd, so determined in securing its goal, which led me to believe that Derek must have felt something more than mere lust for me. At that time I believed emotion flowed from motion, from action, that love was a feeling emanating from a certain routine—sex, shared meals, shopping for Christmas presents—and it seemed to me that Derek's little theft was the first step in such a routine. Now, as I look back on it, it seems to me that I was thinking about love as if it were some kind of by-product. Love is like trash: it's not something you hoard, it's merely something you don't waste, like heat, or water, or paper. Or words, for that matter, for what is more recycled than the language of love? The language of hate, perhaps, or the language of disinterest: *Let's be friends.* Which is what Derek said when he called a few days later. He said Let's be friends, shall we? and I assented innocuously, because I was trying to think of a way to ask him what number he'd just dialled. I never did, and as a result didn't know what my phone number was until my first bill came three weeks later, by which point Derek had called several more times, always during the day, and once or twice a week he stopped by on his way home from work. In the meantime I acquired a bed, a sofa, a table and two chairs, enough dishes to feed as many as four people at the same time, and my flat absorbed all of these new acquisitions and still somehow seemed empty, and so, as an exercise, I typed up every single thing in the flat that wasn't attached to it by nails or glue, starting with myself and ending with three loose paper clips I found in the bottom of my computer case, and the entire list, single-spaced, a single entry per line, stretched to seven pages, and I felt a little better then, and reminded myself how deceptive appearances can be. The list went with me on my first trip to the local recycling centre, but the pages I left there were just as quickly replaced by more from an office supply store I'd found which sold unbleached stock made from one-hundred-per-cent post-consumer waste. I had, as they say, gotten my break, and I was working on a screenplay, and also several treatments, and the amount of paper I went through was unconscionable. I wrote at home, all day, every day; the words barely trickled out of me but even so the pages seemed to flow from my printer, the spool of fax paper spewed forth a cataract of queries and comments and suggestions for cutting which seemed to require twice as much new material to fill the gap, and the stacks of paper I took regularly to the recycling centre were embarrassingly large. I'd been...what, not careful, not in the manner of Europeans, but concerned about waste since I was a child. People think I'm lying when I say that my earliest memory is of Jimmy Carter appearing on television during the OPEC crisis, but it's true. He sat, as I recall, in front of a fireplace in which burned a few small logs, and in a quiet drawl I still consider the very voice of reasonableness, if not reason itself, he urged Americans to turn their thermostats down to sixty-eight degrees. Put on a sweater, he said, pulling on the placket of the grey cardigan that, along with two destroyed helicopters and seven dead bodies in the middle of the Iranian desert, would become a symbol of his political folly. The cardigan might have been light blue actually, the number of bodies in the desert higher or lower than seven, but the one detail I've never forgotten is the temperature, sixty-eight, if only because it happened to be the year of my birth. Sixty-eight degrees and a sweater—not sixty-seven and thermal underwear, not sixty-nine and a T-shirt. Perhaps the only thing that bothered me about my flat in London was that the thermostat was scored in Celsius, and, several months into my stay, in my own sweater—and scarf sometimes, and open-fingered gloves—I still worried that I was wasting energy, that irretrievable kilowatts were pushing through the warped glass and wind-rattled frame of my living room's big bay window and evaporating into the grey grey *grey* winter sky that hung above London like a shroud, but all I did was buy a set of heavy curtains to help retain the heat. By then I was more worried about Derek, about, I should say, my relationship with him, which had taken on a pattern that seemed a little too familiar for comfort: the phone call from work, the quick fuck between five-thirty and six, the occasional drink at Benjy's, the club where we'd met, or some gay venue in Brixton or Islington or Shepherd's Bush—places, as my guidebook told me, distinctly not on the beaten gay track—and finally I just asked him if there was someone else. Not exactly, he said. Not exactly? I repeated. Well, he said, the truth is that there is someone. *You're* someone else. He didn't call for a week after that, but he did call eventually, and he said he had an extra ticket for a play on the South Bank, Friday, he said, eight sharp. Did I want to go? In the end I was early; he was late. I'd wanted to ask him how he came to possess an 'extra' ticket for a play, but immediately he said Derek's ill, meaning, I realized with a start, the someone measured against whom I was someone else. He grinned sardonically when he said it, and I wondered if he was on to my ruse, if he'd found something with my real name on it in my flat, or if he was merely perpetuating a ruse of his own, but before I could question him we were rushed into the theatre by the usher, just as the curtain lifted. Coffee? Derek said afterward, and I assented, picturing some dark firelit café where jazz would be playing softly, more West Village than West London, but it didn't matter, really, since what I got was one of the garishly bright antiseptic eateries at the theatre complex itself. One espresso later—served in an unbelievably over-designed demitasse made of bleached white paper complete with a glued-on handle whose wings folded open and shut like a butterfly's—and Derek said, I have to be off, and I started to protest but he said, My patient calls, and then he shook my hand with mock formality, winked, and told me to be a good boy and use the loo before I got on the tube. He nodded at a door behind me. Another espresso—the countergirl looked at me strangely when I presented my paper cup to be refilled, They're not free you know, she said, to which I replied, I *know*—and I headed for the door Derek had indicated. It led to a hallway which led to a long, narrow descending staircase which led in turn to another hallway, this one dim, dirty, and smelling of subterranean damp, at the end of which was a door marked Gentlemen. There was no Ladies to be seen. I went through the loudly protesting door, and then, three feet further on, another, just as loud, and found finally a small room containing three sinks and three stalls. No urinals. I almost turned around but by then I really did have to go, so I settled for a stall. What a waste, I thought, addressing Derek in my head, 5.0 litres per flush as the Armitage Shanks commode dutifully indicated in faint periwinkle stencil, all for a thin piddle that would hardly fill one of those ridiculously wasteful paper demitasses used upstairs, and almost at the same time as I noticed the hole chiselled into the wall next to the toilet roll dispenser I heard the delayed double whine of the outer doors, and I knew why Derek had sent me down here. The stalls were partitioned by what looked like granite, a brown stone mottled with black and white and flecked here and there with purple, their doors were oak and heavy—solid, I mean, not mere veneer—and brightly varnished, and they reached all the way to the floor; the toilet was, in fact, rather more grand than the poured concrete structure twenty or thirty feet overhead, a structure which just happened to be the pre-eminent theatrical venue in the country, by which I mean that it wasn't exactly the place one would expect to find a glory hole, let alone one so laboriously, even lovingly constructed: perfectly round, its edges invitingly soft, and placed at an appropriately average height. The door to the stall next to mine opened, shut, its lock clicked. For a moment I heard only the hum of fluorescent lights, then, distinctly, the sound of a zipper opening, but nothing else, no plash of liquid into the bowl, no jingle of coins and car keys as pants slid down thighs, and so, after a moment, I bent over and risked a peek through the hole. All I saw at first was another hole in the wall opposite mine, and then, almost on cue, into the circular frame stepped a pair of dark trousers from whose open fly protruded an erect uncircumcised penis. A brown hand was stroking the penis, which was a slightly darker brown, and when it seemed to me that my own silence had grown conspicuously long my neighbour also bent forward, and our eyes met. I could see just one—it was dark and bright—and a large nose, and a full-lipped mouth which smiled almost immediately, revealing the inevitability of tea-stained teeth. He stood up, and a moment later his penis poked through the hole in the granite partition, but before I could decide what to do with it, or about it, the entrance doors whined in warning and the penis was gone like a mouse retreating into its hole. Faint footsteps, then silence. Then the water began running in the sink and I knew instinctively that we were fine: who washes their hands before they use the toilet? Well, the British probably do, but I wasn't thinking that then. The water ran; the penis reappeared; for some reason the sound was the licence I needed, and without hesitating I took it, first in my hand and then in my mouth. The water continued to run. I closed my eyes against the kaleidoscopic spangles of the granite wall so close to my face. The thing in my mouth seemed to have no odour, no taste even: it simply felt. Warm. Living. Not even human really, just...alive. The granite was cold against my forehead when I let it rest there, and my urine in the bowl gave off a faint stink, making me wish I'd flushed. When the man twitched a bit, a warning or an invitation depending on your point of view, I moved aside; when he came his semen shot straight into the bowl and I couldn't quite suppress a chuckle; when, a moment later, I stepped out of the stall, unconsciously wiping my lips with the back of my hand, I saw a dainty little thing, tight pants, tight shirt, both black and shiny, crowned by a bleached-blond Caesar, standing at the sink where the water was still running down the drain at the rate of one gallon, one British gallon, per minute. I went right up to him and turned off the tap. That's very wasteful, I said, especially given the fact that we're in the middle of a drought. A moment later the man from the other stall joined us. He was Indian, about my age, more handsome than I would have expected from this sort of encounter, and taller than I'd realized; he must have had to bend his knees awkwardly to make it through the hole. As we walked out together the queen at the sink said, Greedy, greedy, greedy, in what I think was a Brummie accent, *Grey*-dy, *grey*-dy, *grey*-dy, and then he turned the water back on. My trick's name was Nigel. He carried a briefcase, wore a loosened tie; he was on his way home from an incredibly late day at the office, he said, and thought he'd check out the cottages on the South Bank before catching the tube at Embankment. My good luck, I said. It's usually busier, he said, but the play got bad notices. The play? I said, barely able to remember. You're American? he said. I assumed he'd noticed my accent, but instead he squeezed my shoulder. Americans are just so big, he said, all that conspicuous consumption, and then, before we'd made it up the long flight of stairs, he'd told me about a few other places, Russell Square, the second floor toilets at Harvey Nicks, Mile End Park on Sunday nights, but the place which caught my ear was the Stoke Newington cemetery. People have sex in a cemetery? I said. What else are you going to do there? Nigel said, and then he made me hold back for a minute so we weren't seen leaving together. He kissed me first, said he was sorry he hadn't returned the favour but the boyfriend was waiting at home, and then he grabbed my crotch. Damn, he said. What a waste. Upstaged then, by not one but two boyfriends, I made my way home. Mile End, as it happened, was the next tube stop past mine, and I decided to ride the extra distance to take a look at the thin spit of trees at the north end of the park across from the station, a tiny copse which, according to Nigel, held as many as two dozen men each Sunday after Benjy's let out. I wasn't looking for another trick, but between Derek and Nigel I felt all worked up and there wasn't anything in particular to rush home to, and it was only a little before midnight when I spilled out of the tube with a large loud number of kids on their way to Benjy's—straight kids, because Benjy's only catered to a gay crowd on Sundays, and then only surreptitiously—and I let myself ride their swell for half a dozen steps until I saw the trees across the street, low scrubby evergreens fleshing out the trunks of some kind of short deciduous with pale shiny bark. Skinny girls in tiny party frocks shivered in the cold October wind while boys with acne on their foreheads tossed their keys up in the air and looked around to see if anyone was watching, and measured against their camaraderie the little grove looked cold and inhospitable, but still, I decided to check it out. The nearest entrance to the park was on Burdett Road, past Benjy's and a busy chip shop and the back of a darkened dingy council block, and after I'd made it through all that—I was sure that everyone I passed knew exactly what I was up to, and walking through them felt like running a gauntlet—I had to walk back up to the trees across a lawn whose grass was so dry it broke audibly under my feet. The papers said it had been, literally, the driest summer in recorded history, and though fall had brought the relief of coolness the grey skies had not yet delivered any rain. Still, the drought had been some kind of vague comfort to me during my several months here. At first I thought it was simply because it reinforced my natural urge to conserve resources and ration them appropriately. Each evening as I washed my handful of dishes with a barely dampened sponge I watched the news on Channel 4 and felt joined with like-minded people all over

England. The lawns of Hyde Park browned like toast, black cabs withered beneath a never-washed patina of dust, and swimming pools—said to be in Oxfordshire, although I had a hard time imagining something as American as a swimming pool anywhere in England—filled at summer's start, were by now nothing more than puddles at the bottom of dirt-encrusted concrete holes, and, as I said, I felt a kinship with these people which had comforted me, or at least I thought it had. I would watch the news and give the taps an extra twist to make sure they were fully closed and imagine my downstairs neighbour doing exactly the same thing, but as I walked across the open lawn of Mile End Park I remembered that New York, like London now, had been in the midst of a drought when I'd moved there a decade earlier, and I realized that it was probably only memory which assuaged my loneliness, not recycled water but recycled thoughts, recycled habits: letting laundry accumulate, showering every other day, putting a brick in the toilet tank to save a quart of water—an American quart—with each flush. The moon was the single light in the night sky bright enough to push through the clouds, and I felt its beam focused on me as I crunched my way across the wide open lawn. When I was on the street the trees had seemed slightly sinister but now they cast friendly sheltering shadows, and as I got closer I could make out several gaps in the low evergreens. I headed for the nearest, pushed aside a few scaly branches, and suddenly found myself on a well-worn path. A mulch of last year's needles and leaves softened my footsteps, which only three or four paces further on brought me to a small oblong clearing, where, like socks on a laundry line, a row of more than a dozen condoms hung over a couple of thin branches. Or flags, I thought. The condoms hung there like a row of welcoming banners in front of a swanky hotel, although that night the clearing was without any guests. It was surprisingly bright though. The branches overhead did little more than filter the moon's glow, and plastic wrappers from condoms and candy glittered like something more precious than mere trash while patiently waiting out their millennia on earth. A flash on a tree trunk caught my eye: a shred of red cloth. I tried to imagine the man who had leaned up against this trunk and what had caused him to tear his shirt, perhaps a startled twitch as a pair of headlights shone through the leaves, or the inevitable shudder as he came, or perhaps the grove had simply held on to a piece of him when he walked away, unwilling to take the tryst as lightly as he had, as had the men who'd draped the condoms across its branches. A pair of voices disturbed me then, and, peering through the trees, I could make out a couple of stout men passing by on the sidewalk, which couldn't have been twenty feet away. Their blond crew-cuts reflected the moon like mirror balls—almost all the white men in this neighbourhood were blond and crew-cut, just as almost all their Asian neighbours wore their hair long, either beneath turbans or, on the younger men, in neatly dressed ponytails—and their East London accent was so pronounced I could hardly make out a word, but the tone was loud and boisterous, drunken but not particularly so, and I imagined they were making their way home from the pub to their wives, and as their voices faded away they were replaced by the memory of another disembodied voice, this one also loud, but angry, shouting actually, I was only taking a *piss*, is what the voice had shouted. Can't someone go and take a piss without you shutting the light off behind them? and I remembered shouting back, I piss in the dark all the time, even though the light I had shut off had been in the living room. Some people, I shouted, don't need to look at their dicks to make them work, and a moment later the voice and the body from which it emanated appeared in my door. Well, some of us should clean up the mess we make beside the toilet in the middle of the night, is what he said. I'm just trying to do my part, I said, to which he replied, This isn't a play. There are no parts, there isn't a script. There are only lights, which we leave on so we can see where we're *going*—and just then a car's headlights splintered the grove of trees, dancing a chorus line of skeletal shadows across the clearing where I stood, and I shook myself and pretended I was shivering. As a memory, it was simply a piece of trash, and, dutifully, I shoved it back in the bin and slammed the lid down on it. I pocketed the scrap of red cloth and headed for home, and when I got there I showered off the coating of dust I seemed to have acquired on my foray into the woods. I felt guilty that I couldn't bring myself to shower as someone told me they did in Germany—a quick spray, a lather with soap that congealed perceptibly as the water evaporated from one's body, and then a second splash to rinse. I'd tried it only once, on what seemed like a hot summer morning, and when I stepped out of the shower my teeth were chattering and my skin was slimy with soap scum, and as I towelled off I looked longingly at the spume of steam which, along with a falsetto caterwaul, rose up from my downstairs neighbour's bathroom window. That night I indulged myself, lingering in the shower for nearly ten minutes, but afterwards I turned the heat all the way down and wrapped myself in a comforter I'd bought when I'd bought my bed, and I said, out loud, defiantly, I *am* doing my part. In the morning I saw that Derek had called the night before, while I'd been in the park, and he came by later that afternoon to make it up to me. It's fucking freezing, he said when he arrived, and with a carelessness, an insouciance really, that I envied, he rotated the dial on the thermostat without even looking at it. By the time he left the sun had gone down and my flat was so hot my eyes watered in their sockets. I turned the thermostat down, blindly, as Derek had turned it up, but it wasn't until I woke up shivering that I realized my place was, once again, freezing cold, and empty, and life went on that way, it got even colder but still neither rain nor snow would fall. I saw Derek once a week on average, a quick meal usually, followed by a quick fuck, although sometimes he sneaked out on a weekend and we would go shopping, Oxford Street, Covent Garden and Soho, South Ken, and I blew hundreds of pounds on those occasions but it didn't really matter because in between days with Derek I was writing the most puerile sorts of advertising copy masking itself as cinematic entertainment, for which money was simply being *thrown* at me, and even at an unfavourable exchange rate I had cash to burn. And so it happened that I woke up one morning after Derek had been there the night before and saw that, Derek or no Derek, my flat was hardly empty. I looked around my bedroom, through the doors to the front room. There were things *every*where. Electronic equipment especially: television, VCR, stereo, computer, printer, fax, phone, the answering machine with its unblinking red eye. Stacks of books grew from the mantel up the chimney, flanked by a pair of candleless candlesticks I'd picked up in the market on Brick Lane, and in the grate itself was a chest I'd bought the same day to hold the British linens I'd bought to cover my British mattress, which, like British paper, was longer and skinnier than the American variety. I remembered then the list of my possessions which I'd made in my first week here, and draped in my comforter I made my way to my desk and sat in my chair and turned on my computer—so many things!—and tried to recreate it. I stopped after thirty pages. I hadn't looked in the closet yet, or pulled open a single drawer, but I didn't need to: it was clear I had somehow managed to stuff my flat as fat as a turkey on Thanksgiving, and I remembered then what Nigel had said about Americans and their conspicuous consumption. For the first time I wondered what would happen to all of my possessions when I left. I tripped on that for a moment, I wasn't sure why, until I realized it was the first time I'd acknowledged that just as surely as I'd come to London I'd leave it one day, I wasn't sure when and I wasn't sure why, but then I wasn't exactly sure why I'd come to London either. I'd thought I wanted to live unburdened by the things which had weighed me down in New York, but as I scrolled through the list on my computer—I couldn't bring myself to waste the paper it would take to print it out—it seemed to me that life was nothing more than a process of accumulation. The only thing you lost was time. But I refused to accept this conclusion, and I resolved, again, to divest myself of as much extraneous matter as possible, months of newspapers that had accumulated and needed to be recycled, the books I'd read, which I sold to a used bookstore for a few pounds, also a nested stack of electronics boxes that took up almost all the space in my closet. Why did I save this stuff, I asked myself as I snapped the boxes' styrofoam packing sleeves into tiny pieces, why did I think a minor act of conservation could repair the damage already perpetrated by the manufacturing process that had belched forth all this shit? Also in my closet were a couple of shirts that had come from New York with me, shirts that I'd rarely worn there and never worn here, and I decided that I would give them to the Salvation Army. The nearest one I could find was in Camden, which required a formidably complex tube journey, but I negotiated it successfully, and handed over the two shirts plus a couple more which I'd bought for Derek and which he'd said he couldn't accept, and a pair of pants he'd bought me which I liked but still shucked out of spite, and as I handed them over I told myself that I was becoming one of those faceless people who provide all the great finds that I'd been adept at sniffing out in my first years in New York. It was an image of myself I liked, and so the circuitous tube route between Bethnal Green and Camden became a regular sojourn for me. I only went when I had bought something, a jacket or a pair of pants or shoes, and all I did was weed out a similar older item to make room for the new thing, and I hadn't realized how frequent a visitor I was until one day when I went in armed with a single pair of green cotton chinos, and, because I felt silly going in to surrender one item, a white button-down shirt that I would have had to replace sooner or later, and the old woman whom I saw most regularly smiled at me and said Simon will be glad you've been in. Simon? I said, and the old woman beamed. He works at the weekend. He's just your size—he usually snatches up whatever you bring in before it makes it to the floor. Says you keep him in clothes, you do. Even shoes. I mumbled something incoherently then, I wasn't even sure what I'd meant my mumbling to sound like, and quickly left the store, but that weekend, after an early meeting with Derek, I found myself in front of the Salvation Army. There was the thinnest coat of frost on the ground—the weatherman tried to call it snow, but no one was fooled—and I'd worn sunglasses to protect my eyes from the glare. I kept them on when I went into the store, thinking they would serve as some sort of disguise, but when I realized that Simon would have no idea who I was I took them off quickly. There was no mistaking him though. The green and brown plaid shirt he wore had come from my closet, as well as the brown corduroy pants, and although I couldn't see Simon's feet I guessed he was wearing a pair of suede boots I'd dropped off on the same day I dropped off the plaid shirt and corduroys. Excuse me, I said then. I was in here earlier this week and I saw a pair of pants I liked. They were green. Canvas, no pleats. Simon looked up from the book he'd been reading. Sorry? Despite myself, I was surprised. He was young—I mean, much younger than I was—and a part of me had expected my own face to look at me from out of my own clothes. Green pants, I said quickly, stammering slightly. I saw them earlier— I don't work during the week, Simon interrupted me. Wouldn't know what was here, but I don't remember no green *pants* in, what was it, *canvas*? He stressed the two words slightly, and I wasn't sure if he was mocking the words or just the way I'd said them, but then he laughed lightly, waved an arm, said, We've got loads of polyester to choose from, and as he spoke he turned his book over and placed it open-faced on the counter, a college textbook, economics. He didn't even look like a younger version of me. His hair was floppy and brown and darkened by a tinge of grease, whereas my hair was crewed like the men in my neighbourhood. Derek had teased me when I first cut it off, asked me if I was trying to score with the skinheads down at the local, but then he'd grown serious and run his hand over my downy head and said, It suits you. It suits you, I guess, though I think you deserve the luxury of hair, but still, I continued to buzz it: I'd bought the clippers after all, and couldn't let them go to waste. I shook my head then, to clear it. I'm sure I saw them, I insisted. I even remember the size: thirty-two in the waist and inseam both. Simon's expression was puzzled and uncomfortable. He shrugged thin shoulders inside the green and brown plaid shirt. Maybe they sold. The collar of the shirt had darkened from the grease in his hair, and he pulled at it now, nervously, and I felt sweat filming my own neck, beneath my scarf. I placed my hands flat on the counter. Could you check in the back? Maybe they were taken off the rack for some reason. Look, Simon said, we don't take stuff off the floor unless we're holding it for— That's it! I said. I asked her to hold it for me. What's her name, the old woman. Trudy, Simon said. His voice was suddenly suspicious. That's right, Trudy. I could feel the sweat coursing down my neck now, wetting my shirt inside my winter coat. I could feel the redness of my face and the pounding of my heart. Trudy put it back for me, along with a white shirt. A button-down. Simon stared at me now, disbelief written plainly on his face. Trudy's holding a pair of green pants for you, and a white shirt? I just nodded my head then. I couldn't bring myself to speak, nor even to meet his gaze. My eyes caught the cracked spine of his textbook, saw a yellow sticker, itself creased into near illegibility: USED. Just a minute, I heard Simon say, and as he walked from the counter I watched for his feet. There were the boots. I felt a thrill up and down my spine when I saw them, and a knot in my stomach as well, and then Simon was back with the same brown bag in which I'd delivered the clothes. It was stapled closed now, and the word *Simon* was written on it in black magic marker, and the man who bore that name, and my clothes as well, dropped the bag on the counter. Here you go. I still couldn't look at him. I grabbed the bag and turned for the door, but Simon's voice stopped me. All right, hold on. I turned slowly. Yes? Simon's face and voice were flat when he spoke, but his knuckles were white where his hands gripped the counter's edge. That'll be a fiver, he said, and I said, I'm sorry? That's five for the pants, Simon said again. He paused. And five for the shirt. I thought of protesting, but didn't. What could I say: But they're mine? I thought of running out of the store then, even jerked a little toward the door, and Simon jerked when I jerked, not as if to follow, not even in imitation: it was as if his body was attached to mine by the threads woven into the clothes he wore. Slowly, I returned to the counter. I pulled two fives from my wallet and fingered them for a moment. They were fresh from a cash machine, crisp, sharp-edged. You could cut your finger on these, I thought. I thought, This is how much it costs. It wasn't very much, even if I was buying something that already belonged to me. I gave the boy called Simon the money. Brazen now, Simon put the money in the pocket of the corduroy pants. I looked at him a moment longer. They all fit you. Even the shoes. Something changed in Simon's face then. Disgust gave way momentarily to shame, and then, quickly, anger rose up again. Aw, go on, get out of here before I call a copper. His voice—young, high-pitched, almost cracking under the strain—wasn't convincing, but I nodded once and left. Outside it was cold and bright and I squinted against the glare until I remembered my sunglasses and covered my eyes. The bag with Simon's name on it dangled loosely in one hand, and as I walked toward the tube station I remembered something else Derek had said not so long ago, when I'd tried to tell him that my name wasn't actually Derek. I'd stuttered my way around the subject until, eventually, I realized that he'd figured it out long ago, and that he hadn't cared. What he'd said was that some things, like names, can be used over and over again—or bodies for that matter. But then he went on. He said, Some things *can't* be used twice. There are some things, he said, that are used up on the first go-round, and whatever's left behind, if anything, is just

pollution. There's no point in saving it, he said, or reusing it, it's just
left over, and as he spoke his hands were on my shoulders and he
was looking me straight in the eye and, although I knew it wasn't
his intention, I still felt as though he were telling me *I* was one of
those things that can only be used once. People like Derek, I thought,
people like Nigel, they were able to have boyfriends and still find the
time for tricks on the side, and trysts, whereas it was all I could
manage to be someone's someone else. They renewed themselves
endlessly, shed the days like skin cells and grew new ones without
even thinking about it, while all I could do was fade away slowly as
though I were simply semi-biodegradable packaging whose contents
had long since been consumed, and suddenly I felt the bag with
someone else's name on it hanging from my arm like a dead weight.
Why did you keep coming back then? is what I'd said to Derek—it
was what I had said in New York—and what Derek had said was I
never left, and the more I thought of his words the less I could make
of them. In New York it had been worse. In New York it had been:
I was never really here, and what can you say to that? I stopped
walking then; I'd gone far past the tube station; I looked around and
saw, in fact, that I had no idea where I was. But even the strangeness
was familiar from my first days here, it brought with it a familiar
elation and a familiar dejection, but I threw all these old feelings
away, and threw away my old clothes as well, dropped them in the
first bin I came across, and then I turned toward what I thought was
the east and set out on foot for my flat. I got lost, of course. Of course
I got lost: for London is laid out as haphazardly as a warren. It is a
myriad of Streets High and Low, of Courts and Cloisters and
Crescents and full Circles, Paths and Parks and Parkways, and Yards,
and Mews, and Quays, Palaces and Castles and Mansions and Halls
and mere Houses (never so mere in reality), and Drives (which sounds
creepingly American to my ears, and suburban at that), there are
Ways to go and Ends to be arrived at, Barrows and Buries—or would
it be Burys?—Moats to be crossed and Bridges to cross them, also
Brydges, which don't seem to cross anything, and Squares, which
rarely are, and all of this (and much, much more) is further
complicated by an unknown feud between lexicography and
cartography, so that what is here a Road becomes, a few feet farther

Dale Peck

on, a Terrace; a Vale might become a Walk or broaden suddenly into a Mall, Groves are treeless, Gardens without plants, Gates nowhere to be found. London is, in other words, a maze, but I was simply amazed, surprised that it had taken me so long to realize I was lost. But it was why I'd come here after all, to lose myself in a foreign place. That seems, now, just another way of saying that I wanted to throw myself away, and if I didn't actually succeed it's only because it's against my nature to litter. □

GRANTA

ZERO DEGREES
Anthony Bailey

A L O N D O N V I E W
The first of ten pieces in which writers
(and two painters) select a city view which
means something to them.

At the top of the escarpment, facing north, the General leans forward slightly. One corner of his tricorne hat is to the front, the folds of his bronze cloak deep-furrowed, his nose prominent, the deeply receding chin not at all a manifestation of wimpishness; his gaze is fixed on the glittering skyscraper two miles away named, appropriately, Canada Square. James Wolfe used to come to this spot when he lived for several years during the 1750s at Macartney House, four minutes' walk from here on the western edge of Greenwich Park. The day before he embarked for Canada in 1759 to assume command (at the age of thirty-two) of British forces there, he went up from

Macartney House to dine with the Prime Minister, Pitt the Elder, and some of his ministers. Wolfe flourished his sword, striking the dining table, while discussing his plans. When he had left, Pitt said, 'Good God, that I should have entrusted the fate of our country to such hands.' Wolfe was never again to see what he called 'the prettiest situated house in England', nor the distant prospect of London from Flamsteed Hill. But Pitt's concern had been misplaced. Wolfe died not long after in Quebec, ensuring that North America would be British, not French. The statue was given by the Canadian people in 1930, and chivalrously unveiled by the Marquis de Montcalm, descendant of the French general Wolfe defeated. Wolfe is buried in St Alfege's, the Nicholas Hawksmoor parish church whose white bell-tower can be seen from up here. The plinth of his statue is pockmarked by shrapnel from a German landmine that exploded on this hilltop during the Second World War.

I have lived in Greenwich for twenty-seven years and walk here three or four times a week. The prospect from the hill is best seen in winter, early on spring or autumn mornings, or during a long summer twilight. The tourists and French schoolchildren and lads kicking footballs have mostly gone home. Scanning from north-north-west to just north of east, I'm presented with foreground, middleground and distant views. In the first, to my immediate left are the handsome yet homely red-brick and stone buildings of the old Royal Observatory, hiding the slopes toward Crooms Hill on the western edge of the Park. Then the slim brick tower of the 1930s town hall (Pevsner-approved, unloved by most), St Alf's, the topmasts and yardarms of the *Cutty Sark* (in permanent dry dock), the buildings of the Maritime Museum and what we still call the Naval College, council flats, the four immense chimneys of the power station (like an upturned billiard table) that used to provide electricity for London's trams and eventually back-up power for the underground, a sea of nineteenth-century houses and twentieth-century flats in East Greenwich, and then the green promontory of One-Tree Hill, our hill's eastern neighbour in the Park, with the early eighteenth-century battlements of Vanbrugh Castle on the skyline. In the middle distance—also left to right—Deptford's tower blocks and ro-ro ferry wharf with a slab-sided newsprint freighter alongside (paper for the *Sun* and *The Times*); snatches of Thames between and beyond buildings, Canary Wharf and the last decade's office-developments in Docklands; and next, on the old gasworks site with the gasometer still standing, our most recent object to focus on, the Dome, a stranded mammoth jellyfish skewered by twelve pylons. In the hazier distance, the City of London: Tower Bridge, NatWest Building, St Paul's (still the dome to conjure with); and, swinging east, the ridge of Highgate, Hackney Marshes, the Lea Valley, Barking, Dagenham... Looked at like this what I see isn't obviously a great city though it is manifestly a great urban sprawl, which seems to lap at the borders of this hill. The viewpoint shapes it as a panorama. Possibly, it is also a series of portraits taken over time.

Over the last quarter of a century in which I've stood up here, changes: fewer ships on the river, less use of the docks opposite, fewer funnels and superstructures passing in front of the Naval College; no sirens now to be heard blaring-in the New Year, although the occasional warship goes up to the Pool, a cruise liner now and then moors to the big buoys just west of Greenwich Pier, and the sludge boats continue to haul London's waste downstream. 'Docklands' has absorbed Fleet Street. Movers of money have replaced cargo-handlers. Mr Pelle's pencil, as a friend of mine calls it—an off-the-shelf skyscraper supposedly designed for Düsseldorf—has gone up on the Isle of Dogs, where Henry VIII may have kennelled his hounds, though the effect hasn't been as disastrous for Greenwich as pundits feared. From here, the building's huge blandness is less apparent. I'm more aware of it as providing a point of concentration in the middle distance, and with the western sun on it in late afternoon it looks like a pillar of fire.

Fewer ships but more planes. Greenwich is a pivot on which they turn for the westward descent to Heathrow. As the squealing 747s and Airbuses slip into and out of low cloud, their passengers—nervously gripping the arms of their seats—look down on us, and then on Battersea, Barnes, Hounslow, the ground, thank God. At a lower altitude, with the wind in the east, the quieter, smaller jets and turboprops line up for the runway at the City Airport, on the other side of the river beyond the Dome. I come from a generation which still, fifty-odd years on, looks up and once in a while thinks, 'Good, one of ours.' My NatWest branch, opposite St Alfege's, used to display a photograph whose original was taken from a German bomber crossing the U-bend of the river, about to blitz the docks. In the autumn of 1940 and the following winter many bombs fell on Greenwich as the Heinkels, Dorniers, Messerschmitts and Junkers flew towards the docks and the City. The Naval College was hit and the Greenwich Power Station (thirteen killed on 25 October 1940) and the Azimuth Building of the Observatory up here. In the big raid of 19–20 March 1941, St Alfege's roof was destroyed, and the church with its Grinling Gibbons carvings gutted. Bill Mullins, the milkman whose shop was opposite the town hall, served as an ARP warden and used to tell of nights when he brushed incendiaries from the town hall roof. Later in the war V1 rockets, the so-called doodlebugs, cut out over the park and landed in Crooms Hill, Burney Street, Stockwell Street and Greenwich Church Street, making space for post-war dereliction, in the form of long-lasting bomb-sites and spiritless new building.

From this vantage point, it is hard not to look back in time. I look down on what was a Celtic fishing village and a Roman resort. Early in the eleventh century longships tied up on the foreshore. In Anglo-Saxon, Greenwich meant green port or green bay. The Danish raiders captured Alfege, the Archbishop of Canterbury, and when he refused to be ransomed pelted him to death with ox bones—they ate the meat first. Despite this incident, the Anglo-Norman crown liked Greenwich. Edward I stayed here. Humphrey, Duke of Gloucester, youngest brother of Henry V, built a mansion named Bella Court beside the river and a watchtower where the Observatory stands. In 1433 Humphrey enclosed 200 acres as a park. Henry VII took over Bella Court and renamed it Placentia, the pleasant place. Henry VIII was born here in 1491 and so were his daughters, the half-sisters Mary and Elizabeth. Henry turned Duke Humphrey's little castle on the hill into a double-towered and battlemented residence four storeys high. A salvo was fired from the castle in 1540 to welcome Anne of Cleves, when Henry brought her—wife number four—from

Blackheath through the park and down the hill to his palace. The castle came in handy for overflow guests and girlfriends. It figured in Puttenham's *Arte of English Poesie* (1589), where a voyage is described that Henry made in his royal barge from Westminster to Greenwich to have a tryst with a lady lodged here. When he saw the castle on the hilltop, Henry challenged his standard bearer, Sir Andrew Flamock, to a rhyming contest about the place and its fair occupant. With royal privilege the king began: 'Within this towre/There lieth a flowre/That hath my hart...' And Flamock continued: 'Within this houre/She will...' But Henry—at least according to Puttenham—broke in to order Flamock to desist, since he was going on 'in such uncleanly terms'.

Henry made love in Greenwich, jousted here, went hawking and deer-hunting in the park, and signed the death warrant here of Anne Boleyn, Elizabeth's mother. She was spotted at a May Day tournament, signalling with her hankie to a lover. Heads rolled.

The pleasant place was away from plaguey London, and the Stuarts went on favouring it. When Placentia fell into disrepair, a site for a new house was chosen halfway between the foreshore and the foot of the hill. The Queen's House, begun for James I's wife Anne of Denmark, is still the immediate foreground feature. A rectangular Palladian wedding cake by the masque-composer, stage designer and architect Inigo Jones, it holds its own to this day despite the grand structures that have grown up on three sides of it. It was the crucial feature of a plan got up after the Stuart Restoration in 1660. Hiring the best talent, Charles II put John Webb and Christopher Wren to work; they paced the ground and took in the view and designed both a new palace to replace Placentia and a new building, an observatory, where the ruins of Greenwich Castle stood. The King also contracted André Le Nôtre, Louis XIV's landscape architect, to lay out the park. Le Nôtre evidently did this without leaving France, for his formal tree-lined avenues, converging on the Queen's House, failed to take account of the hill. Sir William Boreman, Charles's park keeper and man on the spot, planted elms and chestnuts and made twelve terraces or giant steps, forty yards wide, on the face of the hill, to fill the void in Le Nôtre's plan.

The observatory and dwelling house on the hilltop for the first astronomer royal, the Reverend John Flamsteed, rose quickly after 1675. Charles II coughed up £500, acquired from the sale of old gunpowder; the foundations of the Tudor castle were reused and some of the bricks came from the ruins of Tilbury Fort. The result—in Wren's words, 'for the Observator's habitation and a little for Pompe'—was one of the most accessible and enchanting of Wren's creations. Its tall main room is octagonal with high windows that let the astronomer tilt his telescopes at the night sky. However, Flamsteed despite his rheumatism often preferred to descend a spiral staircase one hundred feet into a sort of dry well dug into the hill, where he lay on a mattress looking up at the heavens. Flamsteed was notoriously irascible and argued with Isaac Newton. But on a salary of ninety pounds a year he had to provide his own instruments and find time to teach two boys from Christ's Hospital school while making thousands of measurements to determine the motions of the moon and the positions of the stars, and work out that the earth, so he thought, rotated at a constant speed. Precision was what the scientists were after. Flamsteed's calculations, and the consequent nautical almanacs, together with Harrison's clock, helped make it possible for ships to reckon accurately their positions at sea. Since 1833 a red ball has been hoisted up a pole at the Observatory and dropped exactly at one p.m., so that vessels in the docks and on the river could set their chronometers before departing. Since 1852 a clock here has displayed Greenwich Mean Time. In 1850 a zero degrees meridian was drawn through this spot, thirty yards to the left of General Wolfe, from which longitude is measured east and west, with a brass strip on the cobbled courtyard and across the pathway that runs along the north side of the Observatory. This, marking the world's prime meridian since an international agreement in 1884, furnishes a free opportunity for people to be photographed standing with a foot in each hemisphere.

Next to the Observatory gate is a large twenty-four-hour (in Roman numerals) 'Galvano Magnetic' clock, which bemuses tourists. One such, attempting to set his watch by it a few years ago, was advised by a guard that the clock was a minute slow, since the BBC had been here filming the day before and blown all the fuses. In fact, for some time Mean Time has been calculated by clocks working from the decay of atoms, accurate to one-millionth of a second. Moreover, after Flamsteed decided that the earth rotated at a constant speed, scientists who followed him discovered that it doesn't. Judged by an atomic clock the earth rotates more and more slowly, not with absolute regularity, but taking about an extra three-thousandths of a second each day to get turned around. And so, once in a while, a leap second is introduced in the BBC time-signal, and instead of hearing five short pips preceding a longer one, the listener hears six short pips—and does he notice? The astronomers have long left smoky London for in turn Sussex, Cambridge, Scotland and Hawaii. But the old observatory still sits among the trees on Flamsteed's Hill, looking from below not so much like the home of modern science as like the magician's castle in *Rupert Bear*.

Standing here on the heights of Greenwich, I always feel improved. Maybe it helps that time seems to be going more slowly; our lives are a bit longer every day. Perhaps the quick climb today up the fairly steep north slope has had a therapeutic effect. Taking deep breaths, I admire the view. There are the consolations of the ordered landscape and the buildings below, the English Versailles: Royal Palace, Seamen's Hospital, Naval College, University. Sir John Vanbrugh followed in Inigo Jones's steps as stageman and designer at the Palace-Hospital, and in Christopher Wren's as Architect-in-charge. Castle Howard and Blenheim are Vanbrugh's chief and hefty monuments, but visible from Wolfe's statue, across the southern flank of One-Tree Hill, is the castellated house he lived in for most of his married life. It stands on Maze Hill, the road running up the eastern side of the park. Now called Vanbrugh Castle, it was earlier known as Bastille House, the once-army captain Vanbrugh having been locked up in the Paris prison in 1692 on espionage charges. This gave him time to write the first draft of his play *The Provok'd Wife*.

The provoked wife who here comes to mind is our friend Beryl Knott, formerly a nurse, wife of Alfie Knott, a skilled amateur actor and one-time English teacher at the Roan School, along Maze Hill to the south. The Knotts lived further down the hill, a few doors from a British army major who had served in Northern Ireland. One afternoon, Alfie was in his kitchen about to make a sandwich when the garden window blew in with a crash and Alfie found himself on the floor, blood everywhere. The IRA had taken him for his military neighbour. Fortunately a Knott son was at home; a doctor lived nearby. Alfie, with a bullet in his back, was speeded to intensive care and the nurse who greeted him was Beryl. She said furiously, 'Alfie, what the blazes have you been doing?' before helping to administer the life-saving treatment to a non-explanatory Alfie. I sometimes meet the Knotts in the Park and feel cheered.

The Park was opened to the people in the eighteenth century. Among those who took advantage of this was Defoe, who made Greenwich figure at the start of his country-wide tour, 'the most delightful spot of ground in Great Britain...the best air, the best prospect...' A decade or so later Samuel Johnson lodged in Church Street and composed parts of his verse play *Irene* while walking in the Park. But when Garrick eventually staged *Irene* at Drury Lane it ran for only nine nights. Although Johnson gave up drama thereafter, he came back to Greenwich's 'consecrated earth' on occasion to walk in the Park. 'Is it not fine?' he asked Boswell on one such trip. Boswell, sucking up, replied, 'Yes, sir, but not equal to Fleet Street.' The doctor agreed. I like the idea that the great man once put his natural gravitas aside and let gravity carry him down this hill, rolling, with hands clasped above his head, feet together, over and over.

'Tumbling' on Flamsteed Hill became the eighteenth and early nineteenth century sport, as on hilly paths in the Park skateboarding and rollerblading have become those of the late twentieth, despite prohibitions. Greenwich Fair, generally at Easter or Whitsun, brought Londoners to the Park for the stalls, sideshows, and boisterous exercise. 'After the public houses,' Dickens wrote in *Sketches by Boz*, 'the chief place of resort is the Park, in which the principal amusement is to drag young ladies up the steep hill which leads to the observatory, and then drag them down again, at the very top of their speed, greatly to the derangement of their curls and bonnet-caps, and much to the edification of the lookers-on from below... Love-sick swains...become violently affectionate; and the fair objects of their regard enhance the value of stolen kisses by a vast deal of struggling...and cries of "Oh! Ha'done, then, George!"' Tumbling could be dangerous; the worn-away giant steps made the descent irregular as well as steep. Not only were undergarments exposed but bones broken in collisions with trees, and one girl died of a broken neck.

Two artists came here as the eighteenth century ended, both with major projects. The sculptor John Flaxman had in mind a giant Britannia, to stand on the hilltop as a monument to British naval victories over the French. It was to be, he noted on his proposed design, a 'C'lossal statue 230 feet high with an inscription on the plinth "Britannia by Divine Providence Triumphant"'. Fortunately this monster woman, fit denizen for the new Dome, was never erected. Flaxman's Royal Academy colleague J. M. W. Turner walked through the Park sketching but the viewpoint he chose for his lovely oil painting, *London from Greenwich*, now in the Tate, shows the Park, the deer, and the prospect of the city from One-Tree Hill just to the east. The Turner suggests that what Cobbett called the Great Wen is growing: trains and trams are about to happen; the spaces between the city and the old riverside villages are about to be filled in.

A century on, two writers, well acquainted, separately brooded here. One had birds in mind, the other bombs. W. H. Hudson—a very tall, lean man who (according to Ford Madox Ford) described himself as 'a naturalist from La Plata… [and] not one of you damned writers'—thought Greenwich Park seemed larger than it was because of its 'hilly broken surface'. But it made him melancholy, as he recalled 'the royal wife-killing ruffian and tyrant', and he was depressed by all the 'old, lopped and pollarded trees'. Birds needed more branches. Hudson's friend Joseph Conrad had been talking to Ford about anarchism, and an alleged attempt in 1894 to blow up the Observatory was mentioned. Conrad read the ten-year-old newspapers. He came to the Park and stood on the hill.

On Thursday, 15 February 1894, at four-thirty p.m., a short twenty-six-year-old man, wearing a brown felt hat and brown overcoat, climbed the zigzag path towards the Observatory. He was carrying a brick-sized package wrapped in brown paper. He was about halfway up the hill, roughly forty yards from the Observatory wall, when he tripped, perhaps on a tree root that broke the surface of the path. There was a flash like lightning, a loud bang, and brown smoke rose through the trees. Two boys going home from the Roan School across the Park—as Roan students still do—ran towards the sound. They found the man kneeling, doubled-up, bleeding, and thought he had shot himself. They were joined by several park keepers. They moved the man, scarcely breathing, on to his back. His left hand had gone at the wrist. His trousers were torn and some of his insides were exposed. Glass from a bottle lay on the ground amid several pools of blood; pieces of skin and tendon hung from the path railing. Dr William Willis, who lived in Crooms Hill, was sent for, and so was brandy from the Observatory. Dr Willis dispatched a keeper to the Seamen's Hospital for a stretcher and forced some brandy through the lips of the injured man. The latter said only, 'Take me home.'

He was taken to the Seamen's Hospital and died half an hour later. From papers on him he was found to be Martial Bourdin, an out-of-work French tailor, who lived at 30 Fitzroy Street, London W. Also in his pockets were a British Museum reader's request slip, a membership card of an anarchist organization called the Autonomie Club, a tram ticket, and quite a lot of money: twelve pounds in gold, one pound in silver. It was a time when anarchist 'outrages' were frequent in France and Britain. The newspapers and the police were soon suggesting that Bourdin intended to throw his bomb at the Observatory, a symbol of the powers that be, but others preferred a different scenario. Possibly Bourdin didn't know the package was explosive. Possibly he was on his way to Paris and had gone to Greenwich Park to shake off a police tail. The police certainly acted without urgency. It was a day before they raided the Autonomie Club and took names and addresses; no charges were brought. One group of anarchists insinuated that Bourdin's bomb had been supplied by H. B. Samuels, Bourdin's brother-in-law and editor of the anarchist paper *Commonweal*; a noisy proponent of direct action, he was said by some to be an agent provocateur paid by the police. Bourdin had been observed with another man in Whitehall before he took the tram to Greenwich. Samuels admitted to being this man. Later he was said to have admitted supplying Bourdin with the makings of the bomb. Bourdin, it was claimed in one story, had been on his way to Epping Forest to experiment with the bomb and Samuels had redirected him to a more significant target. Others said that Bourdin had been set up and believed that he was on his way to a rendezvous on Blackheath. Whatever, Samuels was never charged.

When Conrad turned Bourdin's tale into that of Stevie—an unwitting, even witless dupe—the brother-in-law of Adolph Verloc, in *The Secret Agent*, he moved his characters to Greenwich by train. He also moved the incident to 'a foggy morning', and he had poor warm-hearted Stevie blown to pieces. But he preserved the ambiguity of the circumstances—with the anarchists at the mercy of larger forces—and he left the exact cause of the calamity obscure, as it was in Bourdin's case, though Chief Inspector Heat in *The Secret Agent* says, of Stevie, 'We believe he stumbled against the root of a tree.' Stumbling, as well as tumbling, could be fatally dangerous on Flamsteed Hill.

Whether because of the General's presence close at hand or the continuing echoes of explosions, I sometimes find myself up here thinking in military terms. Hilltops are what they tell you to seize, in war games. Time was, not long ago, when the Chinese embassy had a residential annex beyond Vanbrugh Castle and the inmates were let out for periods of mass exercise. They would come across the hilltop in line abreast, lacking only rifles for a convincing show of infantry-in-attack. I felt tempted to fall flat and call up artillery support. But ordinarily my encounters are with tourists asking me to use their cameras to photograph them against the famous backdrop; or Greenwich neighbours, out for a walk, pausing to chat. 'Don't you have Daisy any more?' asks one I haven't seen for a while. Daisy, who had a good life (for a springer spaniel) of fifteen years, used to chase the squirrels on this hill and was uninterested in the view. But no, we don't. Time, that bloody tyrant, passes. The second hand of the Galvano Magnetic clock clicks round. Flamsteed's successors now keep an eye on receding galaxies; our minds reel with light-year immensities. It is important to focus on the nearer at hand: the cars moving along the lower road; the area of flat ground this side of the Queen's House, where fat Henry jousted and cabbages were grown on Victory allotments during the Second World War; the young ash tree my sister and I planted a few years ago in memory of our mother, not far from where the uphill path commences. Nearer still, James Wolfe, his dust in St Alfege's crypt, looks over my shoulder.   □

GRANTA

A LIFE IN CLOTHES

CLOTHES

Ruth Gershon

Ruth Gershon circa 1954

The children of ruling families are born in the purple. Those of Vaudevillians are born in a trunk. But families in the rag trade, what are we? Born in rags suggests merely poverty. Born in garments sounds clinically implausible. Growing up in north-west London, In Schmatters was the term I heard most often.

Most of my relatives were In Schmatters. Papa, my grandfather, owned a workshop, inherited by my father, his eldest son. By the time I was born, at the end of the war, it was in Charlotte Street; a few years later, it migrated to Soho. It provided employment for my father, an uncle, and an aunt, and was the substance of Papa's headship of a large immigrant cousinage in London. Most of my family's friends and neighbours were In Schmatters, too. Just one or two may have been In Furs (winter suits sometimes needed trimmings). My mother's sister married a bespoke men's tailor, my brother's father-in-law was In Coats, my best friends' fathers were respectively In Hats and In Zips.

These trades have a particularly important defining characteristic, which I want you to take seriously. There are many commodities in whose production and distribution a businessman can take satisfaction, but clothes are a special case. No matter how commonplace, how routine their presence in a working life becomes, they retain their capacity to evoke aesthetic pleasure and to inspire pride in workmanship. Despite their literal superficiality, they are fundamentals of our daily existence, our goings-out and our comings-in. And what might seem at first sight a feminized undertaking, unlikely to underpin the authority of the paterfamilias, turns out quite otherwise.

A man In Schmatters did not just provide for his family; he literally clothed them. He brought home garments from his own factory, and from those of his friends. He moved in, was indeed sovereign over, female as well as male worlds. He, rather than his wife, knew what was seemly and suitable, what was conventional and what was Selling Well; he knew what was run of the mill and what was a cut above. You did not wear run of the mill. Even when Business Was Terrible, even when things were *In dr'Erd* (buried), your clothes were at the model end of the trade. Daddy could always do that much for you.

Standards of dress were the common coin of conversation. It was not merely a question of compliments or (*sotto voce*) expressions of bewilderment, mockery, regret or surprise. As children In Schmatters, we could expect our appearance to be commented on in ways that might not be thought normal in other circles. We were advertisements for our parents in more ways than one.

'That's nice dear, very nice. Turn around and let me see the back. Is it one of Daddy's?'

Never shall I forget the disbelieving guffaws when, complimented at Oxford on my 'Mondrian' mini-dress, I guilelessly replied, 'Thank you. It's one of my uncle's.'

It was not Mummy, but Daddy who bought me my first lipstick and eyeshadow and nylon stockings. He brought them all back from a business trip to Paris when I was about thirteen. (I had begun to beg for stockings, but not the other things, as all my friends were coming out of socks at the weekends. 'Don't listen to her,' said my older brothers. 'We never had them, did we?') The stockings were nothing less than Christian Dior, thirteen denier, a beautiful shiny mushroom colour, and as much part of a fairy world as a bridesmaid's dress. The lipstick was a suitable and very fashionable pale pink. The eyeshadow was made up of interlocking sparkling pastel blocks in pink, green, blue, grey and mauve.

Did he choose my mother's make-up for her, too, and her perfume? Today, one or two friends express surprise that at the age of eighteen I still received my clothes from my father, shopped only for shoes and accessories on my own account. I explain that we were in the trade, we were short of money, I was sample size; but of course that is not the whole story. And perhaps the whole story is encapsulated in the memory of the only time I ever refused a garment, a pale blue jersey-knit (possibly made up in crimplene) two-piece. There was something visibly wrong with the revers of the jacket. You couldn't possibly have gone out in it. As I recall the anger, disappointment, indeed near-hysteria of my father's reaction, I realize that this was one of the many occasions on which I shortened his life.

Yes, of course he chose my mother's clothes. I turn to the collection of wedding photographs and there, in the set for Janet's wedding, is Mummy in a devastatingly glamorous cream brocade strapless ankle-length sheath. The photograph is in black and white, but I know that the long gloves are a soft emerald-green suede (I've still got them) and that the drape across one shoulder is a strip of velvet in the same colour.

My mother's face is—well, it's not smiling. It is not that she looks wistful, or absent; her expression is more one of discontent. She looks imposed upon, and only half resigned; she is powered by a kind of passive resistance—to the camera? to the photographer (my father)? Surely not to the costume. We talked about that once, and she said, 'I wanted lamé, but your father insisted on brocade.'

Daddy was for a long time a keen photographer who developed his own film. If he had wanted a smiling model, he would surely have asked for one. Did he ask, and she refuse? No, he must have seen in my mother's bearing an approximation of the haughty disdain affected by mannequins at the very top of the trade: women who had to be, literally, models for the aristocracy, to impersonate them on catwalks, in showrooms and in glossy magazine images, without betraying the reality of changing in cramped back rooms in Great Titchfield Street, and submitting to the touch and scrutiny of designers, manufacturers, customers. With stern, abstracted faces, chins and noses in the air, they pretended to own themselves and the clothes they stood in.

My mother's wardrobe, even when the furs and the jewellery had had to be sold, was never less than elegant, and there were always flashes of gorgeousness—silk blouses, a patterned jacket lining—gleaming on hangers between the darker suits and skirts. But I cannot recall seeing her eyes sparkle at the sight of a particular colour, or her fingers reach out to squeeze a piece of fabric the way my aunts and uncles reached out to pinch our cheeks. When we asked her, she said her favourite colour was green, but she rarely wore it. She seemed to take little pleasure in her appearance beyond the satisfaction of not having got it wrong. She dressed with a frown, as if carrying out a duty, almost as if the accoutrements of womanhood were a form of punishment. All this changed dramatically after she was widowed.

As I entered young womanhood I became, allegedly, 'sample

size'. I put away childish clothes and put on factory samples, often of considerable opulence. I remember swaggering around Hendon Central in a copy of a 1961 Cardin suit in a brilliant blue-and-black tweed with a fur collar; going to the sixth form dance at South Hampstead in an A-line dress in an olive-green plaid wool with a stiffened skirt; preening myself in draughty synagogue halls in a brown dress in a kind of mohair which softened and blurred the large checks of the pattern. Many of these clothes did not suit me and none of them fitted. Perhaps they would not have fitted anyone: the skirts were always a bit clumsy and long, the tops a bit too bloused. Did I realize this? Did I think that perhaps I had not stopped growing; that one day I would, and indeed should be the same size as other people; my mother for example? I could see that these were Very Nice Clothes, Very Good Material, and I felt quite privileged to be wearing them. I must, at some level, have believed that it was me, and not the garment, that was in the wrong.

I was eighteen when Daddy had his heart attack. A few months later I packed my bags, and my samples, for Oxford. Stocks were subsequently replenished from my uncle's factory and there were cast-offs from my new sisters-in-law. In my loss and anger it is easy to forget that the sage-green winter coat was made up from a pattern of my own choosing, and that Daddy had sewn the lapels himself by hand; that he made the painting smock and the costume for the title role in the school play in next to no time when I needed them. There were clothes, made with love, just for me, that fitted perfectly.

Mazeltov

Everyone got married. It happened by magic, but it happened to everyone. First you got engaged, and an announcement was printed in the *Jewish Chronicle* and possibly in *The Times* as well. The girl was given a ring with a diamond on it. A person who had been one alone was now in a couple, and did the circuit of relatives in a different way. Eventually there was a wedding. The preparations, absorbing huge amounts of energy and demanding great powers of financial, social and aesthetic generalship, took months to complete. Afterwards, everything that happened at the wedding was talked about in the minutest detail, at home, in *shul*, and sometimes in the shops, too, for what seemed like years.

My mother knew all about it. She spoke about dressmakers' prices; into this sacred female space the factory did not intrude. Of course, nobody bought a wedding dress off a rail in a shop. I heard about headdresses, trains, bouquets, shoes, fabrics. I learned that velvet did not make up well, and that it was a waste of time trying to design something that could be worn later, with minor adaptations, as an ordinary evening dress. (A wedding dress is what it is, and not some other thing.) I heard about West End caterers, and about halls and hotels for receptions. Keeping my head down, I heard about misbehaviour, imagined slights, family feuds, people not speaking to each other.

My father was one of four siblings and my mother one of six; with nine cousins older than myself I had plenty of opportunities to rehearse these protocols. Even when no relatives were marrying there were other weddings offering lower levels of participation: going to the synagogue ceremony, if not actually to the reception; going to the house before the bride set off for the synagogue, if not to the ceremony itself; as if you had to keep touching the magic to keep it in existence, so that one day it would rub off on you.

There were also bar mitzvahs, and there were other occasions for which you dressed up: Masonic dos, and dances and banquets held to raise funds for charities. But there was nothing like a wedding. This was the pinnacle, the height of glory, the moment when every family made its mark upon the world. This is how we do things, this is our idea of good food, of fine clothes. This is how we enjoy ourselves. This is how we scatter largesse.

Everyone got married.

Of course, not everyone was *still* married. You knew some war widows, and life was tough for them, as they had to go out to work. Then there were the very old ladies whose husbands had died, like Nana, or Mrs Cornfeld in the house opposite who taught me Hebrew, or Mrs Simmons further down the road whom I accompanied to synagogue, making that obligatory sabbath walk, the mile up Station Road to the Burroughs and on to Raleigh Close, whatever the weather. And it was even possible for things to go wrong. You might marry too young, like Sharon Levy, who lived next door to Mrs Simmons. Sharon was only seventeen and headstrong, and ended up getting divorced. Or you might still be walking home from synagogue with your parents when you were nearer thirty than twenty, like Rosalind Meyer, the doctor's daughter, and that was not good either.

Rosalind's best friend Stephanie Leigh married out. Her parents sat *shiva* for her as if she had died. Rosalind did get married eventually. At another wedding, nearly thirty years later, she told me that when she was at college she joined the drama club and was cast as Juliet. Romeo was Indian, the handsomest man she had ever seen. She knew that she could not possibly play opposite him without falling in love. So she gave up the part, and left the club. Of such experiences I, a little girl, did not even dream.

Because so many of my cousins were so much older than me, when it was time for them to get married, it was time for me, too, to have a beautiful dress and shoes, to have my hair done specially, to carry a posy, to be given a present. I, too, went for dressmakers' fittings, heard debates about the relative merits of round and square necklines, saw colour schemes put together with meticulous care. I knew that the costuming of me and my fellow bridesmaids was as important as that of the bride.

I don't remember feeling particularly excited beforehand, nor any shyness or embarrassment during the day itself. The pageant was, literally, normal. Wearing wonderful clothes, posing in front of the congregation and the camera, was something you just did from time to time. This does not mean that I took the clothes for granted. They had all the respect and reverence they deserved.

The first frocks were pale blue, the skirts almost down to the ground. The material of the skirt—the top layers at least—was net. It was a different net from that used in curtains and ladies' hat veils; it was unlike any fabric I had ever seen or worn. It was stiff and strong as well as light as air; it floated around me; it was from another world. I was still at an age when I believed in fairies. My costume confirmed everything I had ever heard about dresses spun from gossamer, about transformation scenes; at the touch of a wand

I was Cinderella going to the ball.

Like Cinderella's, the shoes were the most amazing of all, though not made of glass; the fabric a heavy, deep cream satin brocaded with silver. For Susanne's wedding, two years later, the net was white and covered by a long, wine-red velvet cape; for Leonie's we had white taffeta with velvet sashes in a deep moss green. For Valerie, it was back to pastels: a sugared-almond shade of lavender, with white satin ballet shoes dyed to match.

Everyone was wearing wonderful clothes. It didn't matter if in real life they were old or fat or ugly; here everyone was splendid. All the men had dinner jackets and cummerbunds. The band played, and whoever asked you to dance, whether it was the best man or Mr Posen next door, was Prince Charming. People laughed and told jokes and played games like children. They made a big fuss of you and you could do no wrong. You were a princess for a day, and some day you would be queen. One of these men in dinner jackets would make a move, trigger a switch that would turn you into a radiant cloud of whiteness, create a being of unassailable, supernatural beauty that everyone would want to be nice to for ever and ever.

I can remember no goodbyes, no going-away outfits. I suppose I must always have been taken home early. The bride and groom vanished from my sight as if in a puff of smoke at the midnight hour. Long, long afterwards they returned to earth. We would go to a house somewhere for tea and there would be Susanne or Leonie in ordinary clothes. Everything seemed beige. There would be nothing much to do, and you would look to see if they had the Eiffel Tower in a snowstorm on their mantelpiece. And ages and ages after that, Susanne or Leonie would come to us for tea, and you would see a baby at the end of a big white breast.

Still, there remained the consolation of the photographs, of which we always had our own copies. I was allowed to appear unbespectacled on wedding days, and would spend hours poring over the image of my flawless loveliness, all too briefly released from the bad spell cast upon it by eye tests. And then I would hunt for other photographs, of weddings which happened before I was born. Auntie Lily with four or five grown-up bridesmaids with huge picture hats. Markie and Sadie, Sadie a tiny bride with an enormous train,

Markie smiling in his topper and tails, not a hint that within the hour he is going to be outside, minus both, in a punch-up over the Communist Party, or so the story goes...where are Mummy and Daddy?

I didn't actually ask for years; some Freudian repugnance to knowing too much about my own origins? And at the time it did not register that there were no wedding photographs for Mummy's sisters either; neither Miriam, who lived round the corner, nor Leah and Vera, who went to join Auntie Rosa in America in the 1920s, and got married there. When I finally got round to asking, Mummy said none were taken.

'It wasn't a white wedding. I wore a brown suit.'

It had never quite sunk in that if the wedding day was what all girls aspired to, it was also what all girls' parents put money aside for. That if everyone got married, it followed that everyone had money. Mummy did not speak about this; but she did speak about the fact that she didn't have an engagement ring. This, she told me quite early on, was because she didn't think Daddy could afford it, so she let him think she didn't really want one. She seems to have regretted this, and perhaps to have told me about it as a kind of warning.

Changes

At twelve, I had to fast the full twenty-four hours on Yom Kippur. And I had already started my periods. Progressive for her time and place, my mother invited and answered my questions. It was all very natural and wonderful and it meant that you could have babies.

But growing up into a woman didn't seem very natural and, as I looked in the mirror and then looked around me, it didn't even seem inevitable. It couldn't just happen: being a woman was obviously about being good-looking, which I no longer was. On top of that it required massive professional expertise and a perfect faith in the importance and efficacy of that expertise. There seemed to be a class of girls who did know all about it, who were allowed into nylons and high heels and lipsticks before anyone else, who dedicated hours and hours to setting their hair and applying mascara and nail polish, and who flirted convincingly and successfully with boys. They would leave school at fifteen and could expect a diamond ring by the time they reached twenty-one. Those of us who were staying on at school to take our O-levels and A-levels were the babies, the retarded ones. We weren't competition. We weren't even in the game.

Adolescence came with a set of instructions which did not really help. They were often subliminal, and largely negative. You should not be loud, or unladylike. Don't wave your hands about. Don't be common, flash, spivvy or cheap. (This applied to my brothers, too. They were forbidden suede shoes.) Not too much jewellery. Don't wear loads of make-up. Don't wear high heels with trousers.

If you thought the hidden message was, don't be—horrible word—a *shiksa*, a non-Jewish woman, you were not quite there; for it was just as important not to be a *klafta*, a gross, coarse, unrefined woman who was almost by definition Jewish. The old-fashioned English working-class expression, rough, was also used. Most confusing of all, despite our orthodoxy, our willingness to stand up and be counted over issues such as school dinners and school prayers, was the almost unspoken injunction not to look too Jewish.

This was partly concealed under the rubric of caution—don't draw attention to yourselves; partly under the pious reminder—what one Jew does reflects on all the other Jews. But the fact that my eldest brother was constantly mistaken (by other Jews) for an Englishman was the source of a certain satisfaction, as was the incident when my mother and I went to buy a scarf at Fenwick's, and the saleswoman, seeing my gold *magen David* on a chain, whispered, 'Well, I would never have thought you were one of us.'

By the age of fifteen I was totally confused. You had to grow up, but you couldn't convince your mother you needed a bra until you'd been wearing a more 'developed' friend's cast-offs for months. Your purpose in life was to be beautiful, and the fact that you weren't was simply ignored. You had to be a nice Jewish girl, but not *too* Jewish. Everyone got engaged and married, but for you to go out with boys was a procedure so fraught with hazard that how you ever reached your ultimate destination was a mystery.

I had to find some escape routes. At fifteen I took the one marked religion. I became deeply committed to orthodoxy and joined a youth movement which excluded the possibility of mating games on the dance floor, restricted the scope of flirtation, banned lipstick on *shabbos*, and shorts and short sleeves at all times.

I also joined the Campaign for Nuclear Disarmament, understanding The Struggle largely as an extension of prayer, prayer made manifest in mighty, righteous demonstrations. And I did pray, every night, that the bomb would not drop, that there would be peace in the Middle East, peace in the Congo...but I also wanted to wear that black-and-white badge which I thought looked particularly sharp on the lapel of my school blazer (though I removed it as soon as the uniform regulations were invoked).

Most of my religious group joined the campaign, too, but I identified the real essence of the movement in a small crowd of girls at school who were infinitely more worldly and more knowing than the rest of us. They smoked cigarettes and had urgent grown-up tasks outside. They were in the Young Communist League as well as CND. They had important responsibilities for holding meetings, manning offices, selling newspapers, leafleting and stewarding demos; the school rather tried their patience. They were strikingly beautiful but didn't bother with make-up or nail varnish, as far as I could see. They wore dark duffel coats and black stockings.

I had my camel-coloured duffel coat dyed navy (I convinced my mother that it was a good move: I could now wear it to school). I got my dentist boyfriend to take me to a folk song night at the Partisan and could almost believe that his orthodox beard blended with the bohemian faces around us. Sometimes I went out with my school friends and met their comrades. I was too much in awe of their men (they really didn't seem like boys, even those who were still at school) to be able to speak to them. It wasn't just because they were broodingly, romantically dark and handsome with Russian first names, it was their godlike self-possession, the glowing youthful certainty with which they predicted the end of the world, which struck me dumb.

Very suddenly, without giving formal notice, or telling me privately beforehand, my friends left school and signed themselves up at a poly for their A-levels. I wrote a poem about standing on a seashore, abandoned by two birds soaring into the sky.

The world was in trouble; activism was the black and grey reality of staying out late and making your own rules. Out in the cheerfully lit and coloured suburbs, I kept *shabbos* and *yom tov*, and marched only on Easter Monday. I still loved smart clothes, and I didn't even want to smoke. But I did yearn for the trappings of the gods. Easter Monday 1960 was my sixteenth birthday. My father had let slip that he had friends In Leather; he was going to try and get me a black leather jacket. All day long I marched, and sang. The world was coming to an end. Polaris—*oh-no*. We march to save our children (this made all of us giggle, even the sophisticated immortals), *We* shall *not* be *moved*. The unheard song to which I marched was black-leather-*jack*-et, black-leather-*jack*-et, no one will be more terrific than me...

I got home to a drum of talcum powder. Of course I said nothing—1960 was obviously going to be another bad year at the factory—though in recent years I have begun to wonder how many of the loved ones of my adult life have been made to pay for that particular disappointment. I often tell this tale, apparently to show myself up as a desperately, comically shallow teenager; in reality, to proclaim that not only was I rather hard-done-by and quite a little saint, but also that I was always, always, fashionable, in the swim, and Of My Time.

Acts of praise

You wore your best clothes to *shul*. These included gloves and a hat. You needed a Good Coat, not the one you wore to school, naturally, and Good Suits, and dresses for the very hot summer days, when your gloves were white. You had new clothes for the festivals. The annual cycle of Passover, Shevuoth, Succoth, New Year and the Day of Atonement was marked by a succession of different costumes, though you might pare the significant acquisitions down to a spring suit for Passover (when, to your intense disappointment, it was almost always too cold to go out in it) and a new coat for the autumnal High Holydays, adding hats, dresses or separates for the festivals in between. You might never go anywhere else; there might be no public outings, apart from going to school, in the rest of your year; but you still had to have and replenish your stock of formal costumes.

There were, of course, shoes and, if you were not too orthodox to carry one on a sabbath or holiday, handbags to be thought of, as well as hats and gloves. Absolutely nothing was allowed to clash. Though you might have one smash item, such as the hat, it was important for everything to look as if it belonged with everything else.

The layout of the synagogue afforded the best possible view of these ensembles. Women prayed in an upstairs gallery on three sides of a square; there was no lattice-work or veiling such as more orthodox congregations used to conceal male and female worshippers from each other. Week in, week out, it was possible to appraise, from a good distance, the success of each woman's efforts, to see what colours and materials complemented each other, what shape of hat suited what style of garment. I did these aesthetic exercises constantly, automatically, almost unthinkingly, and without reference to the relative cost of each outfit, for of course in the conventional sense the clothes did not cost anything; they all came from someone's factory.

(These exercises have stood me in very good stead. Since my mid-teens I have known what can and what cannot be worn with what. If you have mastered this trick, no one can tell that you are wearing your daughter's friends' cast-offs, and you can save your money for a proper haircut. The downside is that you cannot switch it off, that you are constantly judging people's appearance, silently adjusting their colour schemes and accessories, and wondering why they dress as they do. If you're going to wear that coat, you need a darker pair of tights. If you're going to wear that hat, you've got to put your hair up. Nice skirt, shame about the shoes. *Nul points. Dix points!* Wish I was tall.)

For men it may have been slightly easier, as there were fewer options. But the suit had to be well cut from good cloth, the shirt and tie had to match, the hat had to be chosen with care if the wearer was not to look like an idiot. Anything cheap or ill-judged threw into question the range of a man's professional and family connections; cast doubt, indeed, upon his ability to manage his own affairs. For men and women alike, to dress well was to show that you knew your business.

But there was a sense, also, that it was owed to God. You did not present yourself in his courts dressed like a sloven. You did not come together with others as a recognizable community of his Chosen without looking a credit to him. It was not so much that we thought of him as the great garment manufacturer in the sky; more that, since he feeds and clothes us, to dress badly would be as impious as to waste food or to make it unpalatable. If food was disgusting, in what spirit would we thank God for it?

On the day that we did not eat, three times the normal congregation crammed into the synagogue. As a child I felt stifled, penned in by all the adult bodies upstairs in the ladies' gallery, overpowered by the smell of powder and eau de Cologne, and the humid air that striped the walls with condensation. The mink stoles of old ladies stared at me with beady eyes and snouts while I acknowledged in my prayers that even the pre-eminence of man over beast was as nothing. Herded together, helpless before an unknown future, we were begging for clemency. People were animals; grown-ups were babies; we were all, in the end, naked.

Something still puzzles me. The general principle applied that we were not to draw attention to ourselves. And yet we made ourselves conspicuous every week of the year, as, obeying the injunction not to use transport on the Sabbath, we trudged along Vivian Avenue or Golders Green Road in our finery. Even if our clothes were decent rather than opulent, with no furs or jewels in evidence, in the late Fifties and early Sixties a good hat and matching pair of gloves stood out oddly among the throng of shoppers scurrying for their groceries. Odder still was the effect of white plimsolls with the rest of your ensemble, if these were the only non-leather shoes which you could find to wear on the Day of Atonement. (These were indeed, if truth be told, the worst of all the mortifications; lucky the Nike-proud Jewish teenagers of today.)

According to the *Drapers Record*, we were living in an era when 'Sunday best' clothes were disappearing from the majority of the population's wardrobes. So we were out of time, as well as out of place. Our clothes, supposedly our protective armour, could even expose us to injury. My brother David, after sitting for his Common Entrance exams, was interviewed in his bar mitzvah suit by a headmaster who rejected him with the pronouncement: you're too neat and tidy; you'll never get your hands dirty; your sort don't know how to work. In bewilderment and anguish my mother threatened to mess up his hair and put mud on his face the next time. It proved not to be necessary; but she could be forgiven for wondering if the reason so many people took my other brother, Alan, for an Englishman was that he could not wear a suit for five minutes without looking as if he had slept in it.

It all comes back to me when I glimpse a Muslim or a Hindu neighbour walking down the street in festival clothes; calm and unhurried, in a different atmosphere from the cars speeding past. Perhaps it is possible for what you wear to create an aura, for you to carry your holiness with you, untainted by indifferent or profane surroundings. But there is always a tension between what you and others are doing. On a boiling hot afternoon, when you are going back to the synagogue in your best dress to organize permitted sabbath games for the younger ones, you can hardly be unaware that everyone else is peeling off in the garden or at the swimming pool. And the longing can grow for the cars not to be there, for the non-believers not to be there; for everyone's looks to mirror your own; for everything around you to belong to the heavenly city. It never surprises me that people who wear strange costumes often throw stones; that theocracies are fashion dictatorships.

I can never walk out in a good hat and coat without thinking: I could be going to *shul*. But my way of dressing changed when I gave up orthodoxy, and the contents of my wardrobe are not restocked as they used to be. These days, if I buy a suit, it has to be in a colour that will see long service in the workplace; anything pastel will get too little wear to repay the investment.

That headmaster grasped the wrong end of the right stick. The clothes were about work, and not about work. They concealed the labour we had put into them; and they were that labour's reward. They were *shabbosdik*, that is, of and worthy of the sabbath. They were designed for celebration and for prayer. They set us apart from the rest of our own lives; and probably from the lives of other people. You could say, they took us to another world.

Mechullo: bankrupt

The Jewish master tailor, with his small workshop or factory, was often one of the pre-war immigrants who, in the early 1900s, were 'sweated' homeworkers but who gradually improved their position by taking contracts for the production of clothing in bulk instead of working on piece rates as homeworkers. Margaret Wray, *The Women's Outerwear Industry* (London, Duckworth 1957).

Up in a lift that wobbles to a vast hall of noise. In a tin cubicle high above Lexington Street is Daddy, with Beverley, his secretary (until she gets married), who used to be a Land Girl in the war—hard to imagine, a Jewish Land Girl; she's not even particularly tall. There is a giant's table for a huge layered slab of material. Joe the cutter moves a wire through it. Later Uncle Louis replaces him. Auntie Lily sits at one end checking buttons and buttonholes. There are also some men who are pressers, otherwise it is all ladies. The noise comes from their sewing machines. Each seam is a roar. Sometimes it looks and sounds as if the roars are synchronized.

...a smaller factory tended to have lower overhead costs per unit, resulting from economies in supervision and simpler record-keeping requirements. ...[it] could...be equipped relatively cheaply, as most of the essential pre-war machinery and equipment was inexpensive, compared with the general run of industrial equipment. Machinery could be hired on easy terms, or bought on hire purchase, and small factories equipped with lockstitch machines could be rented for a small weekly sum.

Some of the ladies are black; a very pretty lady is Greek. The only machinist I ever really get to know is Mabel, who has been with Daddy even before her marriage to Pat. She has always been with Daddy. Even when the others have to be laid off, Mabel is kept on.

...the average factory employee [worked] for only forty weeks in the year. ...the worst seasonal fluctuations were, however, in the London fashion trade. Outdoor factories in London seem to have been in production for only about thirty weeks in the year.

Ruth Gershon

Outside, Berwick Street market where Mummy shops for vegetables on the days she visits. At one point she visits almost every day. She is not like some of the wives, Pat Harris or Stella Lewis for instance, who march in, demand to see the books, and decide that they might as well stay because they couldn't make a worse mess of things themselves. She must be there, literally, to hold his hand. And he must be close to mental breakdown. At Chanukkah, one of my brothers makes a joke of it, buying her 'Letts Businesswoman's Diary'.

...the initial orders for autumn and winter stock [were] placed about May each year and similar orders for spring and summer stock about October. The end of each buying season was marked by half-yearly sales, in January and July...deliveries to the stores generally tapered off some weeks before the sales... For a large part of their seasonal requirements they relied on repeat orders for deliveries from manufacturers at one or two weeks' notice.

I don't understand. We have been rich. I have memories, not all my own, of better days. We still have a television. We go to schools a long distance from home, and wear smart uniforms. How long since we have had a car? We still have paintings on the wall. One is a portrait of me, in a peach organdie frock, with thin blue velvet ribbons bunching my hair. (And that peach material, which did not and does not suit my skin, is still the colour of a lost paradise.) The piano stays on the parquet flooring in front of the French windows until I say I do not want to learn. Beyond the windows is the back garden, and a gardener. In the photograph drawer there are pictures of Mummy and Daddy in nightclubs in New York. Daddy takes me to Covent Garden to see the ballet, and a tray of tea is passed along to us in the interval.

In June 1941, the first Consumer Rationing Order introduced a scheme for rationing civilian clothing (which was retained until March 1949). ...New producers could only enter the industry by buying up the coupon capital of an existing business, or by securing an issue of coupons (known as a 'coupon float') from the Board of Trade, and applications for such 'floats' were generally refused.

Between 1941 and 1949, therefore, the de-stabilizing effect of ease of entry, typical of the pre-war industry, was removed.

In 1949 we take a foreign holiday. My Hebrew teacher sniffs and says there are many lovely places to visit in this country.

...the reason for the manufacturer's prosperity lay in the certainty of his profit margin and the absence of the usual offsetting, end of season, losses. His normal pre-war trading risks were removed, because of the strength of wartime demand and because of the virtual elimination of fashion changes. The impact of the season on production was ended; he could deliver his garments to the distributor as soon as they were ready; he no longer had to hold stocks and the rate of turnover of his working capital (and so his yearly profits) was increased. ...most of his uncertainties about cloth supplies and prices were removed and, at the same time, he had a strong demand for his products and could make his own conditions about delivery dates with the distributor.

We go to France and Italy. The images come mainly from Daddy's photographs. A little girl in plaits and a smocked frock, holding balloons in a gloved hand, with the Eiffel Tower in the background. I know I remember the gloves for myself. Cousin Golda bought them in Galeries Lafayette. They are crochet, a pattern of flowers and fishnet, ecru; they have no weight, and yet I can feel them encasing my fingers and palms and wrists, so crisp, so dry... And at Diana Marino I am kitted out with shorts, a skirt, a bolero, and a little ruched top that can be worn on or off the shoulders, all in the same strong pattern of dark blue and red that stands out in the sunshine but is an unusual selection for a five-year-old... I nag them for a straw hat like a Chinaman's, and they give me one to keep me quiet. I am spoiled rotten.

In 1949 and 1950, the end of rationing and the rush to buy clothing...resulted in an increase in sales which brought consumers' expenditure above the 1938 figure for the first time. This was soon followed in 1951 by a fall in clothing sales, as increased prices and

Ruth Gershon

well-stocked wardrobes combined to reduce demand.

The ten plagues of Egypt are recited at Passover. For each one a drop of wine must be spilt from your cup. We chant as we spill it.

DOM: blood.

1950–51 marked the end of the post-war boom for the clothing industry. Re-armament and the Korean War caused a large increase in raw wool and cotton prices, which affected utility as well as 'general' clothing production, because subsidies for utility cloth had been withdrawn in 1948.

SFARDEYA: frogs.

High cloth prices necessitated considerable increases in clothing prices at a time when the end of shortages and restrictions in other industries was leading to a growing supply of other goods that competed with clothing for the consumer's growing power.

KINIM: lice.

Moreover, with the end of rationing, in 1949, new clothing producers could once more enter the industry and fashion became an important determinant of demand. Manufacturers had to adapt production to trading conditions that they had not experienced for ten years or more.

OROV: wild beasts.

...the smaller producer, particularly the outdoor contractor, was exposed to the full force of seasonal changes in demand. Most contractors made new contracts each season; the volume of work available tended to fluctuate considerably, so that they could not estimate with any certainty the demand for their services.

My father sits with his head in his hands. But I can see the colour of his face and neck. It is bright beetroot red.

DEVER: pestilence.

...they had to cover extra payments for over-time working during the season and for the retention of at least a nucleus of skilled workers in the slack periods...

It is the middle of the night, and there is shouting in the bedroom next to mine.

SHECHIN: boils.

...the seasonal orders soon diminished and they were often left with unsold stocks...

It is early morning and Daddy is being sick in the bathroom.

BOROD: hail.

...they frequently found themselves short of money to meet even weekly wage payments and had hastily to sell their stocks at cut prices.

It is the middle of the afternoon and I come home from school bringing a friend back for tea. Daddy and Uncle Louis are there, sitting on the couch in the lounge.

ARBEH: locusts.

...retail sales were seriously affected by unseasonable weather, as in the summer of 1954.

They are there day after day through the summer, watching the racing on television.

CHOSHECH: darkness.

The result of over-production was considerable instability, which showed itself in seasonal unemployment, in a high rate of bankruptcy...

MACAS BECHOROS: the death of the first-born.

A presser left his machine on all night. The factory has burned out.

In 1960, I think, we had another bad summer. It is not true, Daddy writes in a letter which is printed in the *Drapers Record* and which I pin on my bedroom wall, that the industry's troubles come from the plethora of radical new styles on the market. It is the unseasonal weather which has restrained sales and produced the current slump. The public have taken the Empire line and the A-line to their hearts.

I get a beautiful sample of each. The 'Empire' is in navy-blue velvet, the 'A' is a pink and green cotton print. I wear them to friends' birthday parties and to youth club socials, though the Empire is good enough for weddings. I perch gilt or plastic headbands over my urchin cut and leave my glasses off. By now I have two pairs of shoes with 'potato' heels, one in white leather and one in pinky red, each with a lattice front recalling cross-tied ballet ribbons.

At home I am often blamed in general terms for 'being unconscious'. But I am not really supposed to know what is going on. No one sits me down and tells me. If we do not have a car, I do not question the fact. If things disappear to be sold, I do not notice. It registers with me that we do not go on holidays, but I do not feel hard-done-by. Thanks to Noel Streatfeild, Frances Hodgson Burnett, Edith Nesbit and numberless fairy tales, I know that being poor is almost the precondition for being the hero in a story. I feel that a romantic cachet has descended upon us, and that I am quite as good as the girls I go to school with in Hampstead.

But as I get older, I do become conscious. I go to *shul* with my elderly neighbour, or with school friends. Daddy has not kept up his membership fees, has quarrelled with them all and stormed out when the bills fell due. Mummy is not involved with the Ladies' Association, or with the League of Jewish Women. I get involved: I help to run the Children's Service (I buy a pair of very light brown, chisel-toed lace-ups with my wages, and am going to be able to finance a trip to the

Edinburgh Festival), and I am *madricha* in a youth club that organizes *shabbos* activities for younger children.

I am on my own out there. From somewhere the words come into my head: we have no standing.

I sense that other families may not be lurching from one crisis to the next, that other parents are not necessarily anxious about the exposure of their circumstances. Sometimes we are told not to answer the door, or the phone. At school, I am startled to be called to the headmistress's study to be asked when my music tuition will be paid, but I do not miss a beat; my mouth opens and I hear myself saying that the cheque is in the post.

A school friend is shocked about the *shul* membership business. I make the narrative one of bloody-minded independence (having joined CND, I am beginning to fancy myself as a social critic), but she is aware of the practical implications. You have to be buried some day, and if you are not a member of a *shul*, she says, there is no one to take care of it.

That year, we attend High Holyday services somewhere else: a synagogue founded locally in the 1930s by very Orthodox German refugees. Within this community, we ourselves are almost foreigners. Yet Daddy does have an acquaintance there, Mr Rosenblum, someone for whom Daddy found work when he arrived here with nothing.

Was it only the next spring that Mr Rosenblum came to our door, to tell my mother that she need not worry, that he would take care of all the arrangements?

Apparently things were looking up. He was driving round the provinces, picking up orders. On his way home, not a mile away, he felt very ill. He stopped the car outside the cottage hospital. He had had a heart attack, they said, and kept him in.

He did not look too bad when we went to see him. As the days went by and he rested he began to feel, he told a nurse, better than he had done for ages. He became his old self again at visiting times, sending us all on errands around the ward.

Numbers were restricted for visiting hours. On Tuesday night, Mummy and David went. Alan had to be out of London. I stayed

in and washed my hair. It was very long in those days. It took time
to dry. They came back and we had a late supper. Then the telephone
rang and it was the hospital.

Nobody had expected it. He was fifty-five. He had one son who
was a solicitor, one who was qualifying as an accountant, and a
daughter who had won a scholarship to Oxford. And he thought
business was going to get better. Mummy says that he was even
hoping to make enough money to set aside for my wedding.

We covered the mirrors.

A cousin gave me a black jumper to wear for the week, although
it wasn't strictly necessary. An old woman came on the day of
the funeral to make ritual tears in our garments. A shriek came from
my mother's throat as the razor went through the lapel of David's
new suit. He had worked so hard and saved so long for the material.
And we had, to be honest, been left with nothing but what we
stood up in.

I never said goodbye and I still can't. I see him in every well-
dressed, middle-aged Jewish businessman. I've seen him in a film
sequence of Al Jolson dancing, and I've seen him in a Karsh
photograph of Humphrey Bogart. I see him in a tweed jacket, with
a pipe and a walking stick, clothes and props that were more solid
than he was. I've seen him in every slightly built, dark-haired, childish
and unreasonable man that I've ever fallen for.

I see him in the clothes he made for me, and I buy new ones
that resemble them even if they don't suit me any more. I own and
keep dresses that he made or chose for my mother. I've still got the
satin sash to the black velvet dress with the boat neck, three-quarter
sleeves, tight bodice and full ballerina skirt that he made for me just
after I won the scholarship. I wore it to a Masonic uncle's Ladies'
Night; we danced together in the Charleston competition (he had
taught me how to years before) and we were astounded not to be given
the prize. We had been so confident that we walked up to receive it.

I don't know what would have happened. Schmatters boomed
again in the 1960s, but anyone could get into it then. My brothers
had their professional qualifications, but he might have felt
humiliated at being advised by them. Oxford would for a time have

made me a stranger. If I had had a brilliant career, he might have shrivelled; but my not being a star would have robbed him of his dream life. I don't know. This part of me has come away and cannot be stitched back.

I didn't play with dolls. I can't even recall having any, although friends did: great plastic babies with 'Rosebud' or 'Pat. Pending' embossed on their backs. But I do remember seeing something at a friend's house that I instantly craved. It was a cardboard figure of a girl which came in a box containing dozens of stiff paper cut-out costumes—coats, skirts, jackets, dresses and hats. The girl could be dressed for country or town, for school, shopping, holidays or parties. One day I came home from school and was told 'close your eyes and put out your hands'. There was the box. Same girl, different occasions, different outfits. Life in miniature. Heaven.

It still astonishes me to contemplate this child, so early and so completely adapted to a multiply-persona'd self. I seemed always to have known that one man in his time might play many parts, but one woman had to play many parts at a time.

This may explain both the contradictions of my teenage years and the gusto with which I embraced them. For, even as I gave up (for a time) mixed dancing, polished up my Hebrew and attended theological seminars, I pored over *Paris-Match* and studied pictures of Brigitte Bardot. Even as I contemplated an orthodox marriage which would have required me to cover my head with a wig and make monthly visits to a ritual bath, I was seeking out long men's sweaters to wear over a straight skirt and black stockings, and imagining myself in a Paris club with Juliette Greco.

But there were times when I didn't know what to wear or who to be. Could I actually be myself without looking too Jewish? Could you be the type that passed exams and still be glamorous? At that Masonic evening I had my hair up in a French pleat, and though I say it myself I looked a million dollars. Somewhere behind me I heard my father say: 'And that's what they give a scholarship to Oxford!' as if to suggest that I was nothing but a pretty face. What he meant, of course, was that his daughter had cracked it, got the double. I hadn't; only he would ever think so.

I still haven't found the answers. Is there something within which revolts against being pinned down, which yearns for yet another metamorphosis? There is a disease associated with clothes which is like the gambler's neurosis: the belief that out there, there is just one more purchase to make and you will finally find the one, true, right outfit, the one by which you will be both transformed and restored to yourself; you will be undisputably the fairest one of all and, at last, the real, essential you. Crooked shall be made straight, bumps shall be smoothed. Fastened into that belief, the Wandering Dresser is condemned to the torments of an eternal adolescence.

A m I still where I was when his heart stopped? I think so, yes. No one else has thought me the cleverest and the prettiest girl in the world. No one else has seen me as the embodiment of so many ambitions and fantasies. No one else could legitimize quite so many costume changes. He was the only Other in whose heart it could all be held together.

I wish I'd known it sooner; I wouldn't have tried to pin the job on anyone else. This is the only conclusion I can come to. It fits, and I'll wear it. □

GRANTA

LITERARY LONDON

FOUR MAPS BY
MARTIN ROWSON

FOUR LONDON MAPS
by Martin Rowson

1. CHAUCER's LONDON

As far as anyone can tell these days,
LONDON had *no literary existence* before G.CHAUCER's
"Canterbury Tales". London in those *far off days* was
very different from the bustling metropolis of
today, consisting, from what can be gleaned from
the *surviving text*, of ONE PUB and a ROAD
to CANTERBURY. There was then *no river, nor*
anything else at all, save for VAST TRACTS of
wilderness spreading *NORTH* to the Gawain
Poet's WIRRAL, *WEST* to the Malverns
and Langland's FAIR FEELD FUL OF FOLK,
and beyond there to the huge CAMELOT/
AVALON conurbation.

Here be
Palinodes

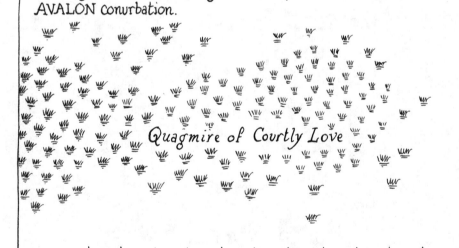

Quagmire of Courtly Love

SCALE: 1cm : 100 lines of Knight's Tale

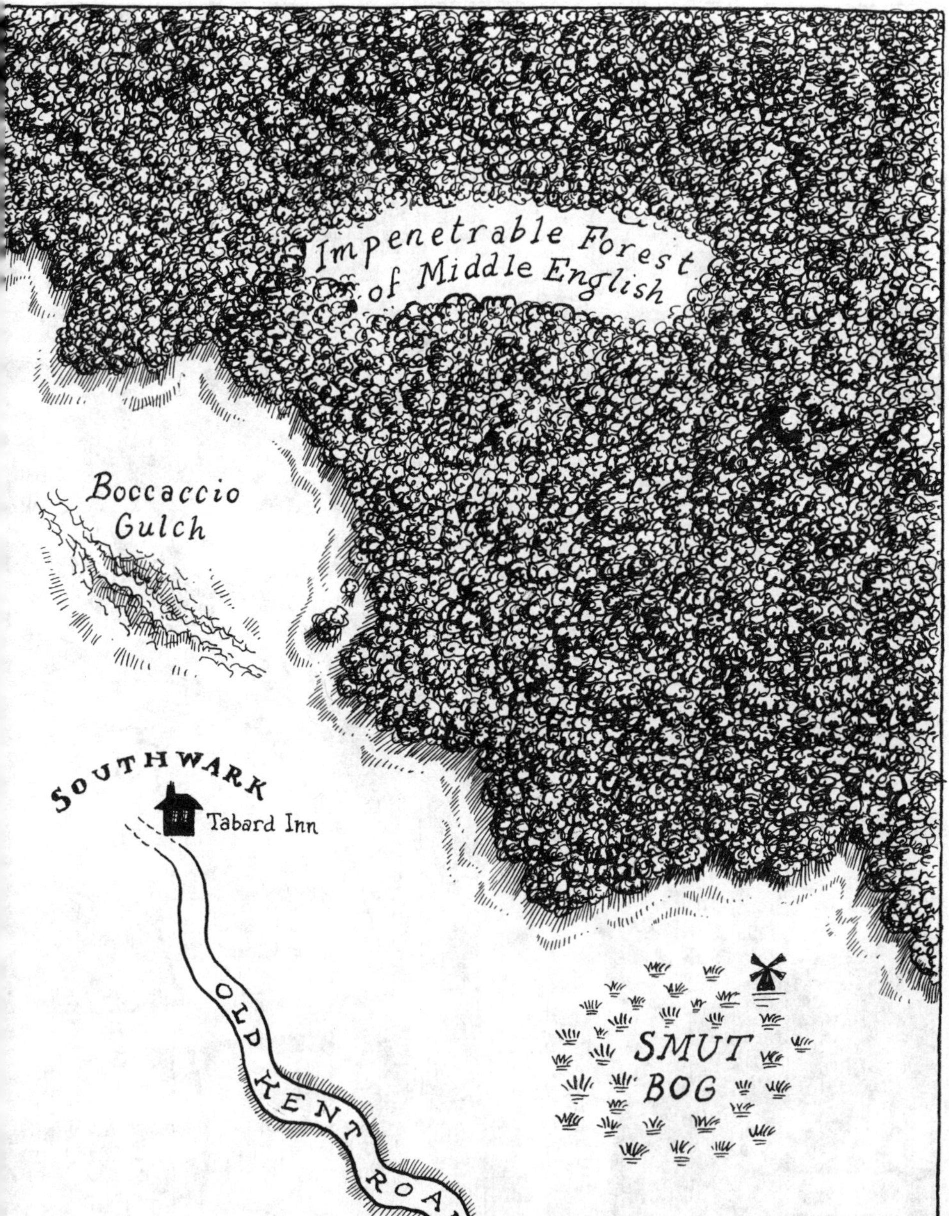

Impenetrable Forest of Middle English
Boccaccio Gulch
SOUTHWARK
Tabard Inn
OLD KENT ROAD
SMUT BOG
To Canterbury

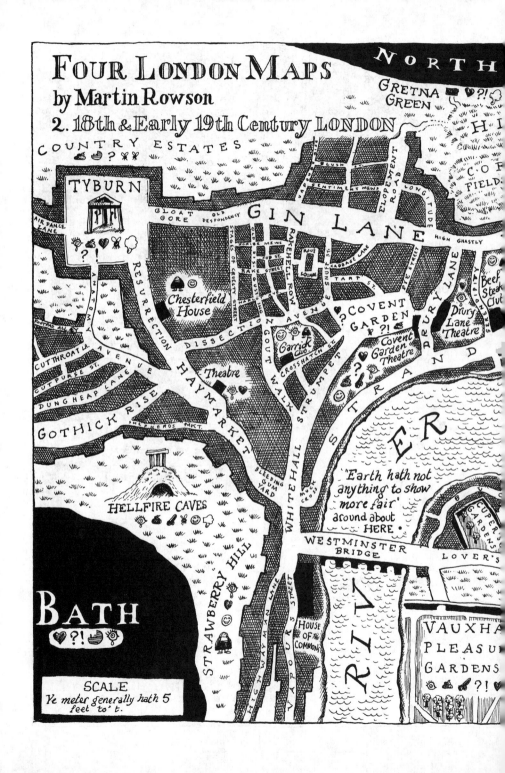

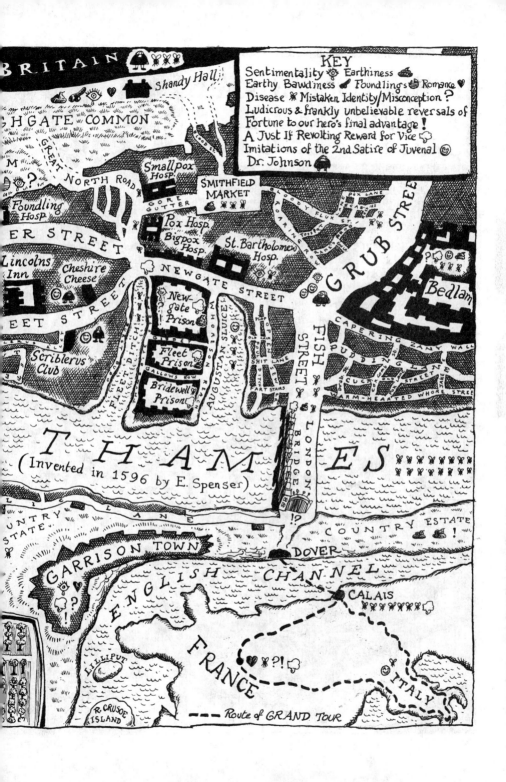

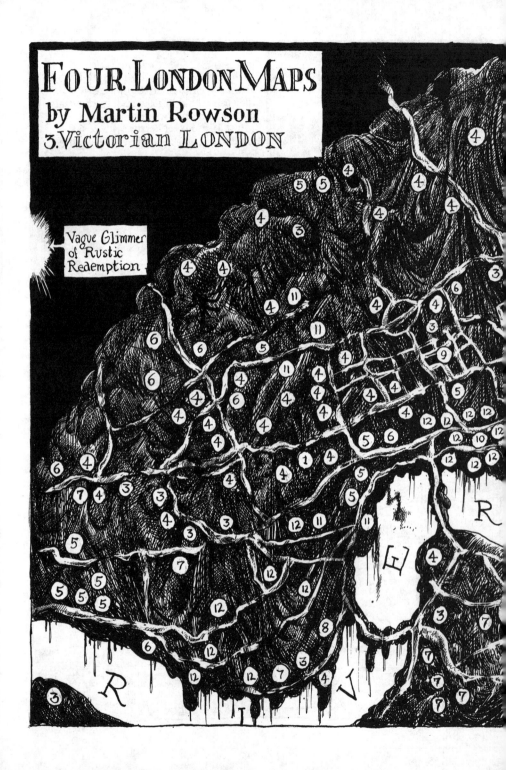

1. CITY of DREADFUL NIGHT
2. FAGIN'S KITCHEN
3. CHOLERA
4. CONSUMPTION
5. DECADENCE
6. DRINK MADNESS
7. THE CONDITION OF THE ENGLISH WORKING CLASS
8. THE HEART OF DARKNESS
9. BRITISH MUSEUM
10. ROYAL COURTS OF JUSTICE
11. CHILD LABOUR/PROSTITUTION
12. PEASOUPER FOG
13. WHERE SHERLOCK HOLMES SCORED HIS COKE

THAMES

Scale
A brute I might have been, but
would not sink i' the scale

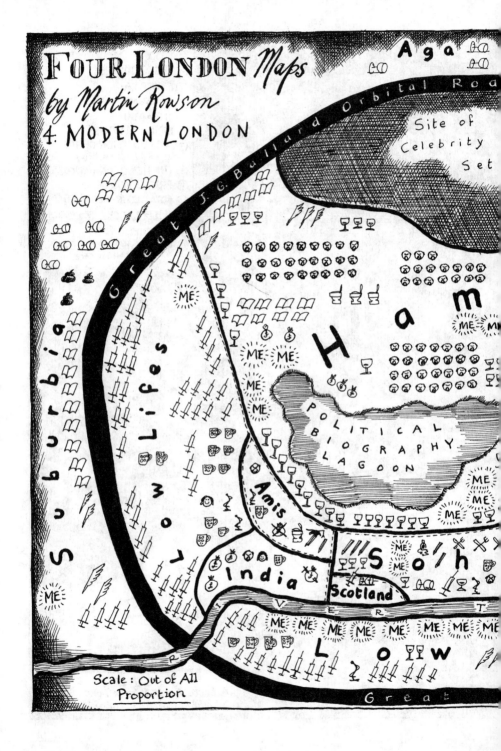

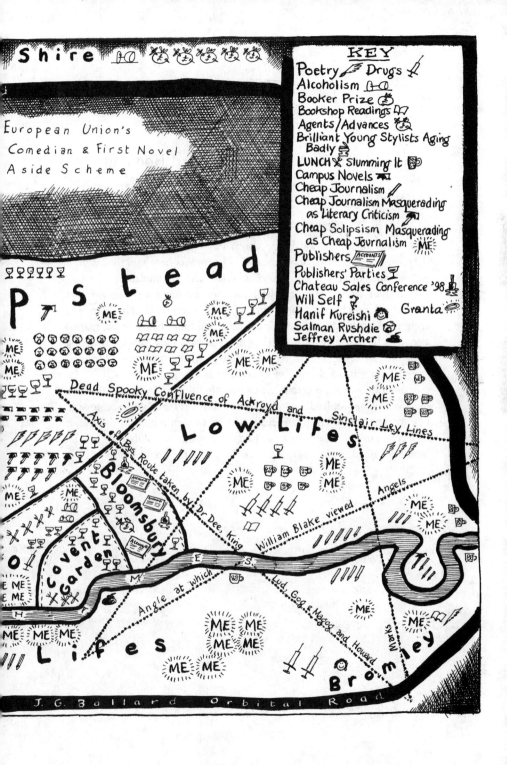

A LONDON VIEW/Howard Hodgkin

Like many other London living-rooms, this one is divided by a square opening, with windows along one wall. The owners have said they want it to look like the inside of a hotel. It does. The accumulation of rather characterless objects and completely out-of-scale furniture, plus a rather morose colour-scheme of dingy greens, adds to the effect. The busts and sculptured heads, also the numerous chairs and other places to sit, suggest a longing for company. It is a view which I always look forward to seeing again, as I sit at the table in the foreground, perhaps being offered tea and sympathy, a glass of champagne or something stronger.

Interior views are certainly more comfortable to look at than those outside. You can sit back and relax with a drink in hand, with someone to talk to. And this room in particular, with its memento mori at the end, is so nicely impersonal, it is as comforting as a room in a club. One mutual friend described it as his favourite bar. Of course the drinks are free.

KATRINA LITHGOW

FREEZING ON THE STREETS

Tonight, at least 2,500 people risk death on the freezing streets. Shelter **must** work around the clock to help them survive. But we need funds urgently. Please, please help. Your £15 donation could help us find someone a warm bed and a hot meal. Your £15 could keep our 24-hour emergency phone lines open. Your £15 could save a life.

For every degree the temperature drops more homeless people are in danger. So please act now.

YOUR £15 COULD SAVE A LIFE

Call us free with your credit card donation on:

0800 95 96 96

Or post your cheque to Shelter, Room 23, FREEPOST, London EC1B 1ND

All money raised will go towards Shelter's campaigning and vital services. Some of Shelter's services are grant aided by the Department of Environment, Transport and the Regions.

Registered in London: 1038133. Charity No: 263710.

98/1/36

GRANTA

BIG DOME
Will Self

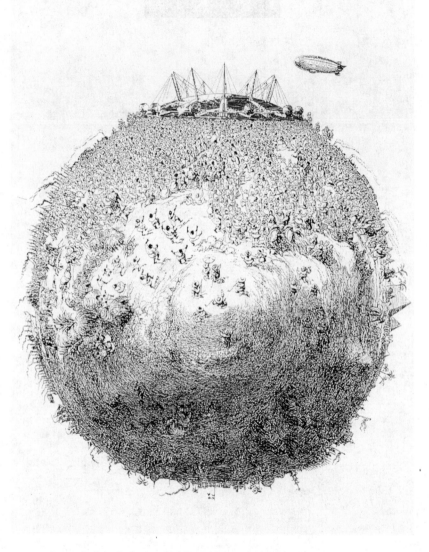

George Cruikshank: the Great Exhibition of 1851. Adapted for the Millennium Dome Experience of 1999/2000 by Anthony Cross.

Big Dome

From where I lie, I can't see much of the world, save for a projecting wall of my own house still fringed by green wisteria, the grey slate line of the next row of houses, and beyond this, the pillbox hat of one of the council blocks on the Wandsworth Road. Of course, if I sat up, I could get a bearing on at least a small part of iconic London—I could see the very tips of two of Battersea Power Station's stacks nestling same-sized among closer chimneys. And from this angle I'd also be able to see the gardens of this terrace, below and to my right; long strips of urban verdancy, most with their own dinky hut, sawn lawn and dwarf terrace: *urb in rus in urb in rus.*

Lévi-Strauss said that all world cities are constructed on an east-to-west schema, with the poor in the east and the rich in the west. Some ascribe this to the prevalent winds; the poor, as it were, being swept into the gutter. I think Claude saw it as a deeper structural phenomenon than this; humanity displaying some of the instinctive, orienting behaviour of the social insects. But I've never experienced London in Lévi-Strauss terms. I inhabit a city within which, no matter where I look, or in which direction I turn, I still find myself hideously oriented. I suffer from a kind of claustro-agoraphobia, if such a thing is possible. I fear going outside in London because it is so cramped and confining.

When you grow up in a great city (and by great I mean a city that is not readily geographically encompassed, even by an adult with mature visio-spatial abilities), your sense of it is at first straight-forwardly crazy—like a film with appalling continuity. (Characters turn the corner of St James's and find themselves standing, grinning foolishly, on the Aldwych.) 'Daddy,' asks my eight-year-old as we drive past Clissold Park, 'Is that Battersea Park?' Poor dog, nodding his way into comprehension, as the jump-cut scenes of the city are projected at him through the windscreen.

Then comes the integration, the coalescence of the 200-billion neurones that will comprise the city-brain. The faux villages of London—the tiny zones around friends' houses, or known haunts—spread over a grey waste of overpopulation, strung out along ribbon developments of short-term memory. And then, in adult life, there is the long, long shading in of the rest, the even adumbration which constitutes regular experience. Even ten years ago, and certainly fifteen, I could patrol central London and still avoid my past self when I saw him coming in the opposite direction. I could take alternative routes to avoid the districts of failed love affairs, I knew short cuts which would circumvent the neighbourhood of an abandoned friendship, I had only to swerve to miss the precincts of a snubbing acquaintance. But now the city is filled in with narratives, which have been extruded like psychic mastic into its fissures. There is no road I haven't fought on, no cul-de-sac I haven't ended it all in, no alley I haven't done it down. To traverse central London today, even in a car, even on autopilot, is still to run over a hundred memoirs.

The irregular, cracked flags of the driveway outside my childhood home in N2 have remained exactly the same for four decades. I know this, because I've been home. Not often, but a few times since the house was sold in the late Seventies. Most recently, after a gap of a decade or so, I took my own children there and was amazed at the continuities of the topiary and the *bricolage*, set against the transitoriness of my own feelings. Of course, my last bitter memories of this house and its environs are of an insufferably stuffy, ultimate *ur*-suburb; Kate Greenaway on Largactil; the sort of place that could grow a J. G. Ballard out of the mildest and least imaginative of psyches. But that's because I was seventeen when I left here. Now, with my own kids chucking each other into the hedges and running on the wide, grass-bordered pavements, all I can see is how green it is, all I can hear is how quiet it is, the soundlessness of the suburbs.

It was on this driveway that we trundled our toys, small-scale precursors of the commuters we would become. It was here that we constructed rooms on the outside, cosy dens containing little stories; here we picked up the trails of our first narratives, worming in the crannies and clefts among the moss. In my childhood home, how many days would I spend, stowed in the hold of the upstairs back bedroom, imagining the oceanic city all around. There—or here, it makes no difference. In either place and time I have the same sense of residing in a permanent mid-morning, of avoiding the workaday world, of being marooned by the audience drain from Radio 4. Beached, here or there, on a grainy mattress, while outside the city hums and beeps and bumps and grinds and pulses and pullulates with

Big Dome

a crazed sense of its own polymorphous perversity, its fanatical ability to construct stories out of its rooms and its streets, its vestibules and its courtyards, its cars and its discarded fag packets. Any object the eye pursues becomes a story, another track scored in time. Any person is a potential Medusa, Gorgon-headed with writhing, serpentine tales.

Which is why I lie here in the spare room, safely barricaded by other people's stories, the tales of other cities. This refuge is almost completely lined with books, most of which have little to do with London. The wall opposite the sunny window is tiled with the spines of some 1,600 battered paperbacks. They are umber, grey, brown and blue, they are as pleasingly textured and involving to the eye as the robes of the couple in Klimt's *The Kiss*, a reproduction of which hangs on the wall opposite me. Their battered backs are a mnemonic of my own history. Despite the gearing of my own book collection into that of my wife, this impression has been enhanced, rather than diminished. It must be because we are both the same kind of trampish bibliophagists. Unlike other, more fastidious types, our collecting instinct is akin to the spirit in which homeless people acquire shopping trolleys then use them to mass everything the verge, the bin, the gutter has to offer, creating small mobile monuments to obsolescence.

Thus we have all the books no one else wanted—as well as most of the ones we did. That's why we have Tony Buzan's *Memory: How to Improve it*, as well as *Extracts from Gramsci's Prison Notebooks*; that's why there are all of my dead mother's Viragos, and the family Penguins, Pelicans and Puffins, paperback generics which have come together in chunks, after generation upon generation of packing them into cardboard boxes, resulting in the evolution of a crude librarianism. But only very crude. J. K. Galbraith still abuts C. S. Lewis abutting Arthur C. Clarke, who in turn leans on *Zen Comics* and a collection of *Helpful Hints* compiled by some upper-class supernumerary. Good cladding—and an entirely suitable housing within which to stay firmly at home. In fact, it is my childhood home—or more like anywhere else could ever be like it again. And looking to the wall outside, its particular pocks, chips and coarsenesses of mortar, I am oppressed by the notion that the bricks may be texts as well, the spines of buried tablets, covered in cuneiform script, which bear, etched into the very

119

mucilaginous matter of the city, the histories of all who live here now, lived here then, or could ever live here.

I can't believe this is exclusively a writer's problem. Consciousness is, after all, simply another story, another string of metaphors, another gag. I think all of us Londoners are like the young schizophrenic man who knocked on the door of my Shepherd's Bush house on a dull winter evening in 1989: 'Could you lend me £13.27,' he said, his voice jagged with the fateful snicker-snack of psychosis, 'and drive me to Leytonstone?'

'All right,' I replied, keen as ever to experience a random act of senseless generosity. As we were scooting under the Euston Road underpass, and his delusional babble was mounting in volume and intensity, I decided that I'd better check out his destination. I pulled over. 'Show me,' I said to him, opening the A–Z to the relevant page, 'exactly where it is you want to go in Leytonstone.' He looked at me warily. 'Come on, man,' he said, 'you know as well as I do that the A–Z is a plan of a city—it hasn't been built yet.'

The A–Z, the colouring book of London. Some of us live in this plan more than we do in the physical reality of London. Some of us even live more in the diagram of the tube than we do in the physical reality of London. After all, the tube imparts a sense of the city that is not unlike the child's unintegrated vision described above: you disappear down a hole in the Mile End Road and then pop out of another one in Chalk Farm. Some people's whole lives must be like that, with no coherent sense of the city's geography; they must find it impossible to circumvent old lovers, defunct friendships.

Of course, I've been orienting myself for a lifetime, which is why it's so hideous, but it wasn't until the mid-Eighties that I had my first epiphany, the first coming together of all these disordered ideas and impressions and imaginings of London. I was standing in Hill Street, Mayfair, on a warm, early summer morning, when the realization came that I had never been to the mouth of the river that ran through the city of my birth. You couldn't have had more solid confirmation of the fact that London's geography remained, for me, exclusively emotional. What would you think of a peasant who had farmed all his life on the banks of a river if he told you he had never been to where that river meets the sea, some thirty miles away? You'd think he was a very ignorant, very insular, very landlocked peasant. There are millions of peasants like that in London; in imagining themselves to be at the very navel of the world, Londoners have forgotten the rest of their anatomy.

I got in the car and drove east. I had an idea, a visual image even, of Southend, the town on the northern bank of the Estuary, though it was someone else's image, smuggled into my memory by photograph or film. But the south bank was unknown, and so potentially the more exciting, although in common with the other peasants, I was certain there was nothing there, only mudflats and defunct industries.

The Isle of Grain, the southernmost extremity of the Thames, was the provider of a parallax, a point of reference that allowed me to sense the overall shape of the city and its peculiar cosmology. Once you've spotted one parallax, you begin to apprehend more and more. Central London may seem curiously flat, but if you drive up the Bayswater Road towards Marble Arch and focus on the very tips of those same iconic, twin chimneys which you can see poking up behind the green swell of Hyde Park to your right, you'll be able to realize the overall shape of the city moving beneath you. Or walk east across Wormwood Scrubs, under the machine eyes of the prison security cameras, but keep your eyes firmly fixed on the Trellick Tower, the block that dominates Notting Hill: you'll have the same sensation. I've now taken so many bearings that I am paralysed, ensnared by my own earlier sightings, lost in a tangled undergrowth of points of view. It took several more years and several more acts of geographic foolhardiness (the worst of which was undoubtedly making a film about the M25), before I could acknowledge the full extent of my own sense of confinement.

I adopted two stratagems to deal with the problem of being a small metropolis boy. The first was to take purposeless walks across the city; the second was to write fictions. The walks, in order to be purposeless, had to unite two parts of London that could not in any way be construed as bearing a functional relationship to one another; they were lines drawn on the *A–Z*: Perivale to Acton; Wood Green to Wandsworth; Hammersmith to Hackney.

This sense of confinement was enhanced by the fact that I was commuting at the time from Shepherd's Bush in the west to Southwark in the south-east. It was my first—and last—proper office job. It came with a company car, a Ford Sierra so new that there was wrapping paper on the accelerator and the interior smelled the way I remember new bicycle brakes smelling when I was a child. The temporal margins within which I had to operate were astonishingly narrow: five minutes too late leaving in the morning could mean another twenty on the journey time. Twenty minutes of giving children asthma, smoking cigarettes, merging with the collective ulcer. Twenty more minutes pinned like some automotive butterfly on the card of the Westway flyover, or the Gray's Inn Road or Blackfriars Bridge. When there were tube strikes—and there were a lot around then—the journey could last three hours.

I was overwhelmed by a sense of the totality of the traffic in the city, and of its complete interconnection. I began to imagine it might be possible to analyse it on a purely physical level, and from this to derive a complete knowledge of traffic flows throughout an entire built-up area. It would be like having an awesomely powered Trafficator computer, but in your head.

I started work on a story that expressed this idea of a metaphoric meta-jam; this world of driverless cars, this ultimate claustrophobia. Soon I was getting up at six-thirty in the morning, rushing through London by car in order to sit down and write about it. I began to work on other stories in parallel—and I began to see their ontogeny, and to see that they were all about London. By this I don't mean simply that they were all set in London, I mean that the city was the main—and possibly the only—protagonist.

Although it seemed as if the city had sucked me in, it was a consummation I had no will to resist. For in order to avoid the massive and destructive sense of irony that I felt whenever I came to the act of writing fiction, I *had* to write about something I knew very well indeed. I was forced on my subject—and it was forced on me. We were locked up together, tapping the monotonous, plastic piano.

Needless to say, my stratagems didn't work. London wasn't going away. Now I was a writer, I thought I needn't actually live in the place. It might be nice to live in the country, to write about London from a position of rural reclusion, or even not write about London at all. What a fool. The country was crowded, noisy and polluted. My infant son's asthma got worse. At night the sky was bruised with the massive explosion of halogen, forty miles away to the south. In the day I fancied I could hear the distant rumble of the Great Wen's traffic, mocking my bucolic idyll. I began writing a novel, most of which was set in London. It was disturbing and involving and I didn't want to get into it. We took a holiday in Morocco and as a piece of *jeu d'esprit* I wrote a novella, a light thing about a woman who grows a penis and uses it to rape her husband. Naturally this took place in Muswell Hill, another theoretically 'anonymous' north London suburb. I scrawled away, with the shouts of Berbers hawking in the Jama Al F'na ringing in my ears, describing a pedestrian narrative around familiar precincts.

Eventually I forced myself back to the novel. The London it was set in was a bewildering place containing many different levels of reality: my protagonist really could turn the corner of St James's and find himself mysteriously in the Aldwych. The city, once again, had usurped the tale, stolen the narrative. In the novel it was 'a mighty ergot fungus, erupting from the very crust of the earth; a growing, mutating thing, capable of taking on the most fantastic profusion of shapes. The people who live in this hallucinogenic development partake of its tryptamines, and so it bends itself to the secret dreams of its beholders.' This was, in fact, my own dark view. It was now not simply a matter of being in a confined, well-known place, it was like being in a confined space with a brooding, potentially violent presence.

My marriage broke up. I moved to the far north of Scotland. I wrote a collection of short stories, most of which were set in the M40 corridor. London was an enormous absence in these stories, but it was there, beyond the horizon, like a giant lodestone, attracting the cars down the motorway and then aligning them like iron filings around the M25.

I moved to Suffolk. It was a tired, eroded landscape which I walked ceaselessly, attempting to map it, but my subject matter, when I did manage to write at all, was exile. My protagonists were all writers who had left the city. I reached a point where my life and my writing life horribly intersected. I started to know people in the locale, there were invitations to gatherings of stultifying chit-chat. I was obliged to 'look in' at the craft shop. After four years, it was over in two days. A van was hired, a house was rented. I went home.

Initially I found myself to be pleasingly disoriented, occasionally even lost. My internal A–Z had faded with desuetude. But soon it was back, and worse than ever. The city was punishing me for my defection. Before I left, my fictionalized London might have been banjaxed and strange, but it exhibited no more anachronism than the real thing. Now this sinisterly altered. I began to perceive the city as not simply filled with my own lifelines and storylines, but choked with those of everyone else as well. I began to write stories set in a London where the opium den that Dorian Gray frequented in Limehouse was still mysteriously open, despite being shadowed by the Legoland of Canary Wharf Tower. This was a predictably more claustrophobic city than the one that had preceded it. It swarmed with humankind: humans running, humans walking, humans scratching, belching, farting, like a pack of apes. I decided to write a novel set in a London entirely populated by chimpanzees. My protagonist found the city to be about two-thirds to scale with the London he knew. That, and the way in which the chimps would ceaselessly and publicly copulate, served to make him feel overpoweringly claustrophobic.

I remarried and we bought this house in Vauxhall, closer to the centre than I've ever lived before. The great paperback miscegenation took place. My claustrophobia was now so complete that in some strange way it wasn't really claustrophobia any longer, more a case of my own partaking of too many London tryptamines: a bit of a bad trip. In the past I would welcome that sensation, familiar to all city dwellers, of suddenly noticing a building that I'd never paid any attention to before, even though it had been in my purview many thousands of times. Now I'm afflicted by a more ominous but related sensation, which involves suddenly noticing a new building and not being able to remember what it's replaced. This is unpleasant. This is like conceptualist burglars breaking into your house during the night and millimetrically realigning all the furniture.

There's only one way to arrest this entropy of the city—keep writing about it. I've learned to accept London as my muse. Initially, there I was, sitting on the tube, when she came in: filthy, raddled, smelly, old and drunk. Like everyone else I wanted to get up and move to the next carriage, especially when she elected to sit down right next to me. But now we're inseparable, going round and around the Circle Line, arm in arm, perhaps for eternity.

The measure of my acceptance is that I'm now prepared to fictionalize an area as soon as I move into it—like a dog marking its territory. I've set a short story in Vauxhall already, and to celebrate the hideousness of my orientation the climax takes place in the hot-air balloon which has recently been tethered here. Tourists pay a tenner to rise up 400 feet over London. On a clear day you can see almost the entire city spread out beneath you. When I did my research ascent, I was struck anew by the immensity of the urban hinterland to the south; it needs a big book, a really long novel. The Great South London Novel has a ring to it, I think.

In conclusion: when I was a child my unhappily married parents would drive us, almost every weekend, to Brighton, where we would stay with my grandparents. My parents would argue all the way there and all the way back; the trip was synonymous with misery for me. In time I came to associate any leaving of London with this wrenching sadness. I began to conceive of the city itself as a kind of loving parent, vast but womb-like and surmounted by an overarching dome. By accepting the city as a source of fictional inspiration I've made this dome a reality—for me. My only wish now is that everyone else should experience the same peculiar sense of interiority, of being in London, that I have. So, my only objection to the Millennium Dome is that it should have been far, far bigger—and I could have told them what to put in it. □

A LONDON VIEW/Ian Sinclair

The point of a good 'view' is that it encapsulates, and gives relief from, the journey that has led up to it. We no longer (unless we're professional location-finders or posey MTV directors) feel the need to traipse around with framing devices, some means of turning landscape into a picture. View is accidental, unlooked for, a breathing space.

Walking the ridgeway of Joseph Bazalgette's Northern Outfall Sewer, slantwise to the south-east, brings the traveller—if he times it right, in the afternoon in winter—up against the glorious absurdity of Beckton Alp, a man-made conical mound that can be ascended by a sequence of zigzag paths (resting spaces thoughtfully provided). The gentle climb allows the weary pedestrian time to remember how he got here. He can play back the drift along the sewage outlet, the savagely chopped verges, the bright blue benches (metallic and indestructible), the mustard brickwork cleaned by community service miscreants for use by the next generation of spray-can bandits. The gothic folly of the pumping station, the muddy vistas of Channelsea Creek (landscaped by spare Euro-loot that cannot be used on schools and hospitals), the electric hymns in the low-slung power cables: all these memories and effects flare and burn out as you pant upwards.

The summit has it all. Now the orange sun-gas is dissolving over the distant glimmer of the unreal city (Canary Wharf and Docklands). This is a post-urban vision seeded by J. G. Ballard and taken to the point of parody: golden browns, flaring scarlet brake-lights on Newham Way, levels and counter-levels of traffic gunning out of town towards the Estuary, hot colours that are absorbed in the grey-blue distance of the river and the Royal Albert Dock. The quiet excitement, the sense of the machinery of metropolitan life, entropy seduced by perpetual motion, is unmatched anywhere within the M25 boundary. The site is mythic, aligned with the lost mound of Whitechapel and the culture of Silbury Hill. It's the best kind of fake. It aspires to the language of television: a non-operational ski-slope that belongs in some lowlife drama, a body slumped in a chairlift. But that's not enough, Beckton wants more. The runway of the City Airport in Silvertown. A floodlit driving range. An ancient, tangled graveyard (now, naturally, made-over into an infrequently opened nature reserve). A business park, more dead than alive. A humming screen: heavy-goods vehicles, commuters, river-taxis freighting an absence of passengers to the airport, water-skis carving patterns in the blue-green algae of the docks, short-haul planes dicing with gravity to scrape the thin skies of the Thames corridor. Black smoke, thick with sugar droplets, from the Tate & Lyle factory.

From the privilege of the alp's viewing platform, leaning on a creosoted railing, the illusion floats before your eyes: that this city makes sense, there is a pattern, a working design. There has to be a word for it. Obscenery. A carcinogenic high. An opportunity to enjoy a panorama of blight and damage. And underneath, the secret rush of underground rivers bearing away all our heavy-metal shit to a processing 'farm'. There's no way back. Better far to remain here, prayers made at the stations of your journey, as by pilgrims crawling on their hands and knees up the rocky path of Croagh Patrick. You've done it, pitched yourself into a molten apocalypse. The river is boiled, the land convulsed.

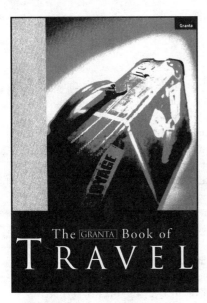
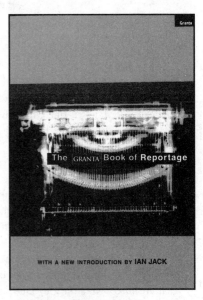

Enjoying yourself?

Then why not subscribe to Granta? You'll SAVE UP TO £40!

(Or treat a friend? A Granta subscription makes a wonderful gift: thoughtful, unusual and lasting.)

Some of the best new fiction, memoir, reportage and photography appears first (and often only) in Granta. Subscribe today, and you will save up to £40 on the £8.99 bookshop price, and get a year's worth (or more) of writing that matters, delivered to your home.

You'll **save £11** (30%) with a one-year subscription (4 issues) for just £24.95.

You'll **save £25** (35%) with a two-year subscription (8 issues) for £46.50.

You'll **save £40** (38%) with a three-year subscription (12 issues) for £67.

The order form is overleaf. It takes a moment to fill it out—then a year (at least!) to enjoy the results.

'Essential reading.' Observer

'This is writing at its very best.'
Scotland on Sunday

'Never take Granta for granted.'
Daily Telegraph

THE MAGAZINE OF NEW WRITING   **www.granta.com**

Order form

Save up to £40!

Your details (we need these even if you're giving a gift subscription)

Name _____

Address _____

_____ Postcode _____

○ I'd like to subscribe for myself, for: ○ One year at £24.95 (£11 off)
○ Two years at £46.50 (£25 off)
○ Three years at £67 (£40 off)

○ I'd like to give a gift subscription for: ○ One year at £24.95
○ Two years at £46.50
○ Three years at £67

Details for a gift subscription

Name _____

Address _____

_____ Postcode _____

Message: _____
(optional: we'll send a letter announcing your gift and, if you like, incorporating a brief message)

Payment details

That's____ subscriptions for a total* of £_____, paid by: ○ cheque (to 'Granta') enclosed
○ Visa, Mastercard, AmEx

Card no: / __ / __ / __ / __ / __ / __ / __ / __ / __ / __ / __ / __ / __ /

Expires: / __ / __ / __ / Signature: _____

* **Postage.** The prices shown include UK postage. Please add £8 per year for the rest of Europe,
£15 a year for overseas (airspeeded delivery). C5S65

○ Please tick if you'd prefer not to receive occasional offers from other, compatible organizations.

✉ Post ('Freepost' in the UK): Granta, Freepost, 2/3 Hanover Yard, Noel Rd, London N1 8BR, UK

☎ Or phone/fax credit-card orders. In the UK: **FreeCall 0500 004 033** (tel & fax)
Outside UK: Tel 44 171 704 0470, Fax 44 171 704 0474. E-mail: subs@grantamag.co.uk

GRANTA

GRANTA

THE MAN
IN THE VAN
Lucretia Stewart

Camden Square

The Man in the Van

On Friday 20 March 1998 at ten-thirty in the morning I was lying in the bath, washing my hair. I came up from under the soapy water, finished rinsing out the shampoo, then turned off the shower attachment. In the silence that followed, I realized that I could hear a woman's high-pitched screams and, mingled with them, the sound of angry roaring. I jumped out of the bath, put on a robe, and ran up the stairs to the front door. In the narrow alley leading to the garden, I saw a man with his back turned towards me, holding another person and, apparently, punching this person. The assailant's trousers were down, exposing pale buttocks, and I feared he might also be raping the person he was attacking. I looked around for a weapon and saw a brick lying on the ground. I could only just get my hand round it, but I picked it up and hit the man on the back of his head. When he felt the blow, actually scarcely more than a tap, he stopped punching the person he was attacking and turned to face me.

In that moment, I registered several things: that I knew both the man and his victim; that she was fully dressed and therefore not being raped; that blood was pouring down her face and that her eyes looked staring, as if she were almost blinded with terror, and, finally, that the man had a knife in his right hand. He came towards me— I knew I should run, but I couldn't move—and seized me by my right arm, which he began to stab, mouthing at me all the while. I wasn't conscious of being frightened and I felt no pain; I couldn't hear what he was saying, though I could see clearly that his lips were moving. Then a young man, a stranger, with dark hair and wearing a leather jacket walked down the alley. The man who was holding my arm and stabbing me said, 'All right, John, arrest me then.' He let go of my arm, handed the second man his knife and said, 'Just let me have my dog. Don't do anything to my dog because I love my dog.' I ran back inside and telephoned for an ambulance.

The man was called Geoff; I had known him for just over three years. The woman he had attacked was Nicole—Nicky—who helped me in the garden and had done so for about two years. On the morning of the attack, Nicky had come to measure the back garden for a terrace which I was hoping to have built in the summer. I was supposed to help her, but I had to go to Paris that afternoon and needed to wash my hair before the trip. I gave her my car keys so that she could collect the new plants which were in the car. As soon as she left the house, I got into the bath.

Geoff attacked Nicky as she was walking down the alley into the back garden. She was holding carrier bags containing the plants in both hands. Geoff ran after her, down the alley, shouting, and attacked her from behind, grabbing her hair. Even though she dropped the bags immediately, she could not break free from him. Geoff stabbed her in the back, then twisted her round to face him, still holding her by her hair. He stabbed her in the chest, below her right breast, then again, several times, in the face. Geoff had threaded the blade of the knife through two fingers, the first two, I think, of his right hand; his method of attack was simultaneously to punch and to stab. He stabbed Nicky twenty-two times.

After Geoff and the man had gone, Nicky came back inside. Her face was covered in blood and she was shaking. The front of her jeans was wet where, in her fear, she had pissed herself. We put our arms round each other and hugged one another very hard. I kept saying to her over and over again, 'I'm so sorry.' I heard police cars drive up, brakes squealing, sirens blaring. In the midst of all this, a friend telephoned. I tried to tell him what had happened, but I found I couldn't frame the words. I said, 'I'm sorry, I think I'm going to faint,' and put the receiver down. When the ambulance men arrived, I left Nicky in my bedroom while they examined her and went out into the square outside my house, still in my dressing gown, with bare feet and my hair dripping. There were two police cars and an ambulance. Geoff was standing in the street with his hands handcuffed behind his back.

The square seemed to be full of policemen and passers-by, ostensibly walking their dogs but actually consumed with curiosity. I recognized a man strolling past with a pale, creamy pug on a lead. Even though I knew him—we had worked together at one time— even though he saw that I had seen him, he did not come over to find out what had happened. Another ambulance arrived. Geoff was taken away in a police car. Nicky was carried outside—I think, on a stretcher, though it may have been a sort of stretcher chair—and driven to University College Hospital. I went inside, put on a skirt, a sweater and some shoes, and brushed my wet hair. The police took away Nicky's bloodstained clothes, my pink bathrobe, which was now torn where the knife had penetrated the fabric and covered in blood, and the cordless telephone which Nicky had used to call the police while Geoff was stabbing me. It was sticky with blood from the wounds on her face. One policeman actually used the phrase, a 'frenzied attack'—which I had heard before only on television or in the cinema—to describe what had happened.

Half an hour later, the second ambulance took me to hospital. Nicky's friend Rebecca had telephoned soon after Nicky was taken off, and I had told her briefly what happened. When I arrived at the hospital she was already sitting with Nicky. She was crying. X-rays had revealed that Nicky had a compound fracture to her right cheekbone. She had six stab wounds to her face, including one just above her right cheekbone near the eye; another blow, it turned out, had severed a nerve in her left cheek. Nicky kept saying that she could feel pain at the back of her head, but the nurses couldn't find any wound. Eventually, after looking carefully, combing through her matted, bloodied hair with my fingers, I found the small triangular puncture just above the hairline.

I had been stabbed six times in the upper arm where the skin seems to be quite resilient. The nurse dressed my cuts with suture strips and then bandaged them, but Nicky had to have stitches in several of her wounds. They were puncture wounds, rather than cuts. Geoff had attacked us with the tool on a penknife used for removing stones from horses' hoofs, or possibly for making a hole in a piece of leather. Something like an awl. The damage would have been worse if he had used an actual blade, though if he had pierced an artery or succeeded in stabbing Nicky in the eye, his choice of weapon would have been irrelevant. Because he had been punching Nicky while stabbing her, she was terribly bruised and very stiff. Even the smallest movement caused her pain. By contrast, I felt numb. I left Nicky lying on a hospital trolley and went to telephone my brother. I told him what had happened—he was horrified—and asked him to send Nicky an enormous bunch of flowers. He said that we would get 'some money'—compensation from the Criminal Injuries' Compensation Authority (CICA). I think he thought this would cheer me up. It did.

I went back to Nicky and told her the good news. I remember cracking jokes about the whole business, asking the nurses why they were or weren't doing something or other. 'I've seen *Casualty*, you know,' I said. It wasn't that funny, but we laughed. Nicky and I seemed quite elated by the whole experience, euphoric even. I suppose this was the aftermath of the fear, the adrenaline high. Rebecca kept breaking down in tears. It was clear that she couldn't shake off the thought of what might have happened to Nicky if I hadn't gone out into the alley.

The police said that they would arrange to take Nicky home, but that they couldn't spare a car for me. I went outside to Euston Road and hailed a taxi. All the way to Camden Town, up Camden Road, and into Camden Square where I live, I felt oddly disembodied—if that is the right word. I didn't feel real. I felt utterly detached.

At home, my flat looked as if I—or maybe several people—had left in a hurry. My bed was unmade, the bedside lamp still on. I live in a basement—we like to call it a 'garden' flat—and the bedroom is the darkest room, usually requiring some artificial light. The bath was still full of water—as I had left it—but now cold. I had given a set of keys to one of the policemen, and he had locked up, though he had omitted to padlock the wooden door to the back garden. This door is right next to the front door and opens into the alley, where Geoff had caught Nicky. I went outside. Late March, bright and blustery. It was about three in the afternoon, though it was difficult to have any sense of time. For instance, I had no idea how long the attack had lasted, nor how long before the police had arrived. There had been a big clay flowerpot by the front door. Now shards of terracotta and clumps of soil lay on the ground. The new plants, which included two white *dicentra*, 'bleeding heart' (one of which I had bought for Nicky), were scattered in the alley, where Nicky had dropped them. On the tiled path and the far wall of the alley, near where the passion flower grows, were big patches of dried blood. Back inside, I undressed slowly, put on a nightdress and got into bed. Suddenly my whole back was rigid, frozen solid. I could move only with the greatest difficulty. I stayed in bed for two days.

I met Geoff six weeks or so after I came to live in Camden Square, just before Christmas 1994. I moved to Camden because one of my oldest friends lived four streets away and it had, I thought, an appealing funkiness. The press reports of the attack described the square as 'fashionable', which surprised me. I know that houses there are expensive now (my neighbour, who bought her house in the early 1960s for just under £5,000, was recently offered £600,000 cash), but the area has remained pretty mixed. There is a 1950s block of council flats on the west side of the square and another one to the north. There are no proper restaurants, no fashionable shops. The neighbourhood still has a raffish, bohemian quality which Knightsbridge and Kensington, say, lack. To put it another way, it's still quite rough. Soon after I moved in, the freeholder told me that burglary and vandalism were so prevalent in the area, I should regard myself as 'under siege'. My flat's previous owners were burgled twice; as a result, they installed a burglar alarm complete with 'panic' button. You press this and the alarm goes off.

My flat came with a square of untidy garden in the back and a patch of uncultivated ground in front. I asked the previous owner why there was nothing but bare earth in the front. 'Nothing will grow there,' she said.

I first spoke to Geoff in early February 1995 when one of my cats disappeared. I was walking round the square, distraught and calling her, and I asked Geoff if he had seen her. He said, 'No,' but added that he was sure a local woman named Marcella had taken her. As it turned out, he was right (Marcella was under the illusion that my cat was actually *her* cat and that I had stolen the cat from her).

After this Geoff and I would exchange a few remarks whenever we saw each other. Somehow he had discovered that I was a journalist (perhaps I had told him); once he asked me whether I might be able to get a piece into the *Evening Standard* about the Newbury bypass, to which he was opposed (the papers, at the time, were full of stories about Swampy and his fellow eco-warriors whose protests were holding up the construction of the bypass). I told him that I didn't usually write about environmental issues, so I doubted it. He never mentioned the subject again.

Geoff always stood, or sat, in the same place, next to a green Camden council rubbish bin, on a raised patch of untended grass at the top of the gently sloping square. This position gave him a view of the whole square and was directly across the road from my front gate. I saw him, therefore, very frequently. He would be there most days, from dawn to dusk, a large, blue can of Tennent's Super in one hand, a roll-up in the other, passing the time of day with whosoever happened to be passing—people out walking their dogs, mothers taking their children to school, and other vagrants.

Geoff is a big man, over six feet tall. The top of his head is completely bald, and his remaining hair—reddish-brown—streams to his shoulders. His beard straggles down the front of his shirt. He wore, whatever the temperature, a checked lumberjack shirt and brown cord jeans, the latter slung so low on his hips that they looked as if they might fall to the ground at any moment. I can't remember ever seeing him in a coat. From his appearance, he could have been any age between forty and fifty (after his arrest, I discovered that he was actually only thirty-seven). He was outside in most weather; sometimes his hair and beard ran with water until they looked like wet grass on a river-bed.

Geoff had a wiry, dusty little black dog which barked at cats and which he had trained to jump up and drape itself round his neck like a moth-eaten fur stole. He often rode round the area on a bicycle with the dog hanging round his neck. I think he dealt in second-hand bicycles, two or three of which he kept chained to a signpost indicating the cycle route to Tufnell Park and Holloway, next to where he always stood. When he got rid of one of the bikes, another one, or some part of another one, would be produced from one of two vans, which he kept parked in the road adjacent to my garden wall. One van was hand-painted a bright buttercup yellow; the other was, I think, white with a red trim. It wasn't possible to see into the interior of either as the windows were obscured, but as far as I know, Geoff lived in these vans, though people said that he had a place somewhere, and he himself told me one morning that he had just been 'offered a flat in West Hampstead'.

But, if he had a home, he didn't choose to go to it very often, preferring to spend his days in the square. Geoff seemed to make a point of being aware of all the local comings and goings, acting as a sort of unofficial watchdog. Friends told me that if I was out or away when they called by, he would know and say, 'She's out,' or 'She's gone away.' In some ways, this was reassuring, though I found his interest in my movements oppressive and, after the attack, some friends told me that they had always felt intimidated by his presence, had found him 'sinister'.

Nicky is a striking woman in her late thirties; she has delicate features, dark curly hair and big blue eyes. She worked in the garden of a neighbour, a woman who lived a few houses away. It was through this woman, with whom I had become friendly, that, in May 1996, she came to work for me.

It had taken me a year and a half to decide what I wanted to do with the front garden. My immediate neighbour, who was also the freeholder of the house, had proposed a coolly elegant scheme involving gravel and York stone, the cost of which would be shared by all the occupants. This seemed both expensive and more formal than I would have liked. One night, hearing a noise, I woke around three and looked out of my bedroom window. The front garden, in the full yellow glare of a street lamp, looked particularly desolate. At that moment, I realized that I wanted a rose garden, thorny, wild, overgrown and romantic, a kind of Sleeping Beauty's bower—inasmuch as this was possible in north London.

Nicky began work on the garden soon after. I spent a small fortune in the local garden centre and I read rose catalogues as if they were love stories, lingering over the names of the roses: Veilchenblau, Albertine, Trascadescent, Eglantyne, Scepter'd Isle, Redouté, La Reine Victoria, Russelliana, Dusky Maiden, Compassion. I ordered recklessly, paying little heed to the suitability of my chosen roses to the garden. Appearance was all. I chose from photographs, but rejected those roses, however beautiful, whose names I didn't like. I wanted white, blood-red and pale blush-pink, old-fashioned roses, with complicated structures, heady fragrances and wistful, rambling shoots.

The garden progressed well. In addition to the roses, we planted peonies (which, according to a magazine article I read on *feng shui*, boded well for long, happy relationships—roses, it claimed, only encouraged short, disastrous love affairs), poppies, hellebores, a purple magnolia, a clematis and a tall evergreen shrub called *pittosporum*. The climbing roses—a Constance Spry, a Bleu Magenta, a Complicata and a Rambling Rector—began to entwine themselves through the iron railings and the wire fence separating my property from that of my neighbours. By midsummer, the front garden was beginning to look just as I had imagined.

And by then, Geoff was in a bad way. He appeared to be having some kind of breakdown. If ever I asked, 'How are you, Geoff?', he would complain of being depressed; he said that *they* were 'out to get him,' that *they* were everywhere: 'people' were spying on him, invading his brain, exerting a malign influence, that the forces of evil were all around. Most days, he would simply stand at the top of the square, in silence, head bowed, still drinking, still smoking, but no longer in a mood for conversation. One Saturday morning I asked him how he was feeling. He said that he was having a bad day and I invited him in for a cup of tea. I can't remember exactly what he said, but the gist of it was clear. He was unhappy; he felt persecuted by dark forces. I feared that he might be suicidal and, after he had gone, I telephoned Social Services. Though it was a weekend, someone answered, but he said that we would have to wait until Monday for anything to be done.

Nicky had always been friendly to Geoff in that she would greet him when she arrived, say 'goodbye' when she left, and sometimes stop for a brief chat. But even in the summer months, when the garden most needed attention, she never came more frequently than once every two to three weeks, and not regularly. Rebecca would often accompany her and the two women would work flat out all day, stopping only briefly for cups of tea or something to eat. In the winter, after the bulbs had been put in and the leaves swept up, I hardly saw Nicky. Geoff could hardly claim to have become a friend of hers in any usual sense of the word. He had never spent more than a few minutes with her, nor had he seen her that often.

Nevertheless, Geoff's interest in Nicky was developing rapidly. He began to shout, as I came out of my front gate, 'You planning on having any gardening done?' and, one morning, he rang my doorbell. He asked me to telephone Nicky and tell her to come to see him. 'She cheers me up,' he said. I didn't call her, of course. On the days that Nicky did come, Geoff was a real pest. He would wander, uninvited, into the garden and follow her as she worked, ranting and raving about Nazis and other demons. One day, when I came back from the supermarket, I found him slumped over her motorbike, which she had wheeled into the front garden. 'What are you doing?' I asked. 'I used to have a bike like this,' he said. 'I don't think Nicky wants you sitting on her bike,' I said. 'I used to have a bike like this,' he repeated. He only got off the machine when Nicky started to become angry and told him to go away. She felt sorry for him, but now her anger overcame her pity.

The incident with the motorbike seemed to mark the beginning of Geoff's obsessive interest in Nicky. Another day, he told her he had dreamed that he had seen her 'murdered and covered in blood'. Geoff's attentions became too much for her; she told me that she didn't think that she could carry on working for me because he was upsetting her so much. So I had a word with him, explaining that Nicky couldn't get on with her work if he kept distracting her and asking him to leave her in peace. He took this calmly—which was a relief. And, just days after my conversation with him, I came home to find a book on my front doorstep. It was a nice old book called *The ABC of Flower Growing*, which had been published in 1947.

'Did you get the book?' Geoff asked the next morning. 'I just thought it might be useful to someone who was interested in gardening.' Some days later, I found an arrangement of cut flowers— which, I imagine, had been professionally done—half-dead on the step. When I saw Geoff, he asked me if I had got them. I thanked him and he said, 'I thought someone might be able to plant them in a garden.'

I said to my neighbour, 'Doesn't Geoff realize that he doesn't stand a chance with Nicky?' 'For goodness' sake,' she said, 'you of all people should know that love is no respecter of logic.'

Despite all this, I still didn't think of Geoff as dangerous. Annoying, yes; frightening, no.

When I think back to that summer, when all this began, I remember meeting Geoff bicycling in Camden Square, his dog around his neck.

'I'm thinking of leaving,' he announced.

'Leaving? Why would you do that? Where would you go?' I asked.
'I might go to Clapham,' he said.
'Clapham? Why Clapham? I mean, what could be better than Camden Square?' I said.
'Paradise perhaps.'

I don't think that we ever exchanged another light-hearted word. In fact, by the spring of 1997, Geoff no longer addressed a single word of any kind to me or to Nicky or to Rebecca. He also made a point—or so it seemed—of cutting dead my neighbour (the one who had introduced me to Nicky), her daughter, her son-in-law, two friends of hers who had also become friends of mine—they had a dachshund, which they would walk in the neighbourhood (one of these women reported that Geoff had told her to 'fuck off')—and finally, the friend of mine who lived four streets away. She owned a fox terrier and she and Geoff had always exchanged a few friendly, dog-related words. But not any more.

I wouldn't go so far as to say that I minded being shunned by Geoff, but nor was it exactly comfortable. Hitherto he had been—ostensibly, at any rate—a benign presence. I didn't miss my conversations with him, but, as I scuttled to and from my car, I disliked feeling that I had to avoid his eye, as if I were somehow at fault. It was difficult to ignore Geoff. He knew how to make his brooding presence felt. On the other hand, I was away a lot—I spent six weeks out of London in the winter of 1997—so Geoff, or rather what seemed now to have developed into Geoff's antagonism towards me and towards anyone I knew, didn't really make much of an impact.

I returned to London in the middle of December 1997. On 21 December, the Sunday before Christmas, Nicky and Rebecca came to tidy up the garden. All the leaves had fallen from the trees; my beautiful rose bushes, denuded, looked stark and bare, and the ground was a sea of mud. The women left around four, just as the light was beginning to go. I walked out into the street with them, and kissed them both, wishing them Happy Christmas. Geoff was in his usual position; I remember noticing that he was watching us. The following morning, when I came out of the house, I found that

I had a flat tyre. I drove my car, a twelve-year-old red Citroën 2CV, to the garage in the nearby mews where they put the spare on for me. Grove Tyres, round the corner in Agar Grove, was closed over Christmas and New Year; I didn't know where else to go, so I wasn't able to get the damaged tyre repaired.

That afternoon I developed a sore throat. By the next morning, I had the beginnings of a cough and a temperature. I spent 22 and 23 December in bed. On Christmas Eve, a couple of friends came for supper, and, on Christmas Day evening, three more friends came for what turned out to be a long night. They left around three in the morning.

I spent most of Boxing Day clearing up the debris left by my entertaining and nursing my sore throat. When I finally left the house around six-thirty in the evening, I discovered that I had two more flat tyres. I called a minicab, reflecting that, this way, at least I wouldn't be drinking and driving.

On the morning of 27 December I called National Breakdown to come and do something about my tyres—three of them were now useless. The mechanic told me that the tyres had been punctured in the side with a sharp instrument—probably a knife—and were irreparable. I would have to buy three new tyres. Grove Tyres was still closed so he towed the car to the nearest branch of Kwik-Fit, off the Holloway Road. I rode with him in the cab of his tow truck. At Kwik-Fit, the guy told me that they had no appropriate tyres in stock and would have to order them, also that they weren't going to be cheap. I caught a bus home and went to bed.

At this point, perhaps because of the flu, perhaps because of the boredom of dealing with all this, my memory of events becomes a little hazy. On 21 February, I wrote in my diary, 'We have a problem with Jeff [sic]. I've had 5 car tyres knifed since just before Christmas; T. [my neighbour] has had paraffin put through her door and Nicky had her motorbike seat spat all over. Plus the bags of dog treats & huge dog bones that keep coming over the fence. Last night at about 10.30 I heard something thud on to the flat roof. This morning I went out to look: it was a packet of dog treats.'

One morning I came out to find that the canvas roof of the car had been slashed. The replacement cost around £250. I reported the problems with the car and Nicky's fouled motorbike seat to the police; I also told them, feeling faintly foolish as I did so, about the small yellow bags of Pedigree Chum dog treats and the bones which kept appearing in the garden. Up to twenty such bags had now appeared. Having made sure that none of them had been opened, I gave them to my friends' dachshund who gobbled them up. My neighbour, the one for whom Nicky also gardened, reported the paraffin which had been poured through her letter box. The police took statements and went to talk to Geoff. He said that he knew nothing about either my tyres or the paraffin, but did describe us (me? Nicky? Rebecca? my neighbour?) as those 'fucking bitches'.

Sergeant Mortimer from the Community Policing Unit (which has now been renamed the Community Safety Unit) in Kentish Town told me that, while the police suspected that Geoff might be responsible for these incidents, they were unable to take action without proper evidence. He also told me that Social Services had apparently never heard of Geoff. I speculated on Geoff's possible motives for the shower of doggie treats; was it because he thought I was such a bitch or because he knew that I had cats and thought perhaps that the cats would enjoy the treats? The handsome young constable who had accompanied Sergeant Mortimer said, 'If I was you, I wouldn't spend too much time wondering about his motives. I shouldn't think he does.'

Sergeant Mortimer had discovered that Geoff had a council flat a couple of miles away in Dunollie Road in Kentish Town; he decided to invoke regulations under the Road Traffic Act which would permit him to have Geoff's vans moved. He reasoned that, if the vans were gone, then Geoff would follow. He advised me to park my car elsewhere while the vans were removed, so I arranged to leave it some ten minutes' walk away in a makeshift car-park next to the car-wash run by some Africans. This arrangement suited the Africans rather better than it suited me. I had to pay them ten pounds a night.

It was now late February. I went to Morocco for a long weekend, leaving the car in the car-wash car-park at a cost of forty pounds. When I returned to London, the vans were gone (though my neighbour reported seeing them parked several streets away). Geoff, however, was not. He still occupied his usual spot. Seeing him there, seeing the vans gone, I felt an uneasy mixture of guilt, relief and trepidation.

Two days after I got back, on 5 March, a tree surgeon came to cut down the big lime tree in the front garden. He arrived early with two helpers, one of whom looked exactly like Steve McQueen. Nicky came too. We had agonized for months about the felling of this tree. It oozed a sticky, blackish substance all summer which discoloured and damaged the leaves of the other plants in the garden and was difficult to remove from the paintwork and windscreens of cars parked in the street. It also blocked much of the light that the front garden needed. Despite all this, I hated the idea of cutting it down.

It was a brilliant, cold, sunny day, and the whole enterprise was somehow suffused with a spirit of comradeship and good humour. The tree surgeon, a spry fifty-five-year-old who was lame in one leg, asked first Nicky, then me, for a date. Steve McQueen, who abseiled up and down the tree effortlessly as if he were simply climbing stairs, told Nicky that he often got work as a Steve McQueen double. The third man, who I don't remember so well, was quiet and had some teeth missing. It took most of the day to cut the tree down and dispose of the wood; a steady stream of people came to have a look, to ask for some of the wood, and so on. Geoff watched the proceedings from his patch, watched—and I don't think I am being fanciful here—Nicky laughing and joking with the men. I remember we talked about Geoff that day. Nicky told the men how he had chased her down the street one day, shouting 'You cunt.' This was the first I had heard of this incident. The quiet man said that we should get some big men to warn him off.

The next time I saw Nicky was on 20 March.

On the evening of the day of the attack, a young policeman came to take my statement. I was in bed, stiff and sore. He sat on the bed and wrote down—or attempted to write down—what I told him. After fifteen difficult minutes, he said, 'Would you rather do this?' 'No, I wouldn't,' I said, 'for three reasons. One, my right arm hurts; two, it's your job; and three, it clearly has to be written in a language with which I am totally unfamiliar.'

It took two and a half hours for him to take my statement. It took a policewoman, Alison McCleod, seven hours to take Nicky's, which eventually ran to twenty-one pages.

The telephone rang frequently that weekend as news of the attack spread. At first, I found that I rather enjoyed telling the story, but before long it left me exhausted and irritable. I took to referring concerned callers to someone who already knew the details; sometimes I asked people who had heard the story to tell other friends. My friend, who lived nearby, asked what had become of Geoff's dog. When I told her that I neither knew nor cared, she said, 'There's no need to be like that. It's not the dog's fault.' My teenage godson inquired why I hadn't pressed the 'panic button'. I said that I hadn't remembered its existence. I spoke to Nicky a few times who told me that she kept reliving the experience, imagining herself trapped in the alley, fighting off Geoff and wondering why I didn't come to help her. My mother came to see me; I couldn't move my right arm, so she planted all the plants, swept up the spilled earth and the fragments of the broken flowerpot and washed Nicky's blood from the wall and the tiled floor.

On Monday 23 March Geoff appeared at Clerkenwell Magistrates' Court charged with Attempted Murder. A criminal barrister friend sent his junior along; she produced a report which he passed on to me. It said: 'Mr Bevan [Geoff] was in a poor psychiatric state—his solicitor had clearly experienced difficulties in taking instructions from him and, in fact, special provision had to be made for instructions to be taken in court with his mother present, since she was not allowed to be with him in the cells. Mr Bevan's solicitor made a bail application, mentioning the psychological pressure caused to him by continuing detention in custody... The application was refused by the stipendiary magistrate on the grounds that he might commit further offences whilst on bail and that he should be kept in custody for his own protection...'

That afternoon, Nicky and her two sisters, one older, one younger, came for tea, bringing with them a large chocolate cake. Her elder sister gave me a card in which she thanked me for 'saving her sister's life'. We all went out into the garden—it was another bright, windy day—and stood in the alley. I thought how brave it was of Nicky to come back there, but I didn't have any sense of having been brave myself. My main emotion was guilt—if I had not selfishly wanted to keep Nicky as a gardener, she would never have been exposed to this danger. When people told me that I had saved her life, I protested. No, no, it was nothing. But, then I began to see that by reacting in that way, by diminishing my action, I was also diminishing Nicky's danger and her fear.

The truth is, I do believe that if I had not come out and hit Geoff he would have killed Nicky, not necessarily because he was trying to kill her (I don't know what he thought he was trying to do), but because he was attacking her so frenziedly that, sooner or later, he would have punctured something vital, such as an artery, a lung or an eye. Nicky herself believes that if she hadn't managed to remain on her feet, she would have been finished. She says that, during the attack, she kept thinking, 'I mustn't go down. I'm finished if I go down.'

My god-daughter wrote to me, saying, ' I hope you're not still frightened,' and my eighty-nine-year-old aunt sent me a cheque for £100 and a note telling me that I had 'earned the Red Badge of Courage' and that she wished she could send it to me.

The following week I went to New York. I stayed away for two weeks and when I returned home it seemed as if a hundred years had elapsed since the attack. Life, for me, returned to normal. Geoff was locked up somewhere—some people said that he was in Pentonville; others said it was Brixton. Someone else had heard that he'd had a nervous breakdown. I didn't feel sorry for him. I was glad that he wasn't around, glad not to have to avoid his gaze as I left my home, glad not to be the recipient of any more dog treats, glad not to have to worry about my car.

It was more difficult for Nicky. She had been the focus of Geoff's obsession and she found this very hard to accept. In her rational mind, she knew that she had not done anything to encourage this, or to provoke the attack, but she had to hang on to that knowledge with all her might. She had also been the primary target during the attack; Geoff's extreme proximity to her alone (remember, I had thought she was being raped) must have been terrifying, let alone his rage. Her fear and her pain had been so much greater than mine.

Both of us were advised to contact our local branch of Victims' Support. Nicky went to see them and found it quite helpful; I went—

reluctantly—when I needed help in completing the claim forms from the CICA. To my surprise, I found going over the details of the attack reduced me to tears. It made me wonder how much I was, if not exactly repressing, certainly controlling. I had already noticed that the mere sight of a tall, bearded man carrying a can of beer made me extremely nervous. Nicky had talked about getting in touch with Jayne Zito (whose husband, Jonathan, was stabbed to death in 1992 by a schizophrenic) whom she had met somewhere; the counsellor at Victims' Support gave me the details of her organization and I thought about contacting it. In the end, I didn't have the time. I didn't feel like a victim.

The Plea and Directions Hearing, at which Geoff was to enter a plea and a trial date be set, had originally been scheduled for 26 May. It had to be postponed twice because Geoff was not in a fit state to attend and finally took place on 17 June. The trial date was set for the week beginning 12 October at the Old Bailey, very nearly nine months after the attack. Geoff entered a plea of Not Guilty.

Snippets of information about Geoff began to leak my way. I already knew that his last name was Bevan; now I learned that his parents lived round the corner from Camden Square, and had done so for many years. This went a long way towards explaining the master-of-all-he-surveys air with which Geoff used to look around as he stood at the top of the square. Mike, the mechanic who had fitted the new roof to my 2CV, turned out to have been at school with Geoff at Acland Burghley comprehensive in Tufnell Park. Mike didn't remember much about him from those days, only that he had always been a 'loner'. Mike said that he thought Geoff had been 'hanging around Camden Square' for about twelve years, but that he had 'gone downhill' in the last few years. He said that Geoff used to wave at him, but that he hadn't done so for some time. And, one Sunday, at a lunch party in North Kensington, a woman who had heard about the attack told me that she knew of a woman in Camden who had had an affair with Geoff. When it ended, Geoff had, this woman reported, 'turned nasty'.

Then I heard that some local residents had got up a petition in support of Geoff. A friend was stopped in the street and asked to sign it. She refused and told the person who had stopped her that they clearly didn't know the true facts of the case. Word was bound to have reached me about the petition sooner or later, but I didn't want Nicky, who had come back to the garden, to hear about it. I rang Detective Sergeant Rob Anderson, the officer in charge of the case at Kentish Town CID. 'There's nothing we can do,' I was told, 'It's a free country.' And so it is. And so it should be. But the discovery of this petition made me uneasy, following, as it did, on rumours that had come my way, rumours which people who had visited Geoff in prison brought back with them. Geoff had apparently told people that I wanted to sell my flat and had thought that the presence of his vans would reduce my chances of a good sale—that was why I had wanted him and his vans moved. This was his justification for his violence. I had—I have—no intention of selling.

It had all seemed so clear to me before: Geoff had harassed, then attacked us. He had been arrested; he should be punished, or at least detained and given medical treatment. What had happened was an accident, a horrible accident, but not something that either Nicky or I had provoked or deserved.

However, it had become obvious as the weeks went by that dealing with the effects of the attack wasn't going to be easy—or straightforward. I found myself getting into arguments with my neighbour, who seemed convinced that Geoff would be let out as soon as the trial was over, and be back on the street to haunt and frighten us all. Every time she expressed this view, even though it was obviously merely an articulation of her own fears, I got angry. I didn't want to have to contemplate that possibility. One of the problems was that I couldn't seem to explain to anyone how I felt; another was that, because Nicky had been hurt so much worse, I felt left out of the general outrage and sympathy; I felt that I was expected to bounce back quickly.

My strongest feelings were guilt and a consequent desire to protect Nicky, who, though her wounds had healed (except for the nerve in her face), was making slow progress emotionally. I also felt a kind of irritable impatience about the whole thing, which sometimes extended even to Nicky. One of the side effects of the attack was that, for months afterwards, neither Nicky nor I could bring ourselves to say Geoff's name, even to ourselves. We would call him 'him' or 'the man', 'the man who stabbed us'. Then, one day, I heard Nicky say 'Geoff' and I realized that she was getting better. And one day Geoff's rusty bicycles disappeared.

As the date for the trial approached, I began to get nervous. I had thought that I would breeze through it; I had almost been looking forward to it, but now I found myself dreading it. I began sleeping very badly. Once I dreamed that it was the day of the trial, that Nicky and I walked into court arm in arm, then waited and waited for Geoff, but he didn't turn up. Eventually, in the dream, we heard a rumour that he intended to run through the courtroom at eleven-thirty (the trial was scheduled for ten-thirty) and cause a riot.

The Friday before the Monday of the trial, Geoff changed his plea to Guilty and the charge was reduced from Attempted Murder to Grievous Bodily Harm with Intent. Nicky was so overwhelmed by the news that she wouldn't have to give evidence, she had to lie down for an hour. I was more ambivalent; on the one hand, the fact that there wasn't now going to be a trial meant that I would be able to take a holiday. On the other hand, I felt that I had been cheated of my day in court.

On the eve of the trial I bumped into a woman in Sainsbury's. 'Hello,' she said, 'you don't recognize me. I'm Caroline.' As she said her name, I immediately remembered her. She was—by an odd coincidence—the sister-in-law of my first real boyfriend, and she lived nearby. On the day of the tree-felling, of all the interested parties, she had been the most vociferous in her concern for the tree and her requests for pieces of wood, stipulating that they should be cut just so and asking whether it would be possible for the tree surgeon to deliver the wood to her. Finally I got so fed up that I had asked her to stop bothering the men and let them get on with their work. The wood she wanted was cut to her specifications, but she never came back to collect it. Subsequently I had heard that she was one of the people responsible for the pro-Geoff petition.

'Yes, I remember you,' I said.

'What's going to happen—you know, about Geoff?' she asked.

'Well, the trial's tomorrow, but Geoff has changed his plea to

Guilty, thank God, so we won't have to give evidence. You know, it's incredible, some idiot who can't possibly have known the true facts got up a petition. I mean, Geoff stabbed Nicky twenty-two times.'

Whenever I remembered this statistic (not that I was likely ever to forget it), I would find myself getting angry. This must have been apparent; Caroline and I stood for a moment in uneasy silence by the tinned vegetables. Eventually she said, 'I hope it all goes OK,' and we went our separate ways.

I arrived early at the Old Bailey. Since Geoff had changed his plea, Nicky and I weren't legally required to be there, but we had both decided that we wanted to attend. Nicky couldn't face being in the courtroom itself, with Geoff, and was going to sit upstairs in the public gallery. The case was late in starting, just like in my dream. Eventually we went into court about an hour late—there had been some difficulty in 'producing' Geoff. I was anxious to sit where he couldn't see me, but I found I could barely hear. Rob Anderson suggested I move. 'But then he'll see me,' I said. Rob looked quizzical. I thought for a minute, 'So what? What can he do to me?' I moved to a bench further forward where, as it turned out, I could still barely see Geoff, or be seen by him, but I could hear better.

Geoff appeared in the dock, almost as if by magic. The defendant's box is reached by an underground staircase which leads straight up into it, the sort of device you might get in a production of *Faust* or *Don Giovanni*. I managed to see his hands as he was led up; he was handcuffed.

Geoff refused to answer to the name of Geoffrey Bevan, insisting that his name was Geoff. The judge agreed to go along with this, also to postpone the hearing for half an hour so that he could read the petition which had apparently been signed by 350 of Geoff's neighbours and the scores of letters also written by neighbours, which were being submitted as part of the defence. We all trooped out of the courtroom and Rob and I went to have a cup of coffee in the canteen, where we talked about *NYPD Blue*, of which Rob was also a fan.

Back in court, the prosecution barrister stood up to present his case. Apart from the fact that he appeared not to have grasped the geography of the situation (he claimed that I had looked out of an upstairs window and seen Nicky being attacked), he made a good speech. He then called on Dr Anthony Akinkunmi, the psychiatrist at Camlet Lodge, the secure unit where Geoff had spent the past five months. Dr Akinkunmi testified that Geoff suffered from delusions and believed that 'he was the subject of persecution by a conspiracy, an organization, of which he believed the victims in this case [Nicky and me] to be members'—Geoff also believed Dr Akinkunmi to be a member of this cult, which was called 'The Order of the Black Sun'. Dr Akinkunmi's evidence revealed that Geoff had actually been treated thirteen years before for psychiatric problems. In 1985, he had been admitted to St Luke's Woodside Hospital as an informal patient, but he had 'absconded from his treatment there, which was voluntary, and refused to return'. The doctor testified that Geoff had twice tried to escape from the secure unit. On the second attempt, he 'removed security screws from a window', and on another occasion he had also punched a fellow patient whom he believed was 'staring at him in a manner he found suspicious'. Dr Akinkunmi's main point was that, because Geoff had 'little or no insight into the fact that he has an illness and this is an illness for which he requires treatment,' he stood little chance of being cured.

Then it was the turn of the defence. In his mitigation speech, the defence barrister, a QC, read out the petition. It said: 'We, the undersigned, have known Geoff for many, many years and know him to be a truly kind and caring person who has helped and assisted very many people. He has lived in the area for twenty-five years, and is valued, loved and trusted by the community. We have always known him to be an essentially calm and peaceful person, with a great deal of kindness and concern for everyone—and, indeed, all living things; and, to our knowledge, he has never shown any sign of violence towards anyone.' The barrister then told the court that Geoff 'specifically did not use the blade of the knife because that obviously would have caused very serious injury'; he said that Geoff 'used the point in question because he felt that it would cause far less injury and not be very serious'. He added, 'The defendant believes that he should not be in any hospital at all...he says that he does not have any persecution complex and that his beliefs are not delusional—his beliefs are based on facts...' These last remarks, he told the court, were made on Geoff's specific instructions.

Four character witnesses—all local people—were called. The first was the Reverend Eric Greer, a bearded American, who had been at the Vicarage in Camden Square for two years. Then followed another man and two women. They all said pretty much the same thing: Geoff was 'an extremely kind, helpful and supportive individual' who had 'an unusual but very special place in the local community'; he was presented as a Gentle Giant, a kind of idiot savant, who wouldn't hurt a fly and looked after children and damsels in distress ('...women particularly have gone to Geoff if their husband hasn't been about...'). The second man told the court that Geoff was a practising vegetarian and someone whom he was 'proud to call a friend'. The first woman said that Geoff had made sure none of her kittens were running off; the other, middle-aged and sounding middle-class, claimed that she, too, 'could do something nasty and violent' if she 'had undergone the same stresses'. They said that with Geoff around, they felt it was safe for their children to play in the street, that he deterred burglars and had, in fact, saved at least one old lady from being mugged.

As I listened to this, I was leaning forward, right on the edge of my seat, my nails digging into the palms of my hands. When the judge said that he had no option but to order that Geoff be detained indefinitely at Her Majesty's Pleasure, under Section 41 of the Mental Health Act, because he was a danger to the public (in other words, a hospital order), I felt relief sweep through me.

There were three reporters in court—all women, two from agencies, one from the *Daily Telegraph*. I spoke to them briefly in the street before going for a drink with Nicky, her family, and Alison McCleod, the policewoman who had been such a support to Nicky. But I wasn't at all prepared for the level of press attention that the case generated.

That afternoon, a journalist from the *Daily Mail* telephoned. The next morning, Tuesday, I was called at eight-thirty by a friend from the *Evening Standard*. He had been deputed to ask me to write an account of my experiences. I agreed, then thought it over, and changed my mind. About an hour later, a reporter from the *Standard* rang my doorbell. I let him in. We talked, then I directed him across the square to the Reverend Greer and to the woman who had said she, too, would have acted violently under the same circumstances. During the morning I was telephoned by the *Express*, the *Daily Telegraph*, the *Daily Mail* and the *Mail on Sunday*, each making larger and larger offers. 'And would no amount of money change your mind?' said the man from the *Mail on Sunday*. I was also called by the local papers, the *Ham & High*, the *Camden New Journal* and the *North London News*. They didn't offer me any money.

At four o'clock, the man from the *Mail* appeared on my doorstep. I wouldn't let him in. That afternoon there were two pieces in the *Standard*, and the next day there were reports in *The Times*, the *Telegraph* and the *Mail*, all of them taking basically the same view. They stressed the fashionability of Camden Square (one paper used the phrase 'ultra fashionable' and described its inhabitants as 'one of Britain's wealthiest communities') and marvelled at the 'naivety' of the 'do-gooders'. Nicky, who had been very upset by the petition and the testimony of the character witnesses, was enormously cheered. I, by this time, felt completely exhausted. On Wednesday, the deputy features editor of the *Guardian* telephoned just before lunchtime. 'What took you so long?' I asked.

That evening, at about half past eight, there was a ring on the doorbell. I wasn't expecting visitors and was already in my dressing gown. I had been watching television and wondering whether there was anything to eat in the fridge. Standing on the doorstep were a man in his thirties and an older woman. I have forgotten their names. They were my neighbours and they wanted to talk to me. I invited them in and offered them a drink. They said that they didn't want anything. They sat one on either side of the fireplace looking around: the man in the velvet-covered Chippendale throne, the woman in the cane-and-teak chair from Indonesia. I curled up on the sofa and sat with my feet tucked under me, facing them. Minouche, my little blue Burmese cat, twined herself round the woman's legs. When I force myself to remember that evening, to remember our conversation, I get so angry that I can barely speak. I don't know why I imagined that telling my side of the story would help them to understand exactly what Geoff had done and why his incarceration was not only inevitable, but also just. Anyhow, it seemed to me that they didn't really want to listen to what I had to say. What they wanted—the man in particular—was to tell me what I had done to Geoff. He did most of the talking; the woman seemed content to sit quietly, watching Minouche play.

The man said, 'Geoff has lost his liberty, his life, because of you.'

I said, 'Geoff forfeited his right to stand on the square, to drink beer and to chat to his friends when he stabbed Nicky. He stabbed her twenty-two times.'

'She wasn't hurt badly,' said the woman, 'the hospital let her go home the same day.'

The man accused me of 'egging on' the police to remove Geoff's vans; he said that I had no definite proof that Geoff was responsible for the tyre slashing and the dog biscuits (this was true enough, but I was, as I told him, one hundred per cent convinced that Geoff had been responsible for these things; also nothing of the kind had happened since Geoff had been arrested).

They barely accepted that the Order of the Black Sun was a delusion of Geoff's (the woman asked me what it was—I told her that it didn't exist), and seemed incapable of understanding—or unwilling to understand—that my alleged persecution of him was part of the same delusion. They had not liked the tone of the press coverage and were convinced that I was employed by the *Daily Mail*.

The woman asked me how I would feel if in six months Geoff was back on the square. I told her that I wouldn't like it at all, but that if she really believed that there was any chance of Geoff being released in six, or even twelve months, she was almost as delusional as he was. The man was worried because Geoff didn't like his psychiatrist (I imagine that he was referring to Dr Akinkunmi), but added that he hadn't liked the two previous ones, either. I was past being careful by this time and said, 'Well, then I wouldn't hold your breath for his chances of release.' He wanted to know how I would feel about meeting Geoff—good work had, he said, been done in encounters between victims and perpetrators. No chance, I said. He told me—and I interpreted this as a threat—that Geoff would hear what was being said about him in the outside world. I said, 'Fine, and let me make one thing clear, I have no intention of moving.'

They stayed for an hour and a half. The conversation went round and round. By the time they left—I had almost to push the man out of the door, he seemed to be enjoying himself so much—I had all but lost my voice. Trying to make them understand that Nicky and I were the victims had been a waste of time and energy.

A few days later, I was telephoned by a Greek woman who lives in Kentish Town. She had read about the case in the papers and got hold of my number. She told me that Geoff had an identical twin brother and not one, but two council flats in Dunollie Road, both filled with old tyres, both of which he had set fire to. I discounted her stories as hysterical fabrications. The secretary of the Camden Square Residents' Association called to say that he had noticed lots of 'strange' people (I think that by strange, he meant mentally ill) hanging around the area and he wondered what *we* could do to prevent another such incident happening. I told Sergeant Mortimer about my visit from the neighbours. He said, 'I know, it's amazing. I've never come across anything like it. I would say it was unique to Camden.'

But it was a one-week wonder. I went away for ten days, then returned to peace and quiet. Geoff is still in Camlet Lodge, which is a regional secure mental unit in Enfield, Middlesex. He shows no signs of being aware that he is ill (Nicky, Dr Akinkunmi and I *are* members of the Order of the Black Sun and we *are* persecuting him). I have been assured that I will be informed if there are any plans to release him. □

GRANTA

CASH IS KING
John Lanchester

What do you call a man with a seagull on his head? Cliff. What do you call a man with a spade in his head? Doug. What do you call a man with no arms and no legs in the ocean? Bob. What do you call a man with ten rabbits up his bum? Warren.

Mr Phillips is lying face down on the floor of Barclays Bank. His arms are spread above and on either side of his head, and his jacket has ridden up and bunched so that it feels as if his circulation is being cut off around his shoulders. Also it is very hot. But Mr Phillips does not want to adjust his position and make himself more comfortable, because four men with shotguns have taken over the bank and it is on their orders that he is lying on the floor looking at the Barclays carpet and trying to keep calm. When the men communicate they do so by shouting and their threats are easy to believe. They have said that they will blow the fucking head off any fucker who moves.

Funnily enough, Mr Phillips saw the men come into the bank just as he noticed a sign saying NO CRASH HELMETS PLEASE. About two seconds later four men wearing jeans, windcheaters and crash helmets walked into the bank, and there was a split second in which Mr Phillips was noticing and remarking on the coincidence—oh look, there are men in crash helmets, who I don't suppose will know they're not meant to come in here dressed like that—before the men started shouting commands and making everyone lie on the floor. One of the crash helmets then picked a middle-aged woman in a perm up off the floor and held what appeared to be a sawn-off shotgun, an object about a foot and a half long with a double barrel, at her head. He told the cashiers that if they did not buzz him through to their part of the bank, behind the glass partition, he would blow her face off. So the cashiers had buzzed him and one of his companions through while the other two robbers stayed outside and patrolled the banking hall.

How many hairdressers does it take to change a light bulb? Five—one to change the bulb, four to stand around saying 'Super, Gary.' How many yuppies does it take to change a light bulb? Two— one to change the bulb, one to organize a skip. How many therapists does it take to change a light bulb? None—the light bulb can change itself, but only if it *wants* to. How many feminists does it take to change a light bulb? One—and it's not funny. How many feminists does it take to change a light bulb? Two—one to change the bulb, the other to suck your cock.

That was one of his son Martin's.

It is all Mr Phillips's fault that he was caught in here. He had not really needed to come into the bank at all. In fact, all day, on and off, he has been deliberately not-thinking about going to the bank and asking for an up-to-date statement of his financial position, checking his balance, which is about £500, and his savings account, which is about £3,000, before he gets his three months tax-free redundancy, which would come to about £14,000. But this was something he simply could not face doing, so he had not-thought about it until what seemed at first to be a happy accident had happened.

This is the way it went. Mr Phillips had been wandering down Shaftesbury Avenue on his first day as a fifty-year-old redundant accountant. As the day went on London seemed to be getting busier and busier—more people, more rushing about, more cars, more tourists, more cycle couriers and motorcycle messengers, more red buses and black taxis, more coaches and coach parties and more girls and more men carrying things and in a hurry. It was a quarter to four. Mr Phillips had to use up another two and a half hours before he could plausibly arrive home in Battersea. It occurred to him for a brief mad moment that he could even walk the distance...but that would be daft, he was tired enough as it was. A couple of hours more walking would finish him off.

He crossed the road and began walking towards Piccadilly. About fifty yards along a temporary bus stop had been erected, compensating for the fact that the permanent bus stop was submerged under a pile of scaffolding where something was being built or demolished or painted or cleaned. As he walked up to the stop a Routemaster bus, spewing black diesel fumes, pulled up beside him and twenty or thirty people began to get off it, the younger and nimbler of them not waiting for the bus to stop but hopping off and hitting the ground running. When he had had things to do Mr Phillips had not noticed how busy, how urgent, everybody in the city seemed.

Mr Phillips got on the bus. He went upstairs to the top deck and sat down at the front.

This bus went through all the glamorous parts of London. First it went down past the Trocadero, down Haymarket, then back up Regent's Street to Piccadilly, then along past the Royal Academy, past the Ritz, past Green Park, round Hyde Park Corner, and towards Knightsbridge. By and large these were all parts of London that Mr Phillips never visited. They belonged to other kinds of people. The feeling of wealth and prosperity was thickly present in all these places, and it made Mr Phillips wonder what the city would look like if, instead of bricks and mortar, concrete and cement, buildings were made out of piles of stacked cash, wadded and glued together into bricks. A house out in Leytonstone would be, say, eight feet high, a sort of wattle hut made out of fivers, whereas one in Knightsbridge would be a skyscraper of twenty-pound notes. And the people, too: if they were nothing more than their total capital value they would vary from tiny bunches, hardly visible, of rolled-up notes, to towers thousands of feet high, stretching up into the clouds, causing trouble for air traffic control and weather balloons, vulnerable to lightning. Mr Phillips himself would be a respectable man-size pile of cash, if you counted the unmortgaged part of 27 Wellesley Crescent, though he would soon start shrinking fast. If you excluded the assets held jointly with Mrs Phillips and the ones in her name, and deducted debts such as the unpaid part of the mortgage, he would be much less healthy—barely a briefcase-full.

Mr Phillips likes to think about people's time and what it costs. The ideal is the taxi meter, ticking away to show how much the customer is spending, every penny accounted for and all above board. The red numerals travelling in one direction only. Everyone should have a little meter on them, in Mr Phillips's view—lawyers in court, politicians on the television; a special lightweight one for footballers and athletes; bus drivers, housewives, Mrs Phillips during her piano lessons and Mr Phillips himself at the office. Only the off-duty and the unemployed would be exempt; perhaps they would wear meters that had been switched off, or meters stuck on their last reading. Or should they show average earnings across time, so that even people on unemployment benefit would tick slowly along? The whole point would be the way people chug along at different rates: Mr Mill, who earns £45,000 a year, would clock along at 45,000 divided by 250 (working days per year) divided by eight (hours per working day) equals £22.50 per hour, whereas Mr Phillips's secretary, the beloved and much-fancied Karen, would tick along at £18,000 divided by 250 (working days per year) divided by eight (hours per working day) equals £9 per hour, with everyone else at work ticking away at their own personal rates, the whole process giving an added point or edge to all interpersonal transactions in the office, something to notice and think about, though it would no doubt become quickly invisible as everyone got used to it, as everyone always does.

The system could get elaborate. For instance, actors might have to wear two meters, one showing their rate and the other the rate of the characters they were playing, indicated perhaps by green numerals as opposed to red ones. Sometimes a famous and highly paid actor would be playing a penniless waif, and the difference between the two meters would become horribly distracting—so much so that films would start to cast poor actors to play poor characters, and successful actors would be restricted to impersonating rock stars, business tycoons, lawyers and, yes, famous actors. Musicians would tick away as they played on *Top of the Pops*, newsreaders and politicians while they talked, beggars as they sat on the street, nurses, waiters, yellow-hat construction workers, everyone. The meters would have different settings to reflect earnings this day, earnings this task, and lifetime earnings. The Prime Minister was paid £100,000, but of course how much he ticked away at per hour would depend on whether you thought he was on duty all the time, whether his holidays were proper holidays, etc. The President of the USA was paid £125,000 and the same thing applied.

Mr Phillips's bus began heading down Knightsbridge. And now, as the bus went past Harrods, Mr Phillips, who had been looking at people on the pavement in an idle, incurious way, felt a jolt of surprised excitement. He had spotted her! It was Clarissa Colingford, sure as eggs were eggs, the TV celebrity he had been thinking and indeed masturbating about on and off for some months. She had been crossing the street, coming out of a clothes shop with a parcel labelled CHEZ GUEVARA under her arm, tripping along at a near-run, looking pretty, busy, preoccupied. She was shorter than she seemed on TV and less lifelike—less like herself than like the generic idea of a thin youngish blonde woman in expensive clothes. In fact if Mr Phillips had seen her in real life first he might well have been inoculated against her. But he hadn't and he wasn't and, deeply curious to get a second look, he had got off the bus at the next stop, doubled back, picked up her trail further along Knightsbridge, becoming a stalker or private detective for all of about three minutes, until she had suddenly swerved to one side and gone into the bank, a branch of the very same bank that Mr Phillips himself patronized.

A real man shoots his own dog. Mr Phillips decided to be a man: he would go in, draw some cash and request a full statement sent to his home address. If he happened to bump into Clarissa Colingford, their hands brushing together as they simultaneously reached for a deposit slip—no please after you, no I insist, took me a moment to find them it's not my usual branch, yes South London, oh do you how interesting, yes a cup of coffee would be delightful—well, that would just be one of those freak coincidences. Which is how Mr Phillips came to be lying face down on the floor of this bank, ten feet away from Clarissa Colingford, at the business end of a sawn-off shotgun. It was just one of those things.

At this range he can see that it's quite an outfit she has on. Her pale brown shirt, open to only just above where you might be able to peer down at her tits if you got up close in front of her, looks as if it is made out of chamois leather, and her thin-looking cream trousers unfortunately seem likely to pick up all kinds of dirt and smears from the Barclays carpet. From this distance she is more like she is on TV than at medium range. She exudes the same aura of shine and of being almost too good to be true, though she is skinnier than she looks on television, by about ten pounds, which makes her seem more nervous, less voluptuous, but immediately wantable. Her skin is slightly pink in the V of her shirt, she would have to watch it if she didn't want to age there. The neck is the first to go, Mr Phillips could have warned her. She looks, not sweaty, but as if she might, if you got up very close to her, see a faint clamminess at the base of her neck, in the crook of her elbow, her perfume enhanced by her body heat. Mr Phillips feels that he is very much in love.

This carpet however has Mr Phillips worried. Once you are pressed out cruciform on any floor surface—prostrated, they would say in church, in the position priests used to adopt when being ordained—you begin to think about what else has been on that floor before you. In the case of a much-trodden-on urban bank carpet there is the question of dog shit on people's shoes. Also pigeon shit, urine, rubbish, spilt things; but mainly dog shit. It would be picked up, brought here, and then trodden into the carpet that was now an inch from Mr Phillips's nose, a pale blue flooring made out of some industrial substance with a tight nobbly weave, the better to adhere to millions of tiny molecules of transported dog excrement, the sort that made children blind if they ate it. Why would they eat it, you might well ask, to which the answer was, accidents do happen.

Mr Phillips once went through a phase of being worried about dog shit in London's parks, on behalf of the children. For instance Martin would kick the football through some dog shit, pick the ball up without noticing, rub his eyes with the contaminated hand or eat a banana, and become sick. It was something to do with worms. Then the worries had gone away, apparently of their own accord. Now they have come back again. It is as if he can see tiny particles of dog shit everywhere he looks.

Clarissa Colingford had come into the bank and gone straight over to the cashpoint machine. Or not quite straight over, she had stood around looking vague for a moment or two and then gone to stand behind a hugely fat man who was having tremendous difficulty inserting his card into the automatic teller. Mr Phillips knew this fine art well and knew that it was all a matter of timing, but this man's stiff jabbing action—and who knew whether the card was even the right way round!—and the quiet mechanical crunch of the card's being rejected made something obscene out of his failure to insert it. Finally Clarissa Colingford stepped in, coming up beside the man and with the sweetest expression saying, 'May I?'

The big man handed her the card and she slipped it into the purring machine at the first attempt.

'Well, thanks,' he said. She just smiled, as if saying something might compromise his maleness, and stood back as he hunched scowling over the console. Mr Phillips felt intensely jealous. He lurched to one side before he was caught eavesdropping and stood at the counter where you filled in slips, did sums, and took leaflets. It was there that he was standing when the robbers burst into the bank. Of course she could have used the cashpoint outside if it was only cash she wanted. Mr Phillips suspects that he knows the reason why she didn't. This Knightsbridge cashpoint can be relied on to have at least one beggar sitting or standing beside it, plaintively (usually) or aggressively (occasionally) asking for money, usually by saying, 'spare change please?' Today there was a woman, probably in her thirties but looking ten years older, sitting half-rolled-up in too many clothes for the weather—heavy trousers, two or three shirts, a coat, a bobble hat, with a couple of plastic bags strewn around her. She looked pitiful, but in Mr Phillips's experience that doesn't always make you want to give someone money. This beside-the-cashpoint pitch must be a prime spot; Mr Phillips wondered if beggars took turns to occupy it. To Mr Phillips's mind there was something hard to ignore about the juxtaposition of someone asking for money, needing it desperately, even, with a machine that was vomiting money out to people who asked for it. It was as if there was a right way and a wrong way of asking for money: sit on the pavement and ask your fellow humans and you'll be refused, stand up and ask a machine and you can have as much as you want.

Mr Phillips sometimes feels a wave of anger or revulsion as he walks past a beggar. When he gives one money, usually fifty pence since they aren't useful for parking meters and are less expensive than one-pound coins, the emotion he feels is not primarily towards the beggar but towards himself, a warm glow of philanthropic self-congratulation. Similarly, the other feelings are directed at himself too, at his ungenerosity and ability to harden his own heart. It is this that makes people hate beggars, for what they make you do to them— since no one can give money to every beggar he sees, the existence of beggars turns everybody into the kind of person who walks past beggars. It is hard to forgive them that.

The men who are robbing the bank are not asking for money so much as simply taking it, and taking their time about doing it too, in Mr Phillips's view. Though admittedly his ability to judge how much time has passed is probably not at its best. It feels like twenty minutes but is probably more like two. This would be something to talk about when he got home—though if he does he will have to say where he's been, and what he was doing in Knightsbridge at four in the afternoon. This is another subject he prefers to not-think about.

'Check that one,' shouts one of the men behind the counter. Mr Phillips doesn't want to look and see what is going on but can guess that it probably involves stashing bags full of cash. The curious thing is that because the robbers shout all the time—which Mr Phillips knows from watching *Crimewatch UK* is a trick to make it hard for people to identify their voices or accents—they sound a little like the head of department Mr Phillips once had at Grimshaw's, a man called, or rather nicknamed, Knobber. He had shouted all the time too, and had been able to call on a bottomless source of seemingly unfeigned anger. He once described his department's performance in preparing at twenty-four-hour notice for an audit as the worst day in the history of the accountancy profession.

Why are there no aspirin in the jungle? Paracetamol. (Parrots eat 'em all.) Have you ever seen a bunny with its nose all runny, don't say it's funny 'cos it's snot. What do you get if you cross a nun with an apple? A computer that won't go down on you. Have you heard about the evil dyslexic? He sold his soul to Santa. Have you heard about the agnostic insomniac dyslexic? He lay awake all night wondering if there was a Dog. Why did the chicken kill itself? To get to the other side.

This is the closest Mr Phillips has ever been to actual violence in his whole adult life, excluding the occasional scuffle in the street, not that he's taken part in one—God forbid—but which he's occasionally seen out of a car or a train window. Mr Phillips must have witnessed many thousands of violent incidents, shootings and explosions and stabbings and abductions and rapes and fist fights and drive-by machine-gunnings, and assassination style head-shots and cars blown up by shoulder-fired rocket-launchers, and rooms systematically cleared by grenades followed by machine-guns, and petrol stations blown up by deliberately dropped cigarette lighters, but all of these were on television (or occasionally at the cinema). The last proper fist fight he saw was nineteen years ago, when he spent six months commuting to the plant in Banbury, a few years after he started at Wilkins and Co. A foreman from Sunderland had accused a fitter from London, a Cockney wide boy whom nobody much liked—the plant was the first place Mr Phillips had realized how much 'Cockneys', as all Londoners were called, were disliked— of being a thief. Twenty pounds, then quite a lot of money, had gone missing from the Geordie's locker. The Geordie had won by making the Cockney's nose bleed so much that the fight had to stop so that he could go and get it looked at in Casualty. There was no more thieving, though no one ever found out who had stolen the money. As would happen in a film, the two men later became fast friends.

The question of who is engaged in taking this money is less hard to sort out. The four men in crash helmets are taking it. The two of them in the front part of the bank are prowling around the room keeping order. Occasionally one or other of them stands so close to Mr Phillips that he gets a good view of his footwear. Both of them are wearing sports shoes. One of them has on a pair of expensive-looking new trainers, one of the brands that children wear and now, these days, rob and murder to own. The other has on an old pair of tennis shoes that have a slight and very incongruous air of raffishness—the kind of shoes a stockbroker with two homes might wear in the country at weekends, on days when he isn't bothering to shave. Both of them wear jeans.

About a dozen customers are in the bank. Mr Phillips wonders how many of them have recognized Clarissa Colingford and whether any of them feels, not the same way that he does, since that would be impossible, but something faintly similar. Three or four of the customers are men: there are two businessmen, and a scruffy youth who fifteen years ago would have been a punk. Luckily, none of the women has children with her. Perhaps that is an accident or perhaps the robbers have been careful about their timing.

There must be a lot of detail to have to think about, being a bank robber. It would seem like a job for the headstrong and reckless but there must be a great deal of planning in it too. It would attract a curious type of person, willing to risk their own lives and threaten other people's but also prepared to take pains over things like escape routes, what kind of getaway car to use, how to dodge the traffic, best time to rob the bank, how long it would take the police to get there and so on. It wouldn't be the sort of thing where you had a few beers and were suddenly seized with the need to put a helmet on, grab a sawn-off, and go rob a bank.

The rewards must justify the risks. That stood to reason. Enough robbers must do well enough to keep the profession alive. But how well was well enough? It must be hard to be precise about robbers' average wages. Some would do well, some less well, and since doing less well involved spending years in prison there would be no sensible way of averaging them out. How did you compare a year in which you cleared £100,000 (and that free of tax) and took the whole family to Barbados to one in which you got sent to prison for a decade? But presumably if he told the armed robbers that he has worked in an office for more than a quarter of a century, earning a top salary of £32,000, and has just been made redundant, they would think that was hilarious. In fact if you spent eight hours a day for thirty years in an office that was the same as spending ten years in jail for twenty-four hours a day—and it was an unlucky bank robber who actually spent ten years in the slammer, since you always served a good bit less than you were sentenced for, and in jail you could read books, do a degree, that sort of thing.

In films there were people in prison who controlled huge criminal syndicates from the comfort and safety of their own cells. Tell Levinsky if he comes back and asks nicely, plus gives us ninety per cent of the gross, I won't chop his dick off and stick it in his mouth, growls Mr Phillips the mob boss to his quailing deputy, who has brought the twice-weekly delivery of Krug and sevruga in a Harrods bag, right under the noses of the bribed and terrified warders. Tell that kid in Streatham he needs to show a little more respect. Nothing too heavy—break his arms, torch his Beamer. You OK Joe, you look a little pale. Maybe you're not eating right. Or maybe you're staying up too late fucking that little piece of totty you're running on the side. Yeah that's right I hear things, you should show your wife a little more respect. A man who doesn't spend time with his family is not a real man. How are Janie and the kids, I hear Luigi got into St Paul's, you must be very proud. A model prisoner, revered by his fellow inmates in the lax regime of the Open Prison, gracefully accepting their unsolicited gifts of cigarettes and phonecards.

Apparently armed robbers were looked up to in prison. Mr Phillips has read that somewhere. Sex criminals were the lowest form of life, whereas armed robbers were the aristocrats.

How do you tell the difference between a stoat and a weasel? One's weasily recognizable, the other's stotally different. What do you call a man with no arms and no legs crawling through a forest? Russell. What do you say to a woman with two black eyes? Nothing, you've told her twice already. Martin again. Perhaps he should tell that one to the robbers. It might be their kind of joke.

Mr Phillips can hear a woman crying, about fifteen feet away from where he is lying. It is a choking, moaning sort of cry, as if she were making every effort to minimize the amount of noise—which of course makes things worse. Mr Phillips could remember his own efforts not to cry at his father's funeral, and the feeling that his chest would crack open; as if he were struggling to contain volcanic forces. The effort had made his shoulders jerk and his chin wobble, and strangled choking sounds had come out of his mouth. In those days men did not cry at funerals. The feat of suppression involved was in its way as wild and violent as any open grief.

His father once, when Mr Phillips fell and cut his knee on gravel, aged about nine—he can no longer remember where, only his father's words stay with him—told him to stop crying, that it made him look like a girl. That happened forty years ago, and it is still one of Mr Phillips's most vivid memories. It is as if the stream of tears was at that moment diverted underground and has not been seen since. In the meantime it sloshed around out of sight like the run-off from a broken water-main coursing through the foundations of a house. In childhood, as far as he can remember, crying had inside it the idea that this feeling would go on for ever—that the pain, whatever it was, that was causing you to cry, was infinite, and would possess you for ever. Or you would live inside it for ever. It was the first vague intimation of what death would be like—to be in the same state without end.

Mrs Phillips cries easily at films and more rarely at music, but she isn't as much of a crier as Mr Phillips would have been if he had been a woman, or so he feels. She does not shake or heave but tears simply begin to appear in her eyes and waterfall down her face, accompanied by sniffles. It is like a spring or a well or some other non-volcanic phenomenon. Both his sons have inherited this ability, which Mr Phillips has been at pains not to discourage. No doubt part of the reason this woman is struggling is the effort involved in crying when you are lying spreadeagled face-down on the floor. Mr Phillips has not tried that and has no plans to.

Death is another subject Mr Phillips exerts himself, not always successfully, to not-think about. He has got to the stage when it only enters his mind when someone he knows died—Betty his first ever secretary of cancer last year, Finker his friend from accounting school of a heart attack at Christmas, Mr Elton, his younger son Thomas's favourite football teacher, in a car crash in January were the most recent. These deaths always bring a wave of anxiety and of me-too, me-next, what-will-it-be-like thoughts. One of Mr Phillips's least favourite reveries involves the idea of lying in a hospital listening to a beeping monitor, wondering if this time would be It. When you are young sex is It, when you are older death is.

Not so much being dead as dying is what frightens Mr Phillips. This is a question which divides people, and he knows the arguments for the other point of view, not least because Mrs Phillips subscribes to them.

'The awfulness of nothing. To lose all this,' she explained. They were sitting in their kitchen, which was throbbing with the noise of moronic neighbours revving their car engines as per their Saturday norm, but even so Mr Phillips knew what she meant.

Nonetheless, he doesn't see it that way. Not being here in itself is nothing to fear. The moment of transition, though—the moment of breaking through the veil of being-here and going through to not-ness, which presumably involves a terrible rending moment in which you realize what is happening, have full consciousness of what you are going through—now that seems to be worth fearing. If he could have a written guarantee from the responsible parties that death would be something he wouldn't notice—here one moment, gone the next, with no lived transition—he would feel perfectly sanguine, even gung-ho, about the whole business. But the thought that you would be aware of what was going on as you died implied that somewhere in the future was a moment of the purest terror, terror at 200 degrees proof, so that you could have a small taste of the fear every time you let your mind touch on the subject, even for a second or two.

Today, lying here on the floor of the bank, must be the closest Mr Phillips has been to death for many years—perhaps the closest since his friend Tony Wilson, who moved to Dorset to run a minicab company and whom he hasn't seen for fifteen years, had crashed their car on the way back from a wedding in Suffolk. Tony was drunk—not paralytic but tipsy. He had taken a corner too fast, skidded, and gone into a ditch about ten feet from a concrete drainage pipe. If they had hit the pipe they would have been dead.

'You're very lucky young men,' the policemen had told them.

'If we're that lucky what were we doing in the fucking ditch in the first place?' Tony said. He knew that he was going to lose his licence anyway.

Mrs Phillips, who had been at home because she was eight-and-a-half months pregnant with Martin and couldn't face the round-trip drive to East Anglia, had forbidden her husband ever to travel in a car driven by Tony again. That was a quarter of a century ago. Since then the nearest Mr Phillips has come to death is through the usual risks to do with strokes and heart attacks and haemorrhages, the things which can jump up and whack you, take you at any moment, as well as the longer-term more stealthy killers, the ones that creep up on you from behind and kidnap you into the treeless country of terminal illness—the cancers, the degenerative diseases. In that sense he has lived with the same proximity to death as any other sedentary man in his fifties with a white-collar job, the kind of intimacy you could have with an acquaintance who might drop in at any moment but who you would probably at the same time have no reason for expecting on this particular day, or on any other day for a little while yet.

This raises the question of how likely death is, on any particular day. It came up one morning a few months ago, when they were all sitting around before the monthly progress meeting of the accounts department.

'Hang on a minute,' said Abbot, the youngest of them. 'The odds against winning the lottery are fourteen million to one, right?'

'The odds against winning the jackpot,' said Monroe in his Aberdonian voice. 'Six divided by forty-nine times five divided by forty-eight times four divided by forty-seven times three divided by forty-six times two divided by forty-five times one divided by forty-four, which is 0.00000007151 or one in 13,983,816, usually referred to as one in fourteen million. So if the prize is greater than fourteen million quid it becomes a rational bet, as opposed to a stupidity tax.'

'Assuming you get all the money for one winner, which you can't assume,' said somebody else.

'Fourteen million to one that you'll get all six numbers right,' said Monroe. 'There is however another risk here which affects the likelihood of winning. Does anybody want to tell me what it is?'

Mr Phillips, who knew the answer because he had heard Monroe on the subject before, kept silent so as not to spoil his fun.

'No takers. All right. The additional factor that needs to be taken into consideration is the chance of being dead by the time the lottery results arrive—since, obviously, the chance of dying in any given week is much, much higher than that of winning the lottery.'

There was a pause, the sound of six accountants sizing up a mathematical problem in their heads.

'What's the death rate? How many people die every week?' said Austen.

'According to the relevant government agencies,' said Monroe, 'the population of England at the time of the last estimate was 49,300,000. The previous year, deaths totalled 526,650. The death rate per week was therefore 10,128, rounded up to the nearest cadaver. Using these data we find that for an Englishman the chance of dying in any given week is therefore 2.054 times e to the minus fourth, or one in 4,880.'

'So your chance of winning the lottery,' said Abbot at his calculator, 'is, er, 2,868 times worse than your chance of being dead by the time of the National Lottery draw. That's nice to know.'

'But we're assuming you buy the ticket at the start of the week,' Monroe went on. 'In other words, if you buy your ticket at the start of the week and hold it until the draw, your chance of being dead by the time of the result is much better than your chance of winning. But most people don't buy the ticket on Sunday, they buy it in the middle of the week before the draw, and so their odds are better. If you buy your ticket at four o' clock on Friday afternoon your chance of not being dead before the result must be significantly improved.'

They were already doing the sums.

'Assuming the deaths are spread evenly over the calendar—'

—which Mr Phillips didn't feel you could assume. Surely more people died in winter and at weekends, of drinking and fighting and the stress of being cooped up with their families and so on? But he didn't say anything—

'—that means that the chance of dying, for a random member of the population, is 0.0107 per year, or $2.93e^{-5}$ per day, or $1.22e^{-6}$ per hour, or $2.03e^{-8}$ per minute. In other words, each of us has a one in 49,200,000 chance of dying in any given minute. So in order for the probability of winning the jackpot to be greater than the chance of being dead by the time of the draw one would have to bet no earlier than,' Monroe tapped some figures into his Psion Organizer, 'three and a half minutes before the draw.'

'Christ,' said someone.

'But that's averaging the risk out,' he continued. 'Obviously a nineteen-year-old girl who doesn't drink, doesn't smoke, has no familial history of anything and whose great-grandmother is still alive at the age of 102 is more likely not to be dead than a sixty-year-old chain-smoking alcoholic with a private pilot's licence. We'd need to get hold of some proper actuarial tables,' he concluded, giving the word 'proper' a discreet but very Scottish emphasis. At that point Mr Mill, the useless departmental head, came into the room, and the conversation petered out and the meeting began instead.

Monroe, however, did not forget. About two weeks later a notice appeared on the board in the company canteen, saying ATTENTION LOTTERY GAMBLERS and below giving a breakdown, along the lines discussed, of the averaged-out risk of being dead before the lottery result was announced, along with a recommended time after which the chances of winning the lottery were better than those of being dead by the end of the week.

It had lingered in the mind. Mr Phillips wonders what his relative chances of being dead before this week's lottery draw are at this precise moment. In all probability they have never been better. Or worse, depending on your point of view. It would only take a single convulsive motion of one robber's finger. The feeling was the same as the one you sometimes have when you're driving, and it occurs to you that all it would take is a strong twitch on the steering wheel and your car will go across the line into oncoming traffic, or over the kerb into a wall, or through a hedge or a ditch or a shop window, any of those things which people in film accidents do to comic or exciting effect but which in real life involve death. This is like that feeling only more so. All that would have to happen is for one of the bank robbers to conceive a dislike of Mr Phillips as he lies spreadeagled and puffing on the floor, inhaling minute particles of dog shit.

'Right, last one. Fifteen seconds,' shouts one of the men on the other side of the bank counter. Mr Phillips, if forced to guess, would say that the man is a Scouser.

If the robber crosses into the bank lobby with whatever he is using to carry the money slung over his shoulder—Mr Phillips can't see, but the men are clearly jamming banknotes into some kind of bag that they've brought with them—another item that should perhaps be banned from banks, along with crash helmets—if he comes out, points his sawn-off at Mr Phillips and blows his head off, for any reason or no reason, today, 31 July, will be the day that was lying there in wait for him all his life, hiding in the calendar, in secret parallel to 9 December, his birthday. Everybody has this day, hiding in plain sight, the one day out of the 365 which has a significance for us that we aren't here to know about. His deathday will be the day on which Mrs Phillips and the boys remember him, or remember him with particular vividness, Mrs Phillips especially. For her 31 July would be like a returning ache, every year. The boys would make a big effort to be with her, at least for the first few years, but then the practice would be less strict, it would die out like a national custom that people were gradually forgetting. Only for Mrs Phillips would the day continue to have its special weight in the calendar, a day she would always dread, when she wouldn't be able to bear the sound of certain pieces of music.

Today could be the day...any day could be the day, of course, that is the whole point, but today especially. Mr Phillips puts his hands under his shoulders and pushes himself up. Then he gets to his feet. As he does so he realizes he is holding his hands above his shoulders, and that this gesture doesn't really make sense any more, so he lowers them. His view of what is going on in the bank is very much better from up here. In fact there's no comparison. Mr Phillips can see the way people are lying scatteredly in the face-down position, not radiating out from a single point as if they had been blown up but higgledy-piggledy, pointing in all directions. Clarissa Colingford, who is lying with her face turned to the right away from him, has her trousers stretched over her buttocks, not quite so stretched that the material is shiny, but nearly. It is quite a sight. He can also see the two bank robbers in the customers' hall of the bank. Both of them are looking at him with as much of a surprised expression as it's possible to have inside a motorcycle helmet. The two men are quite thin and wiry. Mr Phillips probably weighs as much as one and a third of them. He says:

'I'm not doing that any more.'

'You fucking,' says one of the men, advancing towards Mr Phillips, not pointing the gun directly at him but pointing it past his side. He forgot to shout, and his accent is definitely Liverpudlian.

'Get the cunt down!' shouts the robber behind the counter who seems to be in charge. It has been at least two minutes since he shouted about its being fifteen seconds till they would finish, so perhaps something is going wrong. He does not look at Mr Phillips as he shouts but down at the counter, below which his colleague is doing something out of sight.

'I'm not going to get down,' says Mr Phillips. 'I think everyone should feel free to stand up.'

The other people in the bank are by now all looking at him, their necks doing all sorts of kinks and cricks in order to do so. People's faces are extraordinarily blank. Between them they can't notch up so much as a single expression. There is no way to tell what they are thinking. Even Clarissa Colingford, who has turned her head around and is now lying with her left cheek on the floor—she has turned around in order to get a better view of Mr Phillips!—you can see the red imprint of the carpet on her face—even Clarissa Colingford looks as she might look in a camera that was turned on her while the main camera, the one that was broadcasting live, was following someone else. Her face is off duty.

'If you don't lie down on the fucking floor you're going to get your fucking head blown off,' the nearest robber shouts—he remembers this time. His shotgun is pointed at Mr Phillips's stomach. Mr Phillips does not move.

'I think you should all get up too,' he says to the other people in the bank. 'What's the worst that can happen?'

They all stay where they are. It is what Mr Phillips would have done in their shoes. A little old lady writhes around on the floor and Mr Phillips for a moment thinks she is about to get up, but it turns out she is only manoeuvring to be more comfortable and to get a better view. The others do not make eye contact with Mr Phillips— it is psychologically and physically difficult to make eye contact with a standing man when you are lying face down on the floor, and are looking in his general direction rather than looking at him.

Mr Phillips feels a great sensation of lightness. It is as if his life is a crushing weight, a rucksack filled with bricks, one that he gradually got so used to that he forgot it was there, and he has now managed to shift the burden so that the sense of ease, of release, is exhilarating. He feels that he could hop ten feet straight into the air. Or, more gently, just decide to float upward, so that his perspective down on the floor-people would become steeper, and the bank robbers would crane their necks up at him in amazement, and then he would be up through the roof, looking down at the building and out across Knightsbridge, the traffic, Harrods already visible, and then further up, able to see the Victoria and Albert Museum, the way you can fly in a dream (though even in a dream you always know you're going to fall back down, and Mr Phillips has no such feeling) and then further and further up, the Thames snaking away behind and London turning into an aerial photograph and then into a map of itself, the horizon stretching further and further away, startled birds and pigeons swerving to avoid him, up through the first thin layer of wispy cloud and then further up into the clean blue, the haze of pollution and fug over the city becoming visible as it is left behind, the countryside spreading out and expanding as London shrinks, and then England shrinks, turns into an island as he gets higher and higher up, so that he can see the Channel, the crinkly coasts of Ireland and France, then the blob of Paris, so small from up here, and the Low Countries, and then Europe shrinks, and he can see out over the Atlantic, into Russia, and then the edges of the earth itself would come into view, and Mr Phillips would float free of the planet, out into the clean nothingness of space, and suddenly the earth would seem tiny and fragile and blue and green, shrinking fast, and most of the universe would be darkness in which the stars and planets would seem tiny, decorative, hardly disturbing the beauty and calm of the blank lifeless void. □

A LONDON VIEW/Julian Barnes

Every schoolday for six adolescent years I used to travel by the Metropolitan, Bakerloo and finally District (or Circle) Line from Northwood in Middlesex to Blackfriars. My school was in the heart of London, its main steps across from the Thames; there was just a short walk to St Paul's for the annual commemoration of our benefactors. This transition from calm, green suburbia to vibrant metropolis felt in the main a simple psychological process: from family dullsville to the centre of the world. But there was one thing—one building—one part of one building—which usefully complicated such daily world-turning. Blackfriars mainline station (now demolished) was dismissed by Pevsner in a couple of phrases: 'Opened in 1886. Weak Italianate, of red brick, two storeyed.' Was that all? No, that was not all. On either side of its entrance, incised on rising columns of stone facing, were the names of destinations served by this station. ST PETERSBURG, I remember chiefly, and I think BERLIN, and photographic evidence confirms DRESDEN, BRINDISI, LEIPSIC with a C, VIENNA and LUCERNE; though not PARIS, which had presumably been cornered by some rival terminus across the river. By the time I went to school these continental connections no longer existed: John Betjeman had once straight-facedly asked at the Blackfriars booking office for a return ticket to St Petersburg and had been referred, equally straight-facedly, to Victoria Continental. But still... St Petersburg was where you might run into Anna Karenina, wasn't it? And Vienna... And Cannes... As I stared up at this out-of-date gazetteer, I realized that I did not travel each morning to the centre of the world. Northwood was to London as London was to Europe. My subsequent life has been entirely based in the metropolis; I enjoy the city; but I have always felt it as a place on the way to somewhere else.

GENEVA

LAUSANNE

LEIPSIC

LUCERNE

MARSEILLES

VIENNA

St PETERSBURG

JOHN GAY

Artangel

INNER *CITY*

LANGUAGE ON LOCATION IN LONDON

Recent events by Scanner, Augusto Boal and John Berger/Simon McBurney will be followed up in May/June with commissions by Rachel Lichtenstein/Iain Sinclair, Daniel Libeskind, Janet Cardiff and Lavinia Greenlaw.

Publications in book, video and other media by Rachel Whiteread, Gabriel Orozco, Melanie Counsell, Ilya and Emilia Kabakov, Neil Bartlett, Gavin Bryars/Juan Muñoz, Robert Wilson/Hans Peter Kuhn, Tatsuo Miyajima, William Forsythe/Dana Caspersen/Joel Ryan.

Artangel

36 St John's Lane, London EC1M 4BJ
Tel: +44 171 336 6801
Fax: +44 171 336 6802
Recorded information: +44 171 336 6803
e-mail: artangel@easynet.co.uk
www.innercity.demon.co.uk

GRANTA

WITH A BANG
Helen Simpson

KATE SCHERMERHORN

There had been an unbelievable amount of talk about the weather, not to mention the end of the world and so on. The earth continued to turn round the sun, but only just, it seemed. Never before in all its history had the planet's atmosphere been so heavily matted with information about everything, so clotted with flashes and scoops and entreaties and jeremiads. The air and all its waves were sodden with chit-chat.

Muscae volitantes, or flitting flies; that is the name for the spots that float before the eyes and stop you from reading. *Muscae volitantes* are what aeroplanes look like when viewed from high above. They are worse when you look up at them. On this 228th day of the year 1999, planes like stingray are floating overhead, roaring and screaming, their yellow eyes glaring down at the sleeping landscape beneath.

Seen from the air this ominous August dawn, the Thames is a diamond-dusted silver ribbon. The aeroplanes follow the river faithfully, nose to tail, as they descend over south-west London, giving panoramic views of the individual boathouses, Putney Bridge, the green spaces of the Hurlingham Club and Fulham Palace gardens, straining and whining as they throttle back over the salubrious complacence of Barnes, then whistling on through the malty cumulus clouds issuing from the chimneys of Mortlake's brewery. On they roar, hooting and wrangling across the 400 botanic acres at Kew, from there to shade Richmond's millennial prosperity with their wings; then on down lower still to the shattered concentration of Hounslow, its double-glazed schools and uproarious bedrooms, where those on the ground can if they so desire look up and check the colour of the pilot's tie.

Until at last they touch down at Heathrow. All aircraft coming in to land here must first fly directly across the capital when the prevailing wind is blowing. This is an unusual arrangement which has not been much imitated by other countries, but without being unpleasantly nationalistic about this, the British have always been made of sterner stuff.

The planes still wear their lights like earrings in this no man's land between night and day. Cassie Withers stands in her Kew back garden and watches them cross the sky one after another, counting them instead of sheep. She was woken by the first flight in from Seoul. Today at some point her husband Steven Withers will be returning from his fifth foreign trip of the month. The constant over-arching trajectories of noise accelerate and fade into one another. Two days ago Steven heard about a problem with the new bidets at one of his company's hotels in the Philippines. He tried phoning the local quality manager but got a voicemail because of the time difference.

'Can't it wait ten hours?' asked Cassie.

'I can *be* there in ten hours,' said Steven. 'That's the beauty of living here.'

And he had jumped on the next plane out.

Now Cassie gazes up beyond the planes as the sky grows lighter. Several stars are almost discernible through the dense maroon-tinted vapour of early morning. She'd watched a documentary on stars last night, about how the earth is long overdue a collision with an asteroid or comet, just like the one that wiped out the dinosaurs. She had also learned from this programme that a Grand Cross of the planets is due this month, in the fixed signs of the zodiac—Taurus, Aquarius, Scorpio, Leo—and that flat earthers everywhere are interpreting these signs as the four horsemen of the Apocalypse. Then she had gone to bed and read about Nostradamus—in the last months of this century it is quite hard *not* to read about Nostradamus, sixteenth-century Provençal plague doctor, and his 942-verse history of the world's future. She had lingered for a while over a particularly interesting couplet:

The year 1999, the seventh month,
From the sky will come a great King of Terror.

Nuclear war was joint favourite with an asteroid attack, according to the editor's note. Nostradamus had been right about several things so far, including the death of Henri II in a jousting accident and also the fall of Communism; so there was a strong possibility of *something* awful happening soon, it seemed.

It has been an unnaturally still hot summer, and even this early on Saturday there is no freshness in the garden. Cassie yawns and creaks and wonders whether she has ME or perhaps a brain tumour or some slow-growing cancer. But so many of her friends are dragging round in a similar state that she decides it must be the unrenewing air of these dog days. Verity Freeling dropped dead last Tuesday without warning, extinguished by the three-week chest virus which has rampaged through everyone round here. It's said to come from China, and it simply laughs at antibiotics. Verity's husband is frantically trying to find a nanny for the three children before he loses his job.

Or perhaps it's just sleep. Because of the aircraft she has worn earplugs at night ever since moving to Kew ten years ago. Recently she went deaf as a result of the build-up of impacted wax. For a while she was quite pleased as this removed her from the constant din of aeroplanes and family life, and there were no side effects save the occasional muffled crump inside her head like a footstep in deep snow. Then reason had prevailed and her GP had syringed her ears. Unfortunately this had had a side effect—tinnitus—which is slowly driving her up the wall.

Sometimes this new ringing in her ears changes pitch, as now, and turns into a high silvery singing noise with a squeak to it like the edge hysteria gives a voice, or like the sharpening of angels' knives, stainless, at high speed.

'Mum, what comes after nineteen-ninety-nine?' asks her five-year-old son Peter as she clears up after breakfast. 'Is it nineteen-ninety-ten?'

'No,' says Cassie. 'Would you sort those knives and forks for me like a good boy. No. It goes nineteen-ninety-nine, TWO THOUSAND.'

'Mum,' he says, picking up a fork, frowning. 'Mum, will it be the end of the world then?'

'No, of course not,' says Cassie heartily. 'It's just a number. It doesn't actually mean anything at all. Unless you believe in Jesus.'

'Do you believe in Jesus?' he asks, as he sometimes does.

'I'm not sure,' she says diplomatically. 'Some people do. Auntie Katie does.'

'I believe in him,' he says staunchly.

'Well that's nice,' she says, then can't help asking, 'Why do you believe in him?'

'Because otherwise who *made* it,' he demands crossly. 'Of course.'

Helen Simpson

He marches out of the kitchen in a huff.

She finishes the dishes, then takes a cup of coffee into the front room where Peter is now lining up a row of small plastic dinosaurs behind the sofa while Michael, his elder brother, hunches over homework in front of the television.

'It's only the news,' he says, forestalling her protest. 'It helps me concentrate.'

She sits by him and lets the news wash over her. Plague is spreading up from Greece through the Balkans, and now Venice has succumbed. There is footage of floods in China, drought in India, war in Africa, famine in Korea, fire in Australia, hysteria in America and desperation in Russia. Reports of a mass throat-cutting in the deserts of New Mexico are just starting to trickle in. Record temperatures worldwide, yet again, have led to speculation that the human race will become a nocturnal species in the next century, on the basis that it's cooler at night.

Later that morning Cassie leaves her boys playing Deathwish in the waiting room, and sees her doctor.

'Could it be tinnitus?' she asks as he peers inside her ear.

'Tinnitus is just a word for any noise you can hear that other people can't.'

'So it *is* tinnitus.'

'Idiopathic tinnitus, if you want a loftier label.'

'Idiopathic?'

'It simply means there's no known cause,' he says, finishing his examination. 'No known cure either, I'm afraid. Just try to ignore it and hope it'll go away.'

'But that's awful!'

'At least you're not deaf as well. Deafness combined with tinnitus is very common in old age.'

'Does everybody have some sort of noise?' asks Cassie. 'Because I found myself thinking perhaps it was always there and I just didn't notice.'

'That is often exactly the case,' smiles the doctor approvingly. 'Something occurs in the ear, some small malfunction, and there it is: the noise revealed. Unmasked. There is a visual analogy. You come home one day and notice a neighbour's hideous new purple window frames. You point them out to your husband. He looks at you in amazement and says, they've been like that for three years. Once you become aware of something, you can't easily lose that awareness.'

'Loss of innocence,' says Cassie.

'In a manner of speaking,' he replies. 'Yes.'

Cassie knows nine of her ten minutes are up, and decides not to use the last one trying to describe her recent intense feelings of foreboding. After all, he might feel he has to put her on Prozac.

They take sandwiches to the park for lunch. Cassie wrestles with each shouting boy in turn, applying sunblock, and then warns them not to roll down the grassy slope because of pesticides. She closes her eyes and feels the sun warm her shoulders, kiss her bare arms and knows it is hostile, fake gold, full of malignant power.

Being out in the sun and the open air used to be health-giving. Now the sea is full of viruses, one bathe can leave you in a wheelchair for good; no wonder the fish have turned belly up this summer, bloated, to float and rot. As for sex, she thinks, watching her boys play, by the time it's their turn it'll be so dangerous they'll have to do it in wetsuits.

'You look a bit down,' says her friend Judith as she joins her on the park bench.

'Is it so obvious?' smiles Cassie. 'Talk about gloom and doom. I've got this horrible feeling that something appalling is about to happen.'

'When you think about it, something appalling always *is* happening, somewhere in the world,' says Judith, watching her daughters run over towards the swings. 'That's why I don't read the papers. I used to feel I ought to; that I *ought* to know about these terrible things. Then one day I just stopped. And my knowing or not knowing has made no difference at all to the state of the world.'

'How do you know?' says Cassie. 'We're all implicated.'

Judith merely smiles a smug smile. Pregnant with her third, she has been given 29 December as the date for the baby's arrival, but she is determined it will wait until the new century. She is going to call it Milly if it's a girl or Len if it's a boy.

'Did you hear about Kate Pimlott?' asks Judith, remembering some gossip. 'She handed out Lion bars at Ben's birthday party last week, she didn't realize they had nuts in, and one of the children had a fatal nut allergy and had to be rushed to hospital.'

'No!' breathed Cassie. 'And is it all right now?'

'Intensive care,' says Judith. 'Touch and go. As Derek said when I told him, it makes you wonder what Kate's legal position would be.'

'The number of children I know with a fatal nut allergy,' groans Cassie. 'I live in terror.'

She draws her sunglasses out of her bag and puts them on, but this does not prevent Judith from noticing the tears in her eyes.

'I'm a bit fed up,' explains Cassie. 'The doctor says he can't do anything about this trouble with my ears.'

'It's the colour of your downstairs,' says Judith without missing a beat. 'You should get my *feng shui* friend in. Anyone who has ear trouble, sinusitis, catarrh, that sort of thing, they should never have walls that colour.'

'What, magnolia?' says Cassie.

'Cream,' Judith corrects her. 'Dairy products. Milk. Cheese. Terribly mucilaginous. You should ring my *feng shui* friend. What have you got to lose?'

'This ringing noise, for a start,' says Cassie, smacking the side of her head, exasperated.

She spends the next couple of hours in the park pleasantly enough, watching the children and chatting to her friend, but not for one minute does she lose awareness of the minatory knife-sharpening noise inside her skull.

The official transition from afternoon to evening in Kew is marked at this time of year by the lighting of a thousand barbecues. This Saturday it is Cassie's neighbour's turn to host the road's annual summer party. The seasonal stench of paraffin and hickory-impregnated briquettes hangs low in the muggy air.

The women stand in clumps on the patio, sipping white wine and keeping an eye on the children, who surge around the forest their solid legs provide. The men have gravitated to the end of the garden under the trees where they help themselves to icy cans of lager from the turquoise cool-box standing on the picnic table.

Above them roars a steady stream of package flights and others. It is now at that point in the year when there are always three planes in the visible arch of the sky, lined up like formation gymnasts. Every forty seconds the barbecue guests fall silent without thinking at the peak of the central plane's trajectory, and then carry on as normal. Cassie remembers her first summer here and the way, inaudible through the din, people had mouthed at her like earnest goldfish: 'You don't even notice it after a while.'

She pours herself a third glass of wine and joins a group of women who are talking about what they are going to do on New Year's Eve. Carol has booked a family package to Paris, where it is rumoured the Eiffel Tower will lay a giant egg. Donna, recently divorced, hopes to fly to Tonga for a seafood feast on the night, if she can sort out the trouble with the Air Miles people; then on to Samoa. Christine is hoping to dodge across the Date Line on Concorde so that she can see the new century dawn twice.

'I was just saying to Nigel the other day,' says Amanda from number twelve, 'Wouldn't it be nice to see the sun rise from Mount Kilimanjaro. But I don't know what we'd do with the children, nobody'll be wanting to babysit that night, will they.'

'I really don't see why air travel has to be so convenient and cheap,' says Cassie. 'People should think twice before crossing the world.'

It is exactly as though she has not spoken. Nobody ever *listens* to me, she thinks.

'Frivolous and greedy,' she throws in for good measure.

'Amanda went down to Cornwall for the eclipse last week, didn't you Amanda,' says Donna. 'On that overnight train from Paddington, what was it called; champagne breakfast, the works.'

'The *Fin de Siècle* something or other,' says Amanda. 'Yes, it was a bit gloomy, the actual eclipse, but the rest of it was a really good laugh.'

'My God! Look at those ants!' cries Carol with a faint scream, having caught sight of a swarming insect mass pouring out from an airbrick. 'They've all grown wings!'

She runs off indoors for a kettle of boiling water while the rest of them crouch down to examine the glistening insects.

'They look a lot bigger than normal ants,' says Amanda.

'Probably from France,' says Donna. 'You know, like the Eurowasps. Double the size.'

'Oh, not Europe again,' says Amanda, tutting.

Cassie fills her glass and walks unsteadily off across the lawn towards the men. She has that sense of being able to see everything with perfect clarity, but nobody will listen to her.

The men are talking about whether the new century really only starts on the first of January 2001, as the spoilsport Swiss claim, and are speculating about how many work days will be lost, how long the celebrations and their hangovers will last.

'The good thing about the beginning of the year 2000,' says Christine's husband Greg, 'Is, that January the first is a Saturday so everyone will have the Sunday and the Monday to recover, because of course the Monday will be a bank holiday.'

'By then there'll have been a tidal wave of computer crashes,' says Amanda's husband Nigel, with relish. 'It'll be the El Niño of IT. I tell you, it's unbelievable, half these guys I see haven't even started to address the Y2K problem.'

'Heads in the sand,' nods Carol's husband Terry. 'We're talking global economic meltdown.'

'Worse than that,' says Cassie. 'A thousand times worse.'

'Steven not back from the Philippines yet?' asks Terry, acknowledging her.

'He's up there right at this moment,' sighs Cassie, pointing at the sky.

'Let's hope air traffic control has sorted itself out before next year,' Greg chuckles knowingly. 'Because it's set to be the busiest year in aviation history.' He rubs his hands together and grins. 'Just make sure you're not partying under the flight path on New Year's Eve. Take it from me.'

'They're saying there'll be record levels of suicide attempts on the thirty-first of December,' muses Greg. 'Seems a funny time to do it.'

'I reckon they're including the doom and gloom merchants in those statistics,' says Terry. 'Like the ones camping out in the

Himalayas. I mean, you're going to look a right plonker when the end of the world *doesn't* come, aren't you, so the only logical thing then is to top yourself.'

'You can't afford to worry about these things,' says Greg. 'Listen, we're due a sunstorm next year, which is when the US tracking system goes down. Completely useless. Perfect opportunity for a nuclear attack. Germ warfare. Let's hope the bad boys haven't figured *that* one out.'

He takes a big gulp of lager and shrugs.

'Too late,' says Cassie obscurely, mournfully. She knows anything she says now is mere babbling into the wind.

'Cheer up, Cassandra,' Terry chides. 'It may never happen.'

Cassie looks over to where her boys are laughing and playing. 'That's the trouble,' she insists. 'It will. Any minute now.'

On board British Airways flight 666 from Manila the air is exhausted after thirteen hours of being recycled. It has been in and out of every lung on board and is now damply laden with droplet infection. Steven is grey-faced and crumbling with jet lag. He rubs his eyes, his whole face, and the tired flesh moves back and forth in folds. Bloody wild-goose chase, he says to himself, removing his glasses and rubbing his eyes till they creak. Now he is nearly home, and glad that it's a Saturday. He'll be able to catch up on sleep. There has been a child nearby who has been crying for much of the journey, troubled by a recurrence of the sinusitis contracted earlier in summer while on a transatlantic flight to Disneyland with his father, who is from Boston, then back to his mother, who is English but works in Hong Kong where she met and married his father. Although now they are divorced.

The weary pretty air hostess smiles at Steven with just that quality of sympathetic tenderness he wishes Cassie would show him more often.

'Would you like a drink, sir?'

As she searches her trolley for a miniature Glenfiddich, she thinks ahead to this evening when she and her husband must have sex. Her next set of IVF injections is due next week; she only hopes the airline won't mess her flights around again or that's another month wasted. She'll be forty-one in October, and she's been doing this job for twenty years.

The pilot meanwhile rubs his eyes and takes a message from air traffic control. This descent to Heathrow has become a regular white-knuckle ride since they reduced the distance between incoming aircraft to a mere mile. A little bit of a holding delay here to fit into the landing sequence, he says suavely into the microphone. The planes are stacked up now, and with all that confusion between West Drayton and Swanwick recently too, he can't remember feeling as jittery as this on a routine flight in his entire career.

The sky darkens from ordinary pallor into deep violet-grey. There is yellow lightning, the forked flicker of a monstrous snake's tongue, then a grandiloquent roll of thunder like the tattoo before an execution. Above the general steam and vapour scowls a rainbow arch of refracted brilliance.

The aeroplanes continue to follow the trajectory of this arch on their descent to Heathrow, and now they fly one after the other into an ominously gigantic boxer's ear of a cloud. Lost in this vaporous mass, British Airways flight 666 from Manila follows an instruction from the arrivals controller until it finds itself fifty feet vertically and a hundred feet horizontally from a Virgin Express Boeing 737 acting on a contradictory instruction. Then both pilots become aware of the danger at the same time, and the incident almost becomes another near-miss for investigation by the Department of Transport. But not quite.

There is a noise like the crack of doom. The enormous cloud lights up as though targeted by a celestial flame-thrower. Over in West Drayton a man in air traffic control has a heart attack which leads directly to the mid-air conflagration of a dozen more incoming flights.

Now aeroplanes like stingray are plunging, yellow eyes aglare, roaring and screaming as they explode into the glasshouses at Kew Gardens and decimate the placid domestic streets surrounding. Steven joins his wife and children, but only in a manner of speaking. Piecemeal. Planes plough into the Hogarth roundabout at Chiswick and put an end to the permanent crawl of the South Circular. A row of double-fronted villas in Castelnau is flattened like a pack of cards, then rises in flames, joined by adjacent avenues of blazing red-brick houses. Mortlake is obliterated and Worple Way razed to the ground. East Sheen is utterly laid waste.

Fire consumes the sky and falls to earth in flaming comets and limbs and molten fragments of fuselage, where for two days and nights it will devour flesh and grass and much else besides in a terrible and unnatural firestorm for miles around south-west London.

And of course that—as Cassie would say were she still in one piece—*that* is only the beginning. □

A LONDON VIEW/Andrew O'Hagan

I used to wake up next to Boadicea. They say she's buried under platform
nine. I looked right into the station from my lovely room in Culross Buildings
behind King's Cross. And from the roof garden I thought I could feel the
whole of Britain rising in an instant. The trains were going north; the
Telecom tower buzzed into life. And yet on that roof, on a winter morning,
with the 5.21 to Peterborough sliding out of the station, it was mostly the
past that seemed to speak.

    I really love that place. It's a corner of London still mad with Victorian
grandeur. For years now it has lived with the threat of demolition. But it

doesn't want to go. People believe it will last forever. You see the remnants of a place called Agar Town from up there. It disappeared to make way for the great railway terminals. From the roof of Culross Buildings you can see the world as it used to be: the gasometers built in the 1860s, the Regent's Canal, the arch of St Pancras, the Great Northern Hotel. And down below there's the cobbled streets. The German Gymnasium stands like some beautiful monument to the enthusiasms of the dead. I will always love this secretive London. Britain's industrial past is nowhere more present than this. I still hear the sound of the trains as I sleep.

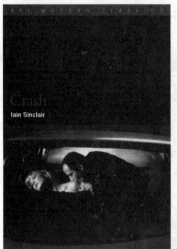

GRANTA

SOHO NOW
Stephen Gill

Above: Brewer Street, looking north
Right: Romilly Street
Over: Frith Street

The Blue Posts, Berwick Street

Above: The House of St Barnabas, hostel for homeless women since 1846, Greek Street
Over: Old Compton Street

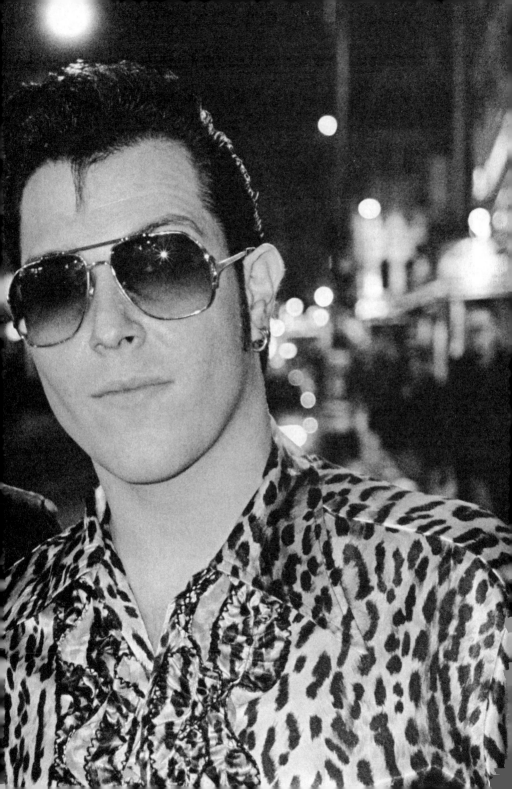

Above: Wardour Street
Opposite: Ingestre Place

W. Sitch & Co. Ltd, dealers in antique light fittings, established 1776

Above: Maison Bertaux, French patisserie, Greek Street
Over: The Moving Picture Company

Agent Provocateur, Broadwick Street

Above: John and Arthur Beare, Broadwick Street
Over: Wonderpark, Great Windmill Street

Above: Soho Square
Opposite: The Groucho Club, Dean Street
Over: Limousine, Wardour Street

The Blue Posts

Above: St Mungo Association for the homeless
Over: Madame Jo Jo's, cabaret club, Brewer Street

Above: Mr and Mrs Santinelli, residents in Soho since 1923
Opposite: Berwick Street
Over: Blacks, Dean Street

A LONDON VIEW/David Harrison

Every day starts with a *si si si*. These blue tits are my friends and we depend on each other. They depend on me to feed them, and I depend on them for the joy of glimpsing a life of natural beauty amid the gloom and destruction of mankind. Blue tits are easy to attract. I only have a window box, but in a very busy part of central London, just off the Caledonian Road, the blue tits quickly learned that this is where they can be fed. I've made them a miniature copy of St Pancras station to hang out on (it doesn't actually look like St Pancras but it does have a gothic feel to it) and in winter I give them fat which can be bought in balls from pet shops.

At breakfast I can see them calling their *si si si*, which I interpret as 'feed, feed, feed'. Always active, they eat, dance and sing. When it's busy, they're joined by great tits, dressed for dinner in their smart black bibs and yellow waistcoats. On rare days there's a harsh screech and a sudden panic and in their place there's a jay, who gobbles all the peanuts in the feeders.

After their breakfast and mine I leave the flat and walk to my studio under the shadow of the station. The main road doesn't have much to offer: a couple of pigeons pecking at last night's curry thrown up over the pavement by some drunk, starlings gathering in the trees. But when I turn down to the canal to give my two poodles a run, it's obvious how much has changed since factories have stopped polluting the water. Melodious and incredibly loud outbursts from deep inside the bushes along the towpath signal a wren, a bird the size of a ping-pong ball with legs. Canada geese hiss at my dogs as they bounce around, barking and wanting to play. An occasional heron stands very still, a posing catwalk model. And sometimes in winter, I see something very special: a small black sphere approaching at great speed about a foot above the water. I stand dead still and watch. As it passes, the sphere turns electric blue with neon orange flashes and then, just as suddenly, it turns black again and disappears along the canal. A kingfisher.

Now I arrive at the car park outside my studio at St Pancras. Once I walked in to see a young girl lying on the ground, looking desperately for the needle she'd dropped among the shit. And there, growing beside her, was a beautiful bright-yellow perennial wall rocket. I stepped around her and the tin cans which people use to smoke crack and saw, over by the drains, another girl pleasuring a man in a suit for her five-quid bag of smack. Then I heard snatches of a sweet, watery sound: the song of the robin, like a rare perfume heralding hope. I looked up and caught a splash of red. Whatever we make ugly, nature will correct.

GRANTA

THE UMBRELLA
Hanif Kureishi

SERGIO LARRAIN/MAGNUM PHOTOS

The minute they arrived at the adventure playground, Roger's two sons charged up a long ramp and soon were clinging to the steel netting that hung from a high beam. Satisfied that it would take them some time to extract themselves, Roger sat on a bench and turned to the sports section of his newspaper. He had always found it relaxing to read reports of football matches he had not seen. Then it started to rain.

His sons, aged four and five and a half, had refused to put on their coats when he picked them up from the au pair half an hour before. Coats made them look 'fat', they claimed, and Roger had had to carry the coats under his arm. The older boy was dressed in a thin tight-fitting green outfit and a cardboard cap with a feather in it: he was either Robin Hood or Peter Pan. The younger wore a plastic belt with holsters containing two silver guns, a plastic dagger and a sword, blue wellington boots, jeans with the fly open, and a chequered neckerchief which he pulled over his mouth. 'Cowboys don't wear raincoats,' he said through a mouthful of cloth. The boys frequently refused Roger's commands, though he could not say that their stubbornness and pluck annoyed him. It did, however, cause him trouble with his wife, from whom he had separated a year previously. Only that morning she had said on the phone, 'You are a weak and inadequate disciplinarian. You only want their favour.'

For as long as he could, Roger pretended it was not raining, but when his newspaper began to go soggy and everyone else left the playground, he called the boys over.

'Damn this rain,' he said as he hustled them into their yellow hooded raincoats.

'Don't swear,' said the younger. 'Women think it's naughty.'

'Sorry.' Roger laughed. 'I was thinking I should have got a raincoat as well as the suit.'

'You do need a lovely raincoat, Daddy,' said Oliver, the eldest.

'My friend would have given me a raincoat, but I liked the suit more.'

He had picked up the chocolate-coloured suit from the shop that morning. Since that most extravagant of periods, the early Seventies, Roger had fancied himself as a restrained but amateur dandy. One of his best friends was a clothes designer with shops in Europe and

Japan. A few years ago this friend, amused by Roger's interest in his business, had invited Roger, during a fashion show in the British Embassy in Paris, to parade on the catwalk in front of the fashion press, alongside men taller and younger than him. Roger's friend had given him the chocolate suit for his fortieth birthday, and had insisted he wear it with a blue silk shirt. Roger's sons liked to sleep in their newly acquired clothes, and he understood their enthusiasm. He would not normally wear a suit for the park, but that evening he was going to a publishing party, and on to his third date with a woman he had been introduced to at a friend's house, a woman he liked.

Roger took the boys' hands and pulled them along.

'We'd better go to the tea house,' he said. 'I hope I don't ruin my shoes.'

'They're beautiful,' said Oliver.

Eddie stopped to bend down and rub his father's loafers. 'I'll put my hands over your shoes while you walk,' he said.

'That might slow us down a little,' Roger said. 'Run for it, mates!'

He picked Eddie up, holding him flat in his arms like a baby, with his muddy boots pointing away from him. The three of them hurried across the darkening park.

The tea house was a wide, low-ceilinged shed, warm, brightly lit and decorated in the black-and-white colours and flags of Newcastle United. The coffee was good and they had all the newspapers. The place was crowded but Roger spotted a table and sent Oliver over to sit at it.

Roger recognized the mother of a boy in Eddie's nursery, as well as several nannies and au pairs, who seemed to congregate in some part of this park on most days. Three or four of them had come often to his house with their charges when he lived with his wife. If they seemed reticent with him, he doubted whether this was because they were young and simple, but rather that they saw him as an employer, as the boss. He was aware that he was the only man in the tea house. The men he ran into with children were either younger than him, or older, on their second families. He wished his children were older, and understood more; he should have had them earlier. He'd both enjoyed and wasted the years before they were born; it had been a long dissatisfied ease.

A girl in the queue turned to him.

'Thinking again?' she said.

He recognized her voice but had not brought his glasses. 'Hello,' he said at last. He called to Eddie, 'Hey, it's Lindy.' Eddie covered his face with both hands. 'You remember her giving you a bath and washing your hair.'

'Hey cowboy,' she said.

Lindy had looked after both children when Eddie was born, and lived in the house until precipitately deciding to leave. She had told them she wanted to do something else but, instead, had gone to work for a couple nearby. She bent over and kissed Oliver, as she used to, and he put his arms around her. The last time Roger had run into Lindy, he had overheard her imitating his sons' accents and laughing. They were 'posh'. He had been shocked by how early these notions of 'class' started.

'Haven't seen you for a while,' she said.

'I've been travelling.'

'Where to?'

'Belfast, Cape Town, Sarajevo.'

'Lovely,' she said.

'I'm off to the States next week,' he said.

'Doing what?'

'Lecturing on human rights. On the development of the notion of the individual...of the idea of the separate self.' He wanted to say something about Shakespeare and Montaigne here, as he had been thinking about them, but realized she would refuse to be curious about the subject. 'And on the idea of human rights in the post-war period. All of that kind of thing. I hope there's going to be a TV series.'

She said, 'I came back from the pub and turned on the TV last week, and there you were, criticising some clever book or other. I didn't understand it.'

'Right.'

He had always been polite to her, even when he had been unable to wake her up because she had been drinking the previous night. She had seen him unshaven, and in his pyjamas at four in the morning; she had opened doors and found him and his wife abusing one another behind them; she had been at their rented villa in Assisi when his wife tore the cloth from the table with four bowls of pasta on it. She must have heard energetic reconciliations.

'I hope it goes well,' she said.

'Thank you.'

The boys ordered big doughnuts and juice. The juice spilled over the table and the doughnuts were smeared round their mouths. Roger had to hold his cappuccino out in front of him to stop the boys sticking their grimy fingers in the froth and sucking the chocolate from them. To his relief they joined Lindy's child.

Roger began a conversation with a woman at the next table who had complimented him on his sons. She told him she wanted to write a newspaper article on how difficult some people found it to say 'no' to children. You could not charm them, she maintained, as you could people at a cocktail party; they had to know what the limits were. He did not like the idea that she shouted at her child, but he decided to ask for her phone number before he left. For more than a year he had not gone out socially, fearing that people would see his anguish.

He was extracting his notebook and pen when Lindy called him. He turned round. His sons were at the far end of the tea house, rolling on top of another, larger, boy, who was wailing, 'He's biting me!'

Eddie did bite; he kicked too.

'Boys!' Roger called.

He hurried them into their coats again, whispering furiously at them to shut up. He said goodbye to the woman without getting her phone number. He did not want to appear lecherous. He had always been timid, and proud of the idea that he was a good man who treated people fairly. He did not want to impose himself. The world would be a better place if people considered their actions. Perhaps he had put himself on a pedestal. 'You have a high reputation—with yourself!' a friend had said. Everyone was entitled to some pride and vanity. However, this whole business with his wife had stripped him of his moral certainties. There was no just or objective way to resolve competing claims: those of freedom—his freedom—to live and develop as he liked, against the right of his family to have his dependable presence. But no amount of conscience or morality would make him go back. He had not missed his wife for a moment.

As they were leaving the park, Eddie tore some daffodils from a flower bed and stuffed them in his pocket. 'For Mummy,' he explained.

The house was a ten-minute walk away. Holding hands, they ran home through the rain. His wife would be back soon, and he would be off.

It was not until he had taken out his key that he remembered his wife had changed the lock last week. What she had done was illegal; he owned the house, but he had laughed at the idea that she thought he would intrude, when he wanted to be as far away as possible.

He told the boys they would have to wait. They sheltered in the little porch where water dripped on their heads. The boys soon tired of standing with him and refused to sing the songs he started. They pulled their hoods down and chased one another up and down the path.

It was dark. People were coming home from work.

The next-door neighbour passed by. 'Locked out?' he said.

"Fraid so.'

Oliver said, 'Daddy, why can't we go in and watch the cartoons?'

'It's only me she's locked out,' he said. 'Not you. But you are, of course, with me.'

'Why has she locked us out?'

'Why don't you ask her?' he said.

His wife confused and frightened him. But he would greet her civilly, send the children into the house and say goodbye. It was, however, difficult to get cabs in the area; impossible at this time and in this weather. It was a twenty-minute walk to the tube station, across a dripping park where alcoholics and junkies gathered under the trees. His shoes, already wet, would be filthy. At the party he would have to try and remove the worst of the mud in the toilet.

After the violence of separation he had expected a diminishment of interest and of loathing, on her part. He himself had survived the worst of it and anticipated a quietness. Kind indifference had come to seem an important blessing. But as well as refusing to divorce him, she sent him lawyer's letters about the most trivial matters. One letter, he recalled, was entirely about a cheese sandwich he had made for himself when visiting the children. He was ordered to bring his own food in future. He thought of his wife years ago, laughing and putting out her tongue with his semen on it.

'Hey there,' she said, coming up the path.

'Mummy!' they called.

'Look at them,' he said. 'They're soaked through.'

'Oh dear.'

She unlocked the door and the children ran into the hall. She nodded at him. 'You're going out.'

'Sorry?'

'You've got a suit on.'

He stepped into the hall. 'Yes. A little party.'

He glanced into his former study where his books were packed in boxes on the floor. He had, as yet, nowhere to take them. Beside them were a pair of men's black shoes he had not seen before.

She said to the children, 'I'll get your tea.' To him she said, 'You haven't given them anything to eat, have you?'

'Doughnuts,' said Eddie. 'I had chocolate.'

'I had jam,' said Oliver.

She said, 'You let them eat that rubbish?'

Eddie pushed the crushed flowers at her. 'There you are, Mummy.'

'You must not take flowers from the park,' she said. 'They are for everyone.'

'Fuck, fuck, fuck,' said Eddie suddenly, with his hand over his mouth.

'Shut up! People don't like it!' said Oliver, and hit Eddie, who started to cry.

'Listen to him,' she said to Roger. 'You've taught them to use filthy language. You are really hopeless.'

'So are you,' he said.

In the past few months, preparing his lectures, he had visited some disorderly and murderous places. The hatred he witnessed puzzled him still. It was atavistic but abstract; mostly the people did not know one another. It had made him aware of how people clung to their antipathies, and used them to maintain an important distance, but in the end he failed to understand why this was. After all the political analysis and talk of rights, he had concluded that people had to grasp the necessity of loving one another; and if that was too much, they had to let one another alone. When this still seemed inadequate and banal, he suspected he was on the wrong path, that he was trying to say something about his own difficulties in the guise of intellectual discourse. Why could he not find a more direct method? He had, in fact, considered writing a novel. He had plenty to say, but could not afford the time, unpaid.

He looked out at the street. 'It's raining quite hard.'

'It's not too bad now.'

He said, 'You haven't got an umbrella, have you?'

'An umbrella?'

He was becoming impatient. 'Yes. An umbrella. You know, you hold it over your head.'

She sighed and went back into the house. He presumed she was opening the door to the airing cupboard in the bathroom.

He was standing in the porch, ready to go. After a while she returned empty-handed.

'No. No umbrella,' she said.

He said, 'There were three there last week.'

'Maybe there were.'

'Are there not still three umbrellas there?'

'Maybe there are,' she said.

'Give me one.'

'No.'

'Sorry?'

'I'm not giving you one,' she said. 'If there were a thousand umbrellas there I would not give you one.'

He had noticed how persistent his children were; they asked, pleaded, threatened and screamed, until he yielded.

He said, 'They are my umbrellas.'

'No,' she repeated.

'How petty you've become.'

'Didn't I give you everything?'

He cleared his throat. 'Everything but love.'

'I did give you that, actually.' She said, 'I've rung my friend. He's on his way.'

He said, 'I don't care. Just give me an umbrella.'

She shook her head. She went to shut the door. He put his foot out and she banged the door against his leg. He wanted to rub his shin but could not give her the pleasure.

He said, 'Let's try and be rational.'

He had hated before, his parents and brother, at certain times. But it was a fury, not a deep intellectual and emotional hatred like this. He had had psychotherapy; he took tranquillizers, but still he wanted to pulverize his wife. None of the ideas he had about life would make this feeling go away. A friend had suggested it would be no bad thing if he lost the 'good' idea of himself, seeing himself as more complicated and passionate. But he could not understand the advantage of seeing himself as unhinged.

'You used to find the rain "refreshing",' she said with a sneer.

'It has come to this,' he said.

'Here we are then,' she said. 'Don't start crying about it.'

He pushed the door. 'I'll get the umbrella.'

She pushed the door back at him. 'You cannot come in.'

'It is my house.'

'Not without prior arrangement.'

'We arranged it,' he said.

'The arrangement's off.'

He pushed her.

'Are you assaulting me?' she said.

He looked outside. An alcoholic woman he had had to remove from the front step on several occasions was standing at the end of the path holding a can of lager.

'I'm watching you,' she shouted. 'If you touch her you are reported!'

'Watch on!' he shouted back.

He pushed into the house. He placed his hand on his wife's chest and forced her against the wall. She cried out. She did bang her head, but it was, in football jargon, a 'dive'. The children ran at his legs. He pushed them away. He went to the airing cupboard, seized an umbrella and made his way to the front door.

As he passed her she snatched it. Her strength surprised him, but he yanked the umbrella back and went to move away. She raised her hand. He thought she would slap him. It would be the first time.

But she made a fist. As she punched him in the face she continued to look at him. He had not been hit since he left school. He had forgotten the physical shock and then the disbelief, the shattering of the belief that the world was a safe place.

The boys had started to scream. He had dropped the umbrella. His mouth throbbed; his lip was bleeding. He must have staggered and lost his balance for she was able to push him outside.

He heard the door slam behind him. He could hear the children crying. He walked away, past the alcoholic woman still standing at the end of the path. He turned to look at the lighted house. When they had calmed down, the children would have their bath and get ready for bed. They liked being read to. It was a part of the day he had always enjoyed.

He turned his collar up but knew he would get soaked. He wiped his mouth with his hand. She had landed him quite a hit. He would not be able to find out until later whether it would show. □

A LONDON VIEW/David Sylvester

The choice has to be Battersea Power Station, not least because there are so many views of it: as you travel around London it's forever turning up, expectedly or unexpectedly, at varying distances, looking when afar like a great steamship ploughing its way through the buildings and the trees. One of the best viewpoints allows you to lean on the wall overlooking the north side of the river a hundred yards or so to the west of Chelsea Bridge. A nice thing about this view is the foreground provided by the wide arches of the railway bridge, the movement of the trains (sliding into and out of Victoria) above and the barges just below you. Another is that, when you turn your back on the view, you're face to face with the Western Pumping Station across the street and its campanile-like tower.

Battersea Power Station is distressing if you focus on its hull with all its evidence of casual demolition. You wonder hopelessly how governments can let their heritage slip away, but the power of what remains doesn't take long to lift you from the dilapidation and make you concentrate on the four corners, where the chimneys, endlessly changing colour between cream and grey without ever being quite white, issue from their chunky stepped plinths, the colour of the bricks ranging, through a mixture of short-term effects of light and long-term effects of weather, across any number of different shades of grey and brown. What is constant is the drama of the contrast between the lightness of the cylindrical forms above and the darkness of the cubic ones below, a contrast that becomes strangely sensual where the light and dark touch.

And, as you go on looking, the whole thing changes every few minutes between seeming to be near and seeming to be far. Does this have to do with the physiology of gazing or the mutability of the light?

The building looks decidedly masculine. Not for any such ridiculous reason as that its outstanding features are upstanding. (How can perfectly vertical forms be interpreted as phallic symbols when in reality phalli tend not to get more upright than the Leaning Tower of Pisa?) What makes for the masculinity is the thickset quality of the blocks and the almost military bearing of the chimney columns. But then that metaphor disappears and the columns become their luminous selves. The luminosity is uncanny. The columns seem to be containers of deep reserves of light. They offer an infinite supply of it. But then you suddenly realize that they're not only radiating but absorbing light. They are feminine, too, soft and yielding. What they yield to

is the light they bathe in, that of the restless skies over the Thames in London.

I can suggest a reason why this upturned table by Giles Gilbert Scott is not commonly ranked among the wonders of twentieth-century architecture, as an alternative to the art of Corbusier, Wright and Mies in much the same way as Elgar offers one to Schönberg, Webern and Stravinsky. I suspect it is because Battersea Power Station doesn't strike us as the creation of an individual mind but as an outcrop of the genius of London itself.

Battersea Power Station photographed in 1933, shortly after it was built. In the late 1940s it was doubled in size and two more chimneys added.

239

GRANTA

TO FEED THE NIGHT
Philip Hensher

They lived in London at the end of the nineteen eighties. His wife was twenty-four. He was twenty-six. In her job, she earned eleven thousand pounds a year, and he earned thirteen thousand pounds a year.

'It's mad,' he said. He and his wife were entertaining two other couples to dinner. One couple consisted of a man she had known in the past, and his girlfriend. The other consisted of an old girlfriend of his, and her new husband. The purpose of the dinner party was to show these four people the flat the man and his wife had moved into the month before.

'What's mad?' the man's wife said.

'The price of property,' he said. 'It's quite scary.'

'I think we got on to the ladder just in time,' she said, for the benefit of their guests. 'I think in another six months, we wouldn't have been able to afford even this.'

'You want to get on to the property ladder,' the man said, as if advising their guests. 'If you leave it too long, you won't be able to afford to buy anything, you'll be left behind, and you'll never ever be able to buy anything at all.'

'It scares me,' his wife said.

'You were lucky,' one of the girls said. 'This is a nice flat. It really is. You were lucky.'

'It's smaller than we wanted, really,' the wife said. 'But it's good for now.'

'It's nice,' another man said. 'It's cosy, really.'

The man did not stop eating as his wife's old friend said that his flat was cosy, but a feeling of wrongness fell over him. He continued to eat the tidy food which his wife had cooked seven times before in the certainty that nothing had ever gone wrong with it, and, saying nothing, felt the narrowness of the flat he lived in. His mind roamed quickly over the sitting room and bedroom and bathroom and galley kitchen. It did not take long. He said nothing.

'I thought that went well,' his wife said when they had all gone.

'Yes,' he said. There was nothing much to say. His wife earned eleven thousand pounds a year. He earned thirteen thousand pounds a year. The amount of money they had borrowed to buy this narrow and depressing place was as much as any firm would lend them. This was all they deserved.

He had drunk too much at dinner, and woke late the next morning. As he walked through the shopping arcade on the way to the underground station, some of the shops were already opening up. They drew his attention. He thought he knew them all. But between the baker's and the newsagent's there was a glossy interior, thick-carpeted and empty. It sold, one might have thought, nothing but photographs. In the window there were photographs of the insides of houses, and next to them, against the dark-painted wood, a sum of money. He paused, although he was late. His eye was drawn upward and into the interior. He had never noticed this estate agent's before. Inside, there was one man, at an empty desk, running a pen along his lips like a harmonica, and watching.

The man, outside the window, dropped his eyes, and they fell against a photograph; a photograph of a quiet empty room, painted white, sunlight against a window; a white room, edged with green tartan, a calm good peaceful room. The man stood there and looked at the photograph for a while. He was late for his job. He looked at the sum of money. It was barely more than he and his wife had paid for the constrained flat in which they lived. He went in.

'How do you do,' the agent said, rising from his desk. He was narrowly built, hungrily mid-twenties, with the rudiments of a smile underneath the startling blue eyes, a brisk smile of wet white teeth.

'Hello,' the man said.

'I am Mr Bell,' the agent said. 'I saw you, looking at our properties. We have some good properties in, at the moment.'

'Yes,' the man said. 'I don't know—'

'Yes?' Mr Bell said.

'I mean,' the man said, 'I've only just bought a flat.'

'But you saw a flat of ours,' Mr Bell said.

'It looked so nice,' the man said, helplessly.

'The Elgin Avenue flat,' Mr Bell said. 'Or so I imagine. A very nice property. I wonder if you would like to see it? You are in luck. It only came on to the market late yesterday. A feeling I had, to put it into the window immediately. You are the first person to notice it, and I imagine it will not be in the window for very long. I wonder if you would like to see it?'

'I've only just bought a flat,' the man said.

'So you will not have settled, not quite yet.'

'No,' the man said. It was as if he had been defeated in some way.

He went with Mr Bell to the flat illustrated in the window of the shop he had never seen before. The road was so thickly wooded it seemed no road but a bridge, floating in a dense green firmament, and heavy with quiet. The empty flat was on the first floor. He followed the agent into the flat, and was struck by the pleasant and clean air it had. The rooms were larger than the flat he had bought with his wife, and he followed the agent, with hopeless pleasure, from the central hallway into the kitchen, sitting room, bedroom, bathroom. Mr Bell paused, and with a smile opened the last door. It was a second bedroom.

'It's a very nice flat,' he said to Mr Bell on the way back to the shop. 'But we've only just moved.'

'That needn't be a problem,' Mr Bell said.

'And it is more than we paid for our flat,' he said. 'And that was really at our limit.'

'I see,' Mr Bell said. 'But house prices are shooting up all the time. You may even make a profit.'

'And it is bigger than our flat,' the man said. 'We might need more space.'

He told his wife about the flat. She listened, her lips closed. When he had finished, she said nothing for a while.

'Why not?' he said. 'It's very nice. And we could do with more space.'

'What for?' his wife said.

'If we had a child,' he said. 'For instance. It's very nice. It's a real bargain.'

'If you think it's a good idea,' she said, in the end.

The purchase of the flat was not a problematic one. Mr Bell was very helpful, and found a buyer for their flat whose offer matched the price of the new flat. On the day they moved in, the man and his wife followed each other round the flat, running their fingers round the walls of each room.

'I'm amazed we can afford this,' his wife said. 'We made a mistake, really, paying more than we needed for the other flat.'

'It was what was on the market at the time.'

'It's so nice. And the spare bedroom.'

'It won't be spare for long,' he said. He stood there with his hand on the door of the second bedroom. The expansion of their lives had begun. The touch of the cool-painted door against his hand, her impressed gaze, the moment, the lacuna, as they stood in their acquired silence, was like an embrace. He earned thirteen thousand pounds a year; she earned eleven thousand pounds a year, in London in the late nineteen eighties. Things were possible.

They had another dinner party, and asked the same people to come.

'I can't believe you moved again so soon,' one of their guests said.

'We saw this,' the man said, 'and it seemed too good to pass up. It was an amazing bargain.'

'We keep expecting the walls to collapse, or the Hell's Angels neighbours to come back from holiday,' his wife said.

'But it hasn't happened,' the man said quickly.

'How did you find it?' his old girlfriend said.

'It was in the window of an estate agent's,' the man said. 'I don't know if you know the one. It's in the arcade by the tube station. I just saw the photograph.'

'And we had to see it,' his wife said. She made a new gesture with her hands, a fountaining upward wave, and her teeth shone.

'And once we'd seen it, we had to buy it,' the man said. 'The last place had gone up fifteen thousand in three months, and this was so underpriced we actually made money on the deal.'

'I don't know it,' one of the male guests said.

'Sorry?' the wife said.

'I don't know the estate agent's,' he said. 'I thought I knew that row of shops, but I don't remember the estate agent's.'

'They're very good,' the man said. 'Ask for a Mr Bell.'

'Mr Bell,' the guest said, nodding in thought.

It was eighteen months later when the man saw Mr Bell again. The estate agent was in the street, standing, stroking his chin, as if waiting for someone. He recognized Mr Bell immediately—the azure flash of the eyes, the abrupt smile—and Mr Bell, it seemed, recognized him. Mr Bell took a couple of steps forward, his arm outstretched to shake hands; a gesture from an office, but unfamiliar and peculiar when executed in the street.

'Your flat,' Mr Bell said. 'I remember your flat, how nice it was. And happy there, are you?'

'Yes,' the man said, vaguely. Eighteen months after buying the place, it had become merely the place they lived, and he and his wife walked through the flat without admiring it, without expending appreciation on the walls, no longer feeling joy as they contemplated each doorknob, each cupboard, contemplated their ownership of everything they could see. 'Yes, very much so.'

'Still,' Mr Bell said. 'I expect you'll be thinking before long of finding somewhere with a garden?'

'I'm sorry?' the man said, but immediately he knew that that was what he wanted; that whatever the agent's reason for saying this, he was right; that a garden was what they wanted now.

'For your children,' Mr Bell elucidated.

'We don't have any children, I'm afraid,' the man said.

'I'm so sorry,' Mr Bell said. 'I thought you were moving into your present flat for the child.'

The man shrugged. They had no children; he had no plans to talk about having children.

'Forgive me,' Mr Bell said. 'My mind was wandering, I expect. Perhaps it was just that I was thinking about this property we've just seen. It's not often that you see a property as interesting as this one.' Swiftly he extracted a file from inside his coat. 'Do you see what I mean?' he said.

The man looked at the photograph. It was as if a dream he had always had but never quite made flesh, never quite recalled on waking, had now been presented to him, in image: a quiet empty room, great double doors opening on to a garden and light streaming in, golden light electric with dust.

'It looks lovely,' the man said.

'And a bargain,' Mr Bell said. 'The old lady died, and her family live in America. The instruction was to price it low and sell it quickly. They came up with a price and—well, frankly, I think they can't have any idea what it could fetch, but they were insistent on a particular figure. Very odd. I've never heard anything quite like it.'

'How much are they asking?' the man said. He steeled himself, but he was still unprepared for the shock when Mr Bell said the figure. He almost gulped.

'Would you like to see it?' Mr Bell said. The man nodded.

'We don't need to move,' the man's wife said, that evening, over dinner.

'I still think,' the man said carefully, 'you might like to have a look at it. It really is extraordinary. All that space.'

'We don't need any more space,' the wife said.

'But it's an amazing bargain,' he said. 'And think of the investment. Don't you want to live in a house bigger than you could possibly need?'

She got up and scraped the remains on his plate, the brown and sordid ends, on to the remains on hers. She had no particular response, he could see that.

'At least come and look at it,' he said.

'What would you do with it?' she said.

'It would be wonderful to have a piano,' he said. 'I always wanted a piano. And the children. I mean, we don't have to talk about this, but—'

'At some point,' she said. 'When we stop worrying about it, I expect. And in the meantime—'

'I always wanted a piano,' he said.

'I never knew you played,' she said. 'You're full of surprises.'

'I don't,' he admitted. 'I always wanted to learn.'

The garden; the spare bedroom; the room for the piano; a room for—what?—for the kitchen machines, for a study, for a dining room, for some purpose. To have so many rooms, to have more rooms than ready purposes. Mr Bell stood at the door, and waited, kindly, for them to get through the empty rooms, remarking only that the house's furniture had been removed only two days before, and sold. When they were home, they shut the door behind them and, in the suddenly little sitting room, looked at each other, and in her shining eyes he could see his eyes, shining, with possibility, with space, with greed.

'What do you need all this space for?' the man's old girlfriend said. It was their first dinner party in the new house.

'Nothing,' his wife retorted. 'Nothing at all. That's the beauty of it.'

He felt her rudeness. 'We're going to fill it, of course,' he said. 'And it was such a bargain. It would have been a crime to let it go.'

'I just don't see,' the other girl said, 'what the two of you need with all these rooms.'

The man and his wife barely glanced at each other, and with their cleverness did not say what was the case, that no one they knew had amounted to what they, in their acuteness, had amounted to. He earned thirteen thousand pounds; she earned eleven thousand pounds, in England at the end of the nineteen eighties, and they lived, somehow, in a house bigger than the houses any of their friends lived in.

'Nor do I, sometimes,' the man said in the end.

'Mr Bell,' the wife said. 'The estate agent. He's a sort of genius.'

'I couldn't find it,' another man said. 'I went down there but I couldn't see it.'

'You should look harder,' the man said. 'He's well worth it.'

'I was in a bit of a hurry,' the other man conceded.

A year passed in their new house. Outside, the seasons came and went. She sat in her new kitchen, and out of the window the wet green garden made her still inside. There were rooms upstairs she never went into; the air-bright yellow room at the back, lovely but unusable, convincing her that her lovely house had more possibilities than she did, or her husband. There was no piano; they could not afford one, but her husband played records of piano music in their house, and the house sounded of music made by other people. It was almost frightening, the half-empty house they filled with what furniture they had, but here, in England, at the end of the nineteen eighties, with everything changing, with every square inch of carpet, every tiny room doubling in value by the day, there was nothing they could do, nothing but rejoice, self-consciously, in the house, so much bigger, so much more than they, with their puny small movements, could ever think of filling. And the seasons came and went, and in the end there was a day which, in its weather, was precisely like the half-happy day on which she and her husband had moved into their house.

'I went to see Mr Bell,' the man said, as if beginning a conversation he had rehearsed.

'He was amazing, that man,' the wife said, not committing herself.

'Yes,' the man said. 'Yes. I wondered if he could be amazing again.'

She got up and went towards the shelf over the fireplace. On it was a small wooden deer, a solitary ornament, and she turned it, without saying anything, to the wall, as if thinking.

'I thought I would just ask him what was on the market,' he went on. 'He was so amazing last time, and the time before. You never know.'

'And were you in luck?' she asked, dully.

'We might be,' he said. From his pocket he produced a list of particulars. She read them in amazement; the measurement of each room, brazen as a misprint; the legendary street; the radiant adjectives.

'That can't be right,' she said, pointing at the price.

'It is,' he said. 'I can't understand it, and Mr Bell can't either. Let's face it. Maybe we're just lucky people.'

'We've only just moved,' the wife said.

'A year ago,' he said. 'I heard somebody saying the other day that the market's on the turn. It can't carry on going up. It really can't. And the point to be at when the market turns is selling something at a profit. This is an amazing opportunity.'

'Can't we—' she said. But it was hopeless; not because she saw what he wanted, bullying her into submission, but because as she spoke, she felt her own want move inside her like a child.

'You're getting to be my favourite clients,' Mr Bell said breezily, driving them away from the miracle house, the house they, the city, the decade had always dreamed of. 'I like lucky people.'

'No one we know can believe our luck,' the man said. His wife was sitting in the back seat, and he could not see her expression. He dried the palms of his hands on his trousers, smoothing them down confidently. 'That was an amazing house. And you really think we can stretch to that?'

'It's not much of a stretch,' Mr Bell said. 'The house you're in at the moment, you'll have no problem selling that for double what you paid for it. And that more or less covers the asking price for this one. I know it seems extraordinary, but you know what they say about gift horses. Of course, you will have the gift horse surveyed, but I promise you, there's no problem here.'

'None at all?' the wife said, leaning forward between the seats.

'As far as I know,' Mr Bell said. 'Apart from one.'

They sat; the husband could feel his wife hugging the back of the seat he sat in.

'Yes,' Mr Bell said. He seemed a little distracted. 'A small one, though, I think. There is another buyer very interested.'

'Has he put in an offer?'

'He has.'

'We'll match it,' the wife said.

'He's offered the asking price,' Mr Bell said.

'We'll match it,' the wife said. 'And add five thousand.'

'My understanding is,' Mr Bell said, 'that he will match any subsequent offer. Can I drop you near your house at all?'

It proved the case. The man made a formal offer of five thousand pounds over the asking price, and the other buyer made a second offer, of ten thousand pounds over the asking price. The man and his wife talked, and they walked in the now small and sullen rooms of the house they lived in through a whole night; there was not talk enough to fill a whole night, and still they talked, again and again and again, saying the same things, not arguing, not disagreeing, but still, somehow, talking, and behind their talk, the mad recurrence of an invisible man's noise at a piano, repeating the same notes in different order, trapped within the caged monochrome limits of the invisible keyboard. And the next day the man made an offer of what he could not afford, of twelve thousand five hundred pounds in excess of the asking price. And the day after that, Mr Bell telephoned to say that the other buyer had, without hesitation, made a third offer, of a full fifteen thousand pounds over the price the seller had set.

'I don't see what we can do,' the man said. He was in the empty agency. He faced Mr Bell across his desk. There was nothing on it except a single brown folder, the fabulous desired address written neatly on it. Outside, the noises of the street were muffled, and he fixed Mr Bell with a look of what he knew must closely resemble desperation.

'It depends,' Mr Bell said, 'on how much you want this house.'

'It is beautiful,' the man said.

'It is beautiful,' Mr Bell said, as if conceding a point in argument, 'and it is unlikely a house of this quality would ever come on the market at this price again. As I say, it depends how much you really want this house.'

'I don't see what else we can do,' the man said. 'We can't offer any more.'

'Do you need the house?' Mr Bell said. 'Do you really need to move? Do you need that much space? Those are the sorts of questions that, perhaps, you should be asking yourselves.'

It was a surprising thing for Mr Bell to say, and the man was startled. It was only a moment, however, before he saw, with certainty, that Mr Bell was playing devil's advocate, and he replied with confidence.

'But we want it,' he said. 'And now is the right time to buy.'

Mr Bell nodded, as if satisfied at the right response in the catechism from a fast-learning pupil. 'There is something you could do,' he said. 'But it depends how much you really want this house.'

'More than anything,' the man said.

'Then,' Mr Bell said, and with a small gesture he knocked the manila folder to the floor. Beneath it was what, somehow, the man had always known would be beneath it, a small, needle-neat and shining pistol. He stared at it. It was not a surprise. There was a silence between them.

'The other buyer,' Mr Bell continued, in the same even tone of voice, 'has asked to see the house on his own, at four o'clock precisely this afternoon. I have lent him the key to the house, since I will be too busy this afternoon to go with him. He will be there, and alone. If the doorbell rings, his assumption will be that it is the estate agent who, after all, was able to turn up and answer any questions. He will be alone.'

'There will be other buyers, surely,' the man said.

'There will be no other buyers,' Mr Bell said. 'I think I can promise you that.'

He looked at the man levelly, his quiet eyes blue in the shaded face. The man stretched out his hand, and found that the tiny pistol cupped into his damp palm. He stood up, without shaking, and left the shop, Mr Bell's gaze hot on his back. It was only on leaving that it came to him that he had not said goodbye, and now, without returning, he knew it was too late to trouble.

He should go to work. It was a Tuesday. But he did not. He left the estate agent's and walked to the underground. In his pocket was something he had never held before. Its weight in his suit was like heat. He let the station for his office swing past, thinking all the time, thirteen thousand pounds, thirteen thousand pounds, from one year to the next, no more, unpromoted, than that. He went on, at ten o'clock in the morning, barely worrying whether he had been seen, hardly knowing who he should hide from. And after a time he looked up, feeling almost breathless, and saw that he had come to the centre of the city. He got off and walked through the mid-morning quiet halls until he reached the surface and, for no reason, turned right, down the hill, his right hand across his chest, feeling the weight of the weapon in his inside coat pocket. There was a museum there, at the north side of the famous square, and, hardly knowing why, or what else to do, he went into it.

The revolving doors were a momentary shock, and he felt hot in an instant, as if he was passing into some airport, through some detecting device. But the attendants barely shifted at the sight of him, who had no bag, and he carried on, not knowing where he was going. The rooms were not crowded, and at first he walked through them, unseeing.

He stopped for no reason, and in front of him was a painting. Naked people, striking poses, against cloth and a scrap of country and a scrap of sky. Big and hairless and smooth they were, and the whole painting seemed to know how clean it was, how gold and green and blue and fresh. He supposed it was a famous picture. He did not know it, but in some way it was familiar to him. He stood and looked at it, wondering not exactly what it meant, but why it was here; why anyone had troubled; why they could be so sure of what it would amount to in the end. He stood and looked, more conscious of how he must seem to the people walking round him than of what he was looking at, and soon a terrible thought came to him. His eye went up the left side of the painting; along the top; down the right side; along the bottom; and again, around it, measuring it with his eye. It would fit—he was certain of it—on the narrow wall of the sitting room in the new house, the one to the right of the door as you entered.

Cities are big, and cities are empty, and to fill them takes time, and space. He had all day, and it was a long day, from ten in the morning until four o'clock in the afternoon. He walked, with his gun heavy in the inside coat pocket, and stopped, and drank a coffee, and had a cheap sandwich. It did not occur to him to go to the office. He thought only of what he was going to do. And finally it was ten past four and the man was in the street where the house was.

He walked up to the front door of the house, unthinking, almost despairing, and before he rang the doorbell, he saw that his luck was holding; the other buyer had left the borrowed key, idiotically, in the lock of the door. It was confirmation; no one so negligent deserved such a house. He turned the lock, with smooth professional silence, and went into the house.

He stood for a moment in the hallway as the door slid shut behind him. The house was perfectly quiet. On the right, the door to the drawing room stood open, and behind that, the vast purple dining room. At the back, to the left, a small bathroom, and at the back of the long hallway, the glass-windowed door to the back garden. There was no sign of anyone, nor in the cellar, now converted into a terracotta-lined kitchen of cool and massive extent. He returned upward, his little gun in his hand, and on to the first floor.

The colour of the house became paler as he went upward, like blood draining from the head; the dark terracotta of the cellar becoming a rich hallway amber, primrose for the first floor, fading imperceptibly, he remembered, into white by the top of the house. The first floor was just as empty; he looked, almost casually, into a study, a library, two bedrooms and a bathroom. And then he heard a creak, above his head, a muffled footstep. There he was; the man to whom nothing could connect him. It was with an unfamiliar resolution that he turned and walked swiftly up the stairs, not troubling to mute his noise, wanting, rather, to attract the startled buyer, to fix a look of nervous terror on his face, the look of someone disturbing a burglar. But the figure at the end of the landing did not turn, but remained as it was, gazing out of the window, his back to the advancing man. The man made a noise; the noise of one attracting attention, but the noise of his voice failed him, unused all day, and he had to make it again, more confidently, his voice, this time, not breaking. And this time the other man—the other buyer—seemed to hear, and to turn with a movement devoid of surprise, a gesture almost mournful in its slow certainty.

And it seemed to the man, before he shot—because he did not shoot—that the face of the buyer who now turned to him, his wet teeth bared, was not that of a stranger, but that of the familiar and guiding Mr Bell, taking him towards an inevitable conclusion with the same security and benevolence as he had taken them through so many houses, so many unnecessary rooms; and now, seeing that Mr Bell was holding, so surprisingly, the same gun in his hand as the man held in his own, the impossible vision of Mr Bell's face made the man close his eyes to wipe away the error, knowing that when he opened them, the impossible face would no longer be there, knowing the simple fact with perfect trust.

A fterwards, the man's wife returned, not to the house she had shared with her husband, but to the house she had been born in, where her parents lived, where they had always lived. Because she had nowhere else, in the end, to go to. In her hand she held a grey cardboard box. And inside the grey cardboard box was an alabaster urn, nine inches high. And inside the alabaster urn, there were the ashes of her husband, and she held the grey cardboard box, and sat on the end of the bed in the room she had grown up in, thinking nothing. Presently she stood up, still wearing her coat, listening for the noises, downstairs, of people moving around, conducting their daily tasks in unnatural quiet, so as not to disturb the widow, and she leaned forward and opened the top drawer of the chest of drawers, and put the box inside, and pushed the drawer shut. And the urn was nine inches high. And the box was twelve inches by six inches by eight inches. And the drawer was three feet wide and two feet deep, and the wife shut it. And for him that was space enough.

□

GRANTA

DAME SHIRLEY

Jay Rayner

Dame Shirley Porter

Dame Shirley Porter would not agree to talk in her flat in Israel, overlooking the sea. 'People write about gold taps and that sort of thing,' she said, accurately. Instead we would take a trip by boat down the Yarkon River which flows through Tel Aviv on its way from the hills of the West Bank to the Mediterranean and which is indisputably filthy. In 1997 three athletes at the Maccabi Games—the Jewish Olympics—fell into the water when a bridge they were crossing collapsed. They later died, not from injuries incurred when the structure gave way, but from poisoning. The river mud, it was discovered, was polluted with lethal toxins poured in by factories further upstream.

We set off in the boat piloted by Dame Shirley's 'environmental adviser'. It was fiercely hot and sunny. Dame Shirley pulled a floppy straw hat from her shoulder bag, put a shielding hand above her eyes, and scanned the bank like an explorer. Soon she had identified the enemy.

'What's all that stuff?' she said, waving towards the water's edge.

We looked. Plastic wrappers and old bottles, a couple of cans and some dirty paper clung to the damp earth. Dame Shirley had found litter.

'It's from a private picnic,' her adviser said.

'I don't care what it's from,' Dame Shirley said. 'It shouldn't be there. It should be cleaned up.'

Dame Shirley has always hated litter. Crisp packets, fag ends, Coke cans, redundant packaging and human detritus of all sorts—in London, these were the things that turned her into a politician. In Israel, however, litter is only one of her many causes. Further upstream on the Yarkon lie the beginnings of a nautical centre, where schoolchildren will learn to canoe and sail, and possibly swim when—if—the water tests clean enough. It is being built in memory of Dame Shirley's grandson, Daniel, who was killed in a car crash in Israel in 1993 while he was on military service, from funds supplied by the Porter Foundation. Two miles away to the north is the campus of Tel Aviv University, where Sir Leslie Porter, her husband, is Chancellor. It is rich with buildings and projects endowed by the Porters. There is the Porter Institute for Poetics and Semiotics and the Shirley and Leslie Porter School of Cultural Studies. There

Jay Rayner

is the Cohen-Porter Family Swimming Pool at the Elite Sport Centre, the only Olympic-standard pool in the country, where Sir Leslie Porter swims occasionally. The Porters have endowed academic posts and set up scholarship funds and made annual donations for books and equipment. They have given large amounts of money to Israel for the past thirty years, even when they didn't live there, and they continue to give money now that they do.

Until 1994, Britain was their home, the source of their wealth and their titles. Shirley Porter is a Dame of the British Empire, just as the actress Judi Dench is a Dame of the British Empire, as is the novelist Iris Murdoch. From the perspective of Israel (and most other republics) such chivalric orders may look rather quaint; the days have long gone when their various divisions—baronets, marquesses, Knights of the Garter—gave their owners some idea of where they stood in the ranks between commoners and the monarch. Now they are handed out by governments, via the Queen, as honours for services to the nation—in politics, in acting, in literature; stamps of approval from the Establishment. Within the Cohen-Porter family it could almost be called tradition. Dame Shirley's father, Jack Cohen, was made a Knight of the Realm, the male equivalent of damehood, in 1969, because he dipped into the fortune he made from his supermarket business, Tesco, and gave generously to charities. Dame Shirley's husband, Leslie, who became chairman of Tesco in 1973, was made a Knight of the Realm in 1983 because he, too, gave a lot of his money to charity. This turned plain Mrs Shirley Porter into Lady Porter. But that dignity only reflected her husband's glory: she could be forgiven for saying, when she collected her honour in 1991, that it was 'nice to have a title of one's own'.

Why should Dame Shirley and her husband leave this climate of esteem and come to Israel? There are several answers to this question, but one of them is the wish—for a change—not to give money away too easily. According to a ruling reached in December 1997 by the High Court of England—this Realm, this Empire—Dame Shirley Porter owes £26.5 million to a small part of it: the London Borough of Westminster, also known as the City of Westminster (since 1900, when its first mayor was elected). She is in no mood to pay and has appealed against the judgement to a higher court. In any case, she has no assets left in England to pay with. In 1994 she sold her flat overlooking Hyde Park and her weekend cottage in Oxfordshire. Up to that year there had been 5.5 million shares in Tesco registered under her name, worth more than £10 million. In 1994 any reference to Dame Shirley Porter disappeared from the company records, either because she had sold the shares or because they had been transferred to another name. Other of her investments were moved into trusts in Panama and Guernsey.

At the time this money was on the move, a report in the *Sunday Times* estimated the combined wealth of Dame Shirley and her husband at £70 million. However accurate the figure—the Porters did not challenge it—none of that money remained within British jurisdiction, and neither did she. The year the money departed the Porters took up residence in a penthouse apartment at the wealthy seaside resort of Herzilya Pituach, half an hour's drive north of Tel Aviv. They also have a house in Palm Springs, California, to which they retreat from the wind and rain of a Middle Eastern winter. Their links with Britain have not quite been severed. The Porters still attend official functions staged by representatives of her Majesty's Government in Israel. Last June they were at the Queen's Birthday Party, which is held every year at the official residence of the British Ambassador in the hills of Ramat Gan, a suburb of Tel Aviv. But other than on legal business, their visits to Britain are rare.

Dame Shirley does not see herself as a fugitive. She sees herself as a victim of history. She wrote in a letter to me: 'As the years have passed the political nature [of the case against her] has become ever clearer. I am being hounded for who I am, for my unrepentant Thatcherism, for the sins of the Eighties, real or imagined.'

In the 1980s, the three most important women—indeed people—who lived in the London Borough of Westminster—perhaps in the United Kingdom—were: Her Majesty the Queen; Mrs Margaret (now Baroness) Thatcher; Lady (now Dame) Shirley Porter. The Queen and Baroness Thatcher still live there, though there are rumours that the Royal Family might soon leave Buckingham Palace and move full time to their weekend retreat, Windsor Castle, while Mrs Thatcher lost her official residence in Downing Street when she lost the support of her party in 1990 and now has a flat in Belgravia. These two women didn't get on: there were rumours of differences over the Commonwealth (very important to the Queen, rather less so to the prime minister), and perhaps some regal dislike of Mrs Thatcher's regal style. Mrs Thatcher and Lady Porter, on the other hand, were allies in the same revolution. They had the same rhetoric: both believed in enterprise, initiative and 'personal responsibility'; both believed that the state should do less and the private sector more. They hated bureaucracy. They hated, especially, the Greater London Council which until Mrs Thatcher abolished it in 1986 stood out as an awkward, anti-Thatcherite leftist rump in a city being bent to the will of the free market. (According to Lady Porter, the GLC had been using 'the poor, the sick and the frightened people of this city as pawns in their political game'.)

Perhaps it helped that Lady Porter was Jewish. Unlike the Conservative Party at large, which was infected by a genteel anti-Semitism, Mrs Thatcher was thought, in a popular phrase, 'to care more for Jews than Dukes'.

In his biography of Margaret Thatcher, *One of Us*, Hugo Young wrote: 'It was the Jewish belief in self-help which she found most telling. As a moral code for upward mobility of the kind [she] never ceased to preach, Judaism embodied many useful precepts and could produce many shining exemplars, some of whom found their way into the prime-ministerial circle and thence into public positions including the Cabinet itself.'

Lady Porter never got as far as the Cabinet (she was never to become a Member of Parliament), but she saw herself as much more than a local politician. As the leader of Westminster City Council, she believed she was the custodian of the essence of London. Her domain included almost every institution and landmark that defines it: the royal palaces and parks, Big Ben, the Abbey where English monarchs have been crowned since 1066, the Houses of Parliament, Trafalgar Square, Whitehall, Bond Street, the Ritz, the Strand, Madame Tussaud's, the theatres of Shaftesbury Avenue, the restaurants of Soho, the gentlemen's clubs of Pall Mall.

All this to Dame Shirley was 'what foreigners think of as London...the real London', and it was all, for a time and up to a point, hers. Mrs Thatcher occupied Downing Street, and there, a mile away in her offices in Victoria Street, was her lieutenant, Shirley Porter, using Westminster as a testing ground for Thatcherite policies. Two women with sharp features and domes of lacquered hair, each of them dogmatic, each enjoying the hostility that their dogma engendered. 'I think I must epitomize everything that rabid left-wing socialists dislike,' Lady Porter once said. 'They don't like my strength and they don't like my background.'

She reduced local taxation until it was the second-lowest of any borough in the country; she privatized the rubbish collection; she introduced 'one-stop shops' where Westminster residents could settle all their council business—parking permits, litter permits, rates—in one go; she talked about 'customers' rather than residents; she was a pioneer in the war against dog shit (*Keep Westminster free of dog dirt. Clean it up*). Some of her ideas came from the family supermarket business and some would become standard features of local councils throughout Britain. Her personal style, however, was more difficult to emulate.

She would walk the streets, Dictaphone in hand, recording memos to herself about broken street lights and fractured paving stones; about rubbish bins left unemptied and litter left uncollected. Council officers would be forced to accompany her on her daily stroll around Hyde Park to discuss business, or to meet her in her flat nearby, which housed a large collection of teddy bears, each carefully positioned to be tidy.

Publicity stunts came naturally to her. Once, to publicize an anti-litter initiative, she posed for photographers dressed as an Indian squaw, on the grounds that Native Americans have a deep love and respect for the land. In 1988 she gathered together Westminster's executives and the heads of the public utilities in London—the people who ran the gas, electricity, telephone and water services—and loaded them on to a hired bus and drove them around the capital. When they reached dormant roadworks or uncollected rubbish, she stood up at the front of the bus and, using a microphone like a tour guide, ordered those responsible to come forward and confess. 'And whose is that tatty piece of zigzag trench-filling on the left?' she asked as the bus drove alongside the gardens of Buckingham Palace. 'Come

on. Own up. Whose is it?' The man from British Telecom came
forward and apologized publicly for a poorly filled-in hole. In Lady
Porter's Westminster there was penitence, at least.

Where did it come from, this un-English flamboyance and open
ambition? Chutzpah can be only part of the answer. Shirley
Porter is Jewish, but she is also a woman, born rich, and when she
was growing up rich Jewish women like her were not expected to
have careers, whatever their ambitions. Her father, Jack Cohen, and
her mother, Cissie Fox, were the children of Polish immigrants who
came to London's East End in the late nineteenth century. Like so
many other Jews arriving in Britain at that time they set themselves
up in business as tailors and cutters and anglicized their names from
Kohen to Cohen and from Fuchs to Fox. (A small but necessary
disclosure: my family is related by marriage to the Fox family, and
so Dame Shirley Porter and I are also distantly related, though before
our river trip we had never met.) Tailoring had no appeal for Jack
Cohen. Soon after the First World War, in which he served, he began
selling cheap food to market-traders: battered cans of fruit, dried eggs
of unspecified origin, Snowdrop condensed milk from New Zealand,
so thick it could coat your finger like emulsion paint. Shirley was
born in 1930, four years after her sister Irene, and in 1932, Jack
Cohen launched a chain of shops called Tesco, putting together the
initials of one of his wholesaler's names—T. E. Stockwell—with the
first two letters of his own. Today Tesco is worth over £12 billion.
It has 595 stores, 420 of which are in Britain, and in 1998 declared
annual profits of £900 million on sales of just under £16 billion.

In his later years—he died in 1979—he liked to dwell on this
journey from barrow boy to supermarket mogul. He would say
things like 'You can't do business sitting on your arse,' or 'If you lie
down with dogs you'll get up with flies,' to demonstrate his wisdom
of the streets. And as the leader of Westminster council, his daughter
would often quote these earthy sayings in the cut and thrust of
political argument—'My father had a motto...'—though she had
grown up in an entirely different way.

In 1934, the Cohens moved from the East End to a large house
in the north-west suburbs of London. Shirley was sent to The Warren,

a girls' boarding school on the Sussex coast. It was not a happy experience. She was withdrawn by her parents at the age of fifteen because, she said, the school did not want a Jew to be head girl. ('They did not want to see the Cohen name on the roll call,' she told an interviewer in 1993.) When we met in Israel she told me: 'I was a sensitive child and I didn't want to go to boarding school. When I did go, it was the first time I came up against anti-Semitism. I can remember retaliating and saying, "Never mind, I'm better than all of you. I'm a Cohen and Cohens [in Hebrew] are priests."' After this she was sent to a finishing school for Jewish girls in Switzerland. That was not a happy experience, either. 'It was just after the war,' she told me. 'And to me the Swiss had no sense of what war was really like. I only stayed seven months and couldn't wait to get out.' Aged eighteen, she was married to Leslie Porter, who was ten years older and a partner in his family's textile business. Aged twenty-two, she was the mother of two children, Linda and John. She was sitting on the committees of Jewish charities, she was playing golf. She played no part in her father's business.

She had fulfilled the expectations of her parents and of her community. Many wealthy Jewish women of her generation could have ended their biography here, their roles as mother and wifely support fixed to the end of their lives, but Mrs Porter had wider, less homely ambitions. Aged twenty-seven, she became one of the youngest women ever appointed to the board of the Women's International Zionist Organization. She took courses in literature and philosophy at the Workers' Institute in London. Golf became more than an occasional pastime: she joined predominantly Jewish golf clubs, both to the north and south of London, playing in championships and winning trophies. It was golf that led to her first appearance as a news story when, in December 1964, she disclosed to the *Jewish Chronicle* that she had been refused membership of a golf club in north London which the then prime minister, Harold Wilson, had recently joined. 'She was told it would be a waste of time to put her name forward for membership,' the paper reported, 'and she was left in no doubt that she was not wanted because she was a Jewess.' At a time when the Jewish community in Britain was still paralysed by the belief that to make a fuss was to draw attention to Jews and therefore to incite anti-Semitism, her disclosure was a brave piece of behaviour.

By 1974, her children had left home, her husband was chairman of Tesco, and they had moved from the suburbs into their flat in Westminster. Dame Shirley was forty-four. She needed something to do. Through the windows of her flat she could see Hyde Park, central London's largest stretch of grassland. The park was spattered with litter. Something must be done. That year she stood for election as a Conservative councillor for the Hyde Park ward, won easily, and was soon a prominent figure in movements such as the Cleaner London Campaign, the Tidy Britain Campaign and the Find a Bin and Put it In scheme. She also led the Westminster Against Reckless Spending (or WARS) campaign, which portrayed the city-wide authority, the Labour-dominated Greater London Council, as a band of wasteful Trotskyites. In 1983, the year her husband was knighted, she became the leader of Westminster City Council and took the title of Lady Porter. Now came her greatest years, the time when she got things done. There was criticism: her intransigence angered her political opposition and alienated council officers. ('There's no question that she made people cry and bullied them,' said John Ware, who made the first BBC documentary about scandals at Westminster council in 1989. 'I met a lot of officers whose lives had been made hell by her.') Between 1984 and 1988, forty-eight out of seventy senior and middle management staff left the council, including fourteen chief officers. But autocracy alone was not her undoing. This came with a policy blandly entitled Building Stable Communities, known later as the 'homes-for-votes row'.

Fear of defeat proved its inspiration. In the elections of May 1986, Westminster council's Conservative majority dropped from twenty-six seats to four. Lady Porter was distraught. Britain, it seemed then, would live under Mrs Thatcher for ever; the opposition was fragmented and inept, the Thatcherite victory seemed complete and unalterable. And yet here, at the epicentre of her regime (where she lived, where her decisions were made, the capital, 'real London'), was *weakness*. If Westminster had fallen to Labour, Lady Porter would have failed as the city's custodian, she would have let down the boss. Within weeks she was laying plans to ensure that Labour would never again come so close to winning the prize. And so: Building Stable Communities.

At the heart of this policy lay a simple truth, revealed year after year in the demographics of British politics: people who own their homes are more likely to vote Conservative than people who rent them from the local authority. Westminster's task, as Lady Porter saw it, was therefore to increase the proportion of private housing in the borough, not by building more houses, but by converting public housing (owned by Westminster council) into private housing (owned by the occupier). This was perfectly legal; the 'right to buy' policy was an early piece of Thatcherite legislation. More contentious, however, was the plan not to sell to sitting tenants (who might not change the voting habits of a lifetime) but to more affluent, perhaps younger people, who were then more likely to vote Conservative.

By boarding up properties as they became vacant when old tenants moved on or died, Westminster council could designate entire blocks for sale at a later date so that private purchasers wouldn't find themselves living next door to council tenants, whom they might consider undesirable neighbours. Originally the plan had been to designate council properties for sale in only the eight marginal wards that Labour had come close to winning. Lawyers advised that this would be illegal—the council would be spending public funds to advance party interest—and so the plan was extended to cover every ward in the hope that it would achieve the same effect, while being seen as a non-political blanket housing policy. It was clear, nevertheless, that Lady Porter knew her plans were controversial. She ended one memo to her colleagues: 'When you've read the documents and after we've had our discussion, it would be helpful if you swallow them in good spy fashion otherwise they might self-destruct!!' The policy was passed by the council in July 1987.

In 1989, after complaints from both residents and Labour councillors that this policy of 'designated sales' left Westminster council unable to meet its responsibilities to the homeless, an investigation was begun by the council's auditor, John Magill, an accountant from the firm of Deloitte & Touche. He had been district auditor to Westminster council since 1985, a job which, under local government legislation, empowered him to inspect council spending on behalf of the residents. He had already been kept busy with a stream of complaints and objections to council policy from the Labour group, including one against the council's sale of three cemeteries for just fifteen pence. Lady Porter had argued that, as they were located outside the borough and their upkeep was at council expense, getting rid of them was good business. Council officers warned her that it would be bad politics, but Lady Porter ignored their advice. Relatives of the dead buried in these cemeteries were outraged, particularly after the land was sold on by the original purchasers and planning proposals to build on the plots put forward. John Magill castigated the council for its lax administration and the council had to buy back the cemeteries at a cost of over £4 million.

Magill's investigation into the sale of council homes lasted almost seven years, his progress slowed by the difficulties of finding documents and the reluctance of witnesses. He was told that papers he needed had disappeared, or that they had been shredded, until he decided he had no option but to mount a raid on the council's headquarters in Victoria Street. Councillors and council officials proved difficult to pin down for interviews, not least among them Lady Porter. Eventually, in January 1994, he made his provisional findings public. His report was sensational. Four council officers and six councillors, including Lady (by now Dame Shirley) Porter, were found guilty of wilful misconduct. They had wasted large sums of council money in attempting to influence the vote in the marginal wards, and by his calculations they were personally liable to a surcharge of £21.25 million.

One immediate consequence was that Dr Michael Dutt, a former housing-committee chairman who was named and surcharged in the report, took a gun and shot himself. Shirley Porter and her colleagues accused the council's Labour group and the auditor of hounding him to death; the Labour group argued that the other side had put an emotionally fragile man under intolerable pressure. Shirley Porter was by this time no longer the council's leader. In 1991, soon after she was made a Dame, she stood down and took on the ceremonial role of Lord Mayor for a year. In 1993 she quit the council altogether. Then, in May 1996, after thirty-five days of public hearings and an attempt by Dame Shirley to have John Magill removed as district auditor for behaving like 'judge and jury', the final report was published. The list of the accused was reduced to six—three councillors and three officials—but the surcharge was increased to nearly £32 million. According to Magill's calculations, the losses were £15 million from selling council properties at large discounts; £2 million from illegal grants to enable people to buy those properties; just under £8 million in rents and rates that would have been collected if the properties had remained tenanted; £2 million spent on using council staff to push through unlawful policies; £5 million in interest on the amounts spent unlawfully.

Dame Shirley was the only one of the surcharged rich enough to pay; the others were middle-class professionals. In October 1997, she mounted a High Court challenge to the final report. The judges exonerated four of the six of any wrongdoing, leaving Dame Shirley and her former deputy on the council, David Weeks, to pay a reduced surcharge of £26.5 million. But the judgement was damning. Throughout the hearing Dame Shirley had been asked repeatedly whether she had pushed through the designated sales policy for the purposes of electoral gain. Repeatedly she had denied it. According to Lord Justice Rose, Dame Shirley and David Weeks had 'lied to us, as they had to the district auditor, because they had the ulterior purpose of altering the electorate'.

Despite Dame Shirley's proclamation that she would take the case to a further appeal, and that therefore no money was yet owing, calls came from the Labour councillors in opposition for her assets to be frozen. Forensic accountants were hired by Westminster council to track her funds. The search was fruitless. In 1994 Dame Shirley Porter had quietly left England behind and now returned only for legal consultations and court cases. She had resigned from the board of LBC, the London radio company, and from Neurotech Medical Systems plc, and from a charity, Jewish Continuity. She was no longer a director of Lampol Developments, a property company owned by the Porter family. Her only remaining directorship was of the Oxford Centre for Hebrew and Jewish Studies, but that was an honorarium accorded to forty-five others, including Sir Ralf Dahrendorf, Sir Isaiah Berlin and the publisher Lord Weidenfeld. The accountants did discover 1,700 acres of woodland in Scotland, which Dame Shirley owned as a tax-efficient investment, but it was sold soon afterwards. In the autumn of 1997, the accountants reported that there was not a single reachable penny left in Britain. When she was asked whether, should she lose her appeal, she would be settling the bill, Dame Shirley regularly issued the same simple statement: 'I always pay my debts.'

Dame Shirley had not given an interview for more than five years when I first wrote to her in Israel in September last year. She seemed determined to continue this silence. 'I have had time to reflect upon your request,' she wrote back. 'As much as I would like to put my point of view I am advised by my lawyers that this case should be decided in the courts and not in the media. So reluctantly I must say no. I believe it is a miscarriage of justice and we will eventually be vindicated. I intend to fight all the way.'

She invited me to talk instead to Roger Rosewell, who writes right-wing editorials for the *Mail on Sunday* and who for fifteen years has been her unofficial spokesman. Rosewell started his political life as the industrial organizer of the Socialist Worker's Party (a Trotskyist group) in the 1970s and then made the familiar journey to the other extreme. 'The older I get,' he said, 'the more suspicious I become of people who have too many political principles.' His view of Dame Shirley was roughly this: that she was not 'a philosophical Conservative' but someone who believed that local government was about the apolitical business of 'delivering services...of getting things done'. As he saw it, part of the problem was the speed of her rise. 'She'd gone from housewife to litter supremo to leader of the most prestigious local authority under Thatcher, which catapulted her to national fame without going through a long political apprenticeship.' She was not a problems person, she was a solutions person. Rosewell talked in long, clause-heavy sentences, as if he was addressing a public meeting and didn't want to allow space for interruptions. What really defined her, he said, was her desire to speak her mind. As to homes-for-votes: 'Shirley did what the lawyers said. The lawyer who gave the advice has been acquitted. The council officers have been acquitted. But judges say she's still guilty because she had an unlawful motive. They think they know what was going on in her head.'

But if she were convinced of her innocence, why had she left the country? Rosewell said that it wasn't as people thought. Her daughter Linda had lived in Israel for many years, and in 1993 her grandson, Daniel Marcus, had died in a car crash. At the same time Linda had been in the middle of a complicated divorce. 'A great wave of affection and emotion came over Shirley, and she was adamant she had to be at Linda's side,' Rosewell said. 'I think they found a strength there as a family that they did not have here. But she's still a British citizen. She's not hiding. She's not fleeing the country.'

It was difficult to find other people in Britain who, like Rosewell, would admit to being 'fond' of Dame Shirley, though some spoke well enough of her early years as council leader. Rodney Brooke, the council's chief executive during her reign (who was forced to resign, he says, because Lady Porter did not feel he was implementing her policies with sufficient enthusiasm), said: 'She was extremely vigorous and dynamic. No one could withstand the force of her personality. And credit where credit's due, she came up with those one-stop centres. But she was panicked by the narrowness of her victory in 1986 and strayed into activities that were beyond the pale of what's legal.'

It was easy to find those who despised her. Tricia Kirwan, who resigned from the chair of the council's housing committee in 1989, said: 'It was bully, bully, bully. She didn't know how to handle people. She always needed to be told how important or how clever she was. So she surrounded herself with sycophants like Roger Rosewell.' But to Kirwan, her life was marked by failure. 'She has set her mind to do a lot of things and I don't think she ever made it,' she said. 'I think she wanted terribly to achieve something and I don't think she ever did.' The essence of Dame Shirley's character, she said, was in the detail: 'Her flat was indescribably vulgar. She had covers on the loo paper. Her drinks cabinet was gilt.'

John Ware, the BBC producer who investigated Dame Shirley for two years, had tried to understand her. 'I think she experienced quite a lot of subliminal, posh anti-Semitism. When a Tory said "she's just ghastly" you knew what they meant.' The result, he said, was that she interpreted all opposition as unjustified and unfair. 'She was someone who set her jaw against the world. A combination of a doting dad, loads of money, and a chip on her shoulder that wasn't imagined, was lethal.'

Jay Rayner

Neil Coleman, a former councillor who had produced documents that helped prove the scale of the homes-for-votes scandal, said: 'One of the things that makes me most angry is that as a consequence of what she did a number of people have had their lives ruined.'

I was even told by a former opposition councillor: 'I sometimes wonder how anybody can like her, and then I remember that even Hitler had friends.' In Israel, they do not say that kind of thing. In Israel they say the opposite.

I went to Israel in the hope that Dame Shirley might change her mind and agree to see me. On the phone she said she would think about it, but her lawyers were still advising her to refuse such requests. In the meantime, she said, I might make a tour of Porter sites. She would help with the appointments. At Tel Aviv University, I visited the jewel among the family's endowments, the United Kingdom Building of Life Sciences, a six-storey cube of bright white concrete. It is home to an enormous range of academic endeavours (including an entire floor endowed, according to its plaque, by Gail and Gerald Ronson; the latter spent a year in a British prison for his part in the Guinness fraud). There, at the Porter Super Centre for Environmental and Ecological Research, I met Professor Yossi Loya. 'There are not very many donors interested in the environment,' he said. 'Most of them, they just want to put their name on buildings. But here is a lady who has the environment prime among her interests. This is very unusual.' She was always asking questions, he said. She always wanted to know what was going on. 'We have a boat on the Mediterranean and she is visiting the boat.' Also, she wanted to clean everything up. 'She came to the faculty and she looked at the toilets and she gave money to clean them up.'

Yoram Shamir, the university's spokesman, was equally enthusiastic about the Porters. 'There are many projects they give money to but which they don't put their name upon,' he said. When I asked about the Westminster case, he waved it away. 'Most people here believe that this is political; a political attack by the opposition. Everybody understands that this is a civil case.' These things did not interest the university. 'She's willing to do things no other donor would do. She initiates prizes for the cleanest toilet. This is brave.'

Another BBC documentary, screened shortly before I arrived in Israel, had made much of the fact that, while Dame Shirley was not yet willing to pay the money the auditor said she owed, she was still pouring cash into Tel Aviv. The implication, that she was ingratiating herself with the establishment in Israel to make her stay easier, was not substantiated by the records of the Charity Commissioners in London, which showed that the Porter Foundation had been making large donations to causes in Israel since it was established in 1970. More than £15 million was transferred into the accounts in the early 1990s, from the estate of Lady Cohen, Dame Shirley's mother, who died in 1989. Last year the Porter Foundation had assets of over £35 million and made donations of £750,000 to around fifty registered charities, in both Britain and Israel.

Dame Shirley also arranged for me to see the Porter Senior Citizen Centre in Old Jaffa, of which Tel Aviv had originally been a suburb, and where many Jewish immigrants, mostly Sephardic Bulgarians, had made their homes in the 1940s. Now they were in their seventies and eighties. For many of them, Israel had not lived up to its promises; they were poor and isolated and ailing. The day centre, opened in 1993, had clearly been a success, full of local residents from dawn until dusk. It provides workshops, legal advice and companionship. 'Shirley was one of the first donors to give to these people,' said David Altman, the director of the Porter Foundation. 'Why did she give? Because of her sensitivity to older people. To needy people. Because of her experience in public life. She understands what having needy people does to a city. She understands that it is an issue for a city.'

He introduced me in Hebrew to the crowds in the social room, telling them I was a journalist writing about Shirley Porter. Immediately a dozen elderly women jumped to their feet and ululated in greeting, their arms lifted high. 'They don't see her as a nameless figure,' Altman said over the din. 'She is someone they know.' One of the women said, 'Shirley is the mother of this club. She takes care of everything.' 'See?' Altman shouted genially. 'See? For them the Porter name makes them very proud. We are very proud to carry the Porter name. I can tell you fifty per cent of the people here wouldn't be alive today if it wasn't for the Porter Centre.'

And the case in Westminster? 'I have never seen a successful politician anywhere in the world,' he said, 'who didn't have people after their neck. People are always trying to prove you are not as good as you say.'

So it went on. Shlomo Lahat, who was mayor of Tel Aviv for twenty years until he retired in 1993, said he had been to Westminster and studied Dame Shirley's methods. 'I was very much impressed by the way she treated the public and her employees. I copied many things from her.' Such as? 'Denver boots. You know. Wheel clamps. I copied it from her. I wasn't looking to make myself popular. I was looking to bring order to the city. When we used Denver boots they saw that I meant it.'

I was granted an audience, at Dame Shirley's request, with Aura Herzog, the widow of Chaim Herzog, the former President of Israel. We met at the offices of the Council for a Beautiful Israel, of which Mrs Herzog is president and Dame Shirley a patron. 'What binds me to her is that we are both enthusiastic about the environment,' she said. They had worked closely together to cleanse the country of the rubbish that 'littered Israel beyond belief'. 'She has a very quick mind and has a practical view of things,' Mrs Herzog said. 'She likes to know what you are going to do, how you are proceeding. I think she has a very positive attitude to life. I think she wakes up looking forward to every day.'

Eventually, after further snatched conversations by mobile phone in which she restated the risks she felt she would be taking if she granted an interview, Dame Shirley agreed to meet me. In television news reports, during the homes-for-votes scandal, as she had stood on the steps of the London court building, or outside Westminster council's offices intoning statements of defiance, Dame Shirley had appeared solid and square-shouldered in tailored two-piece suits. Here, dressed against the Israeli sun in denim trousers and a long-sleeved floral shirt in matching shades of rust, she looked thin and fragile. Her face was slightly tanned and her hair was tinted light auburn, although the grey roots gave away her age of sixty-seven which the casual clothes, arranged a little too neatly, were perhaps trying to disguise. We took our boat trip and then returned to the restaurant of the Council for a Beautiful Israel, where we had met. She wouldn't discuss the case, she said. Any thoughts she had on that she would give me in a letter. We would have to come at it from other directions, then.

Did she understand why people often reacted so badly to her? 'I live in a very peculiar world,' she said. 'People either like me or hate me. Nobody has middling views about me. The thing is, I hate pretension and in politics you see a lot of it. I need to be involved. I like to improve the quality of life.' She reminded me about the litter we had seen on the river bank. 'So what if it was this or that private picnic? It shouldn't be there. It should be cleaned up. I have this habit inherited from my father. He would go into a shop and he would always find the one dented tin. Well, I'm like that. I'm exactly like that.' She said she thought of herself as a catalyst. 'I am able to empathize. I'm a people person. I think I get that from my father. I like the fabrics of cities, people who make things happen. I don't like pretension. I like encouraging people.'

Once, she said, these qualities had won her friends. 'I used to be the darling of the London *Evening Standard* before Max Hastings became editor [in 1996]. Max seems to hate me.' Why? 'It might be because he came from the snobbish hunting-and-shooting wing of the Tory party. Because I'm a woman, I'm Jewish, I'm wealthy.' The truth was, she said, she didn't have much time for the British Tory party these days. She didn't see a place for herself in an organization that was so set against closer ties with Europe. 'I actually think that the European Monetary Union is inevitable. Individual nations can't stand alone. So I'm not a Conservative in that way.'

This was a major break with the party through which she had made her name. It did not mean, however, that she could throw her lot in with Labour. 'I think Blair's a very clever fellow. Their party management is terrific. But I can't believe they have the extreme Left under control. The odd thing is I like the razzmatazz and sense of fun and excitement that they engender, though when I tried to do the same in Westminster with similar pizazz the opposition were the first to scoff.'

Her irritation that her achievements had been forgotten was a constant theme. She gave me typed lists of initiatives and policies:

the Say No to Drugs Campaign, the Plain English Campaign, her success at keeping local taxes down, her involvement in the abolition of the Greater London Council. 'Basically, I was just interested in cleaning things up,' she said. 'I wasn't a deep thinker. I believe people should be helped if they need it. My own philosophy was about putting the customer first.' Would she still describe herself as a committed Thatcherite? 'Yes,' she said. 'I believed in Margaret Thatcher's policies because she believed in people running their own lives. And she believed firmly in private enterprise and that was the background from which I came.'

I wondered if she missed London. She said: 'I miss my friends and the theatre and the changing seasons. But I'm happy here because I've still got the energy. We've all got high energy levels in my family. This country's very exciting. You can make a difference here and I feel I can contribute.' Which party did she support in Israel? 'Labour,' she said. It made sense. The peace process would reap enormous dividends for the environment. Likud, the party of the Right, appeared to be trying to jeopardize the peace process and therefore the environment. Who could be in favour of that?

I asked if there was anything she regretted. 'I regret having gone into politics and having put my whole life and soul into it. I didn't spend as much time with Daniel [her dead grandson] and Joanna [her granddaughter] as I could have done.' She looked uncomfortable for the only time in our conversation and rapped her fingers on the table. 'Nor did I spend enough time with my parents. And what for? To have my name dragged through the mud. It upsets me that people, out of revenge, tear me apart. I wouldn't recommend anybody to go into local politics unless they understand the risks and are prepared to stand up to the flak. Nobody here in Israel understands what this case is about. They don't understand it in America, either.' Then she said, 'I never want to be at the mercy of anybody else ever again.'

She handed me the letter. 'You can quote from that,' she said. She had a meeting to go to. I walked her to her taxi in the car park. She pulled the floppy straw hat from her bag and put it on against the sun.

The letter ran to eleven pages and was unsurprising. Her designated-sales policy was entirely lawful, she wrote. She had taken legal advice and acted upon it. Yet she was being found guilty because, the judges said, she had an unlawful motive. 'While I never bullied or bribed anyone to do my bidding, I used my strong personality to push through a policy that appeared lawful on the outside, indeed which was lawful on the outside, but which has since become unlawful because of my private thoughts and passions. This is another key issue of my appeal; why everyone else should be cleared and not me.'

She had understood perfectly what was going on: 'Westminster was one of the Left's prime targets. They hated us because we beat them at their own game. We became better organized, we worked harder, we refused to be cowed. Sure they wrecked meetings, spat at me and others, smoked dope in the council chamber, thumped staff and tried to make the council ungovernable. But we hung on.'

The problem, as she saw it, was that the case was being dealt with through the courts. 'Law and politics don't mix,' she wrote. 'Political skills don't count for much in a courtroom. If there had been a vote between myself and the auditor I would trust democracy any day.' And then, not for the first time, she invoked the memory of Jack Cohen. 'My late father was a great fighter. I am the same. Whatever it takes and however long it takes I will clear my name. I will prove my innocence. I have never been a quitter. I am not going to start becoming one now.'

She appeared genuinely to believe that she had broken no law. What is any political policy, she had asked me, but an attempt to win electoral advantage through popularity? What was Margaret Thatcher's 'right-to-buy' policy, but an attempt to do the same through the sale of public housing? If she were defeated at the appeal, she said, she would take her case to the highest court in the land, the House of Lords, and, if unsuccessful there, onward to the European Court.

After I got back to London, Dame Shirley wrote to me, asking if I could help her find a ghost writer for a book she was preparing on her story. Later she asked me to recommend a financial journalist who could help her to simplify the complex accounting of the case. I declined to make suggestions and wrote saying it was not my job to help her pursue her cause. 'Interesting response!' she wrote back. 'I won't take it the wrong way even though I don't think I am pursuing a cause, I think I am trying to explain my point of view.'

One afternoon, not long after my return from Israel, I went along to the National Portrait Gallery. I had noticed from the accounts of the Porter Foundation that it had given substantial amounts of money to the gallery and I wanted to see what it had bought them. The Porter Gallery, on the ground floor, is less a room than a broad alcove of shiny marble, with a tablet of bleached stone carved with the family name fixed to the wall.

Inside was a temporary exhibition of cartoons by Gerald Scarfe, who does cruel things to the human face. There was Harold Wilson, the prime minister who had given Jack Cohen his knighthood, hangdog features drooping to the ground, bags beneath his eyes big enough to carry home the weekly shop. There was Margaret Thatcher, the prime minister whom Shirley so adored. Scarfe had her as a bloody axehead, decapitating her opponents. There was John Major, the prime minister who had given Shirley her damehood, and who was pictured as a grey-faced Dr Death. Scarfe's introduction to the exhibition was attached to the wall of the gallery. 'It is the misuse of power,' he had written, 'from the smallest, crookedest local councillor to the bloodiest Stalins, that fires my political drawings.' There was no cartoon of Shirley Porter. For the time being, she appeared to have escaped. □

GRANTA

LONDON THEN
Sergio Larrain

The Chilean photographer Sergio Larrain came from Paris
to London in 1958 and caught the city at a time of change:
among the smog and bowler hats were new immigrants from
the Commonwealth and young 'bohemians' in jazz clubs,
heralding the city of the next decade.

Bishopsgate

London Bridge station

Portobello Road market

Bethnal Green Road

Hyde Park

Outskirts of London, taken from a train going from Victoria towards Epsom

Party in a house in Archway

Chelsea Arts Club Ball, Albert Hall

Baker Street station

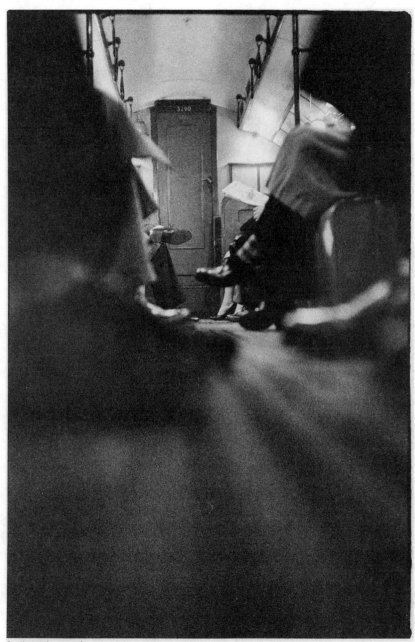

On the underground

Jazz club in Windmill Street, Soho

GRANTA

SOHOITIS

Ian Hamilton

What brings me to this place, this pass? It's four-fifteen in the afternoon on Charlotte Street and I'm thinking of ordering a third bottle of white wine. On the table in front of me I have copies of two books: *War Like a Wasp* by Andrew Sinclair and *Under Siege* by Robert Hewison, both studies of the wartime literary scene. Look at these names: Charles Hamblett, Paul Potts, John Waller, Ruthven Todd, Wrey Gardner, Keidrych Rhys. How many of them now ring bells, or set off even the most distant sirens? I also have in front of me a street map, drawn some fifty years ago by the above-named Rhys, of my immediate environs. 'Fitzrovia', the map is called, and every thoroughfare and passage has been charted with great care, with A,B,C,D,E, etc. marking all the pubs. But I don't need a map. I've been here far too many times before, gripped then as I am now by the big questions: why am I here? how did it get to be so late? And do I really need the bottle of white wine I seem already to have ordered?

In the early 1960s, just down from university and not knowing what to do, I started up a small poetry magazine called *The Review*. It was pretty much a one-man band and for the first few years of its short life I ran it from my home: at first from a bedsit in Oxford and later on from my small flat in Paddington. I was editor, business manager, publicist, distributor, the lot. I did have help from time to time, from friends and relatives. When an issue of the magazine appeared—the thing was meant to be bimonthly—I would organize stamp-licking supper parties, or wrapping-up-parcels supper parties, or getting-it-all-down-to-the-post-office supper parties: not exactly fun events (the supper bit was often overlooked) but conducive all the same, or so I said, to solidarity—a sense that we were all, all four or five of us, in some way fighting the good fight.

In between these supper parties, there was the matter of week-to-week survival. But this was understood to be my problem, beyond help. And of course I wanted it to be this way. Insolvency was part of the romance. If any half-awake money man had happened to check out *The Review*'s accounts, he would have given the enterprise a jocular thumbs-down: you can't be serious. And yet 'serious' was what I thought I was. In my scheme of things, to be serious meant to be seriously up against it—up against it in a way that philistines might tremble to behold.

At the same time, though, I had big ideas. I harboured delusions of ultimate 'success'. At odd moments, I'd soliloquize about some future, far-off date on which the money men would shake their heads and say: 'We don't know how you did it.' Did what, though? To have turned *The Review* into a viable business concern would have been to sacrifice its soul, its *raison d'être*. Magazines like this were surely broke, or they were nothing. Why then wasn't I rejoicing when the writs started to flood in? Why was I so fidgety, so restless? The magazine was as insolvent as could be, and I myself could hardly have been broker. I'd clearly chanced upon a formula-for-failure. Why couldn't I stick with it? The restlessness persisted, though. I wanted something bigger, something better, I would tell myself. Or was it that I wanted something worse?

Looking back, I think my real problem was provincialitis, an allergy to holes-in-corners. Paddington, as somewhere to eke out one's days, was perfectly OK. From where I lived, I had a good view of the station. In the end, though, Paddington was Paddington, the fabled haunt of cheap prostitutes and swarthy nomads, a stopover for yokels from Somerset or Devon. The area, so far as I knew, had no literary background—indeed, the Royal Society of Literature was rumoured to be housed close by on Hyde Park Square. Not for long, it seemed to me, could such a backwater hope to accommodate the world-altering pretensions of a project such as mine. I had to move. I had to move to where the action was, or where the action used to be, or ought to be. I had to make my magazine go metro.

Quite often, in the early days of *The Review*, I used to find myself toiling along the Charing Cross Road, holdall in hand, invoice-book in pocket of black duffel coat: a litbiz man who'd come to town to offer up his wares. In those days, there were three or four booksellers who were prepared to display little magazines. Better Books was the ideal: run by would-be writers, it stocked anything and everything. Also hospitable was Colletts, a Communist-run operation which had a soft spot for publications that resembled pamphlets. Third best was Zwemmers, home now of unbuyable art books but then more of an all-round bookstore with faintly avant-garde susceptibilities. For me, and my magazine, these were the all-important London shops, the places to be seen.

I used to take great pleasure in my bimonthly sales trips to these centres, even though the actual business of offloading magazines was fairly dull, and sometimes humiliating. As well as delivering a gleaming batch of 'No. 10—our latest issue', I also had to pick up a just-as-gleaming batch of unsold No. 9s. Sometimes a sale had taken place and money would change hands—two-thirds of two times 2s. 6d. was thought to be a decent haul. 'Do you think we really need to stock twelve copies when we only ever manage to sell two?' the manager would sometimes ask. And I would say: 'Please, reason not the need.' And he would say: 'I'm sorry...and good luck.' Those were the days. Bearing my armful of returns, I'd hit the streets again. Two copies, eh? Not bad.

Across the road from Better Books was Soho. Bloomsbury was to my right. And half a mile away, beyond Soho, was Fitzrovia. I felt myself connected to the past—or, as some might say, to a continuum of splendid ruin. It so happened that around this time, I was writing a book about the history of literary periodicals. I also served as an extremely part-time adviser to a reprint company which had started up a series on twentieth-century small mags. My head was full of *Windows, Wheels, Now, Now and Then, New Verse* and *Kingdom Come*. Although scarcely any of the magazines I was perusing on an almost daily basis were actually worth reading, let alone reprinting, I still found myself responsive to the aroma of heroic pointlessness which each of them, even the most numbly semi-literate, seemed somehow to give off. One of my reasons for starting *The Review*, I occasionally recalled, had been to inject some critical stringency into the current poetry scene. And yet most of the periodicals I studied stood for just the kind of otiose permissiveness which, as an editor, I was meant to be combating.

Even so, here I was devoting almost every spare moment, so it seemed, to browsing through yellowing ephemera which in truth deserved no more than a quick laugh. What was this strange allure? Could it be that all literary folk, however primly disciplined, yearn in their hearts for a Bohemia? Do even the tamest of pen-pushers dream sometimes of a season on the wild side? I mean why, for example, did I think that there was anything at all soul-stirring in my current plight: standing on Cambridge Circus, bag heavy with spurned copies of my little mag, and staring—with a kind of wistfulness—across the road at Soho, sink of boozed unruliness but home also, as my studies had revealed, to many a botched literary breakthrough? Explain it how you will. All I know is that, within weeks, I'd moved *The Review* from Paddington to Greek Street.

In Greek Street, my magazine's new home was actually a tiny, two-room hovel: poky, freezing and superbly squalid. The amenities were non-existent, or they didn't work. Above me, so my landlord aggressively explained, there was a never-seen Chinese family who would regularly clog the plumbing with 'their fucking rice'. Below me there were tailors—real Soho tailors of the old school, I was told: and certainly their boss-man, a big weary-looking Greek, always seemed to have pins in his mouth. Below the tailors there was said to be a strip club, or a kind of brothel, although no one appeared to visit it, not even me.

The chief zone of activity in my building turned out to be the staircase. There was always somebody sitting on the stairs: caricature villain-types, usually, complete with scarred faces, snappy suiting, two-tone shoes. These lowlifes seemed to wander in off the street whenever they felt like it. When I asked one of them if I could 'help you, in any way?', he answered—without looking up—'No, mate, I'm just here to check the mail.' And so he was. There in his hand was a bundle of what looked like poems. I watched, enthralled, as he placed these manuscripts to one side, on the stairs, and then proceeded to pocket the stamped addressed envelope that had presumably been pinned to them—to the manuscripts, that is. 'You do realize that this mail is meant for me.' 'Don't *worry*, son,' he said, and this time he did look at me, quite kindly.

For weeks afterwards, I would come across poetry manuscripts in all sorts of crazy places: gutters, pub lavatories, street garbage bins. I also came across filled-in subscription orders—minus cheques. I didn't mind too much about the manuscripts. The cheques, though, were our lifeblood. Luckily, this mail surveillance eased off after a few weeks. My staircase thieves presumably decided that my project was too boring and small-time to be bothered with. Having lost interest in me, they would always give me a big smile whenever they passed me on the street, or on the stairs. It was more of a wry, head-shaking chuckle than an actual smile, now I remember it, but all the same it made me feel that I belonged.

Colourful stuff, you will agree. And seemingly just what I wanted: to be part of the mainstream, albeit the mainstream of the misfits, the non-mainstream. This was the Soho life: crooks, tailors, strip clubs, choked-up Chinese drains. And poems from Somerset that ended up in Soho loos. Looking back, I'm sure I liked the idea of it much more than I liked *it* but even so my poet-friends, when I reported back to them, or when they came to visit me from Paddington or Oxford, were mightily intrigued. They too seemed responsive to the myth, although even then I doubted that they wanted to change places.

Meanwhile, my magazine was not getting any better and I was beginning to spend more time in the pub next door than in my so-called 'office'. I also took to wandering the Soho streets, working out how alleyways connected between Wardour, Dean, Frith, Greek and checking also what went on in them. I located numerous small drinking clubs and felt really in the swim when one of them got raided by the cops. My name and particulars were taken—'Oh yeah, what *kind* of magazine?'—and for a few days afterwards I looked forward to a visit from the law, but nothing happened.

My study of little magazines was falling badly behind schedule. I stuck with it, though, if only in the hope of finding out what I was playing at. And in the course of my researches I picked up a newly published book by Julian Maclaren-Ross. The book was called *Memoirs of the Forties* and it had in it an essay called 'Tambimuttu and the Progress of *Poetry London*' in which Maclaren-Ross recounted his meetings with the famous wartime literary entrepreneur, J. Meary Tambimuttu. 'Beware of Fitzrovia,' Tambi had once told Maclaren-Ross. 'It's a dangerous place, you must be careful.'

'Fights with knives?'

'No, a worse danger. You might get Sohoitis, you know.'

'No, I don't. What is it?'

'If you get Sohoitis,' Tambi said very seriously, 'you will stay there always day and night and get no work done ever. You have been warned.'

I knew a bit already about Tambimuttu and I had studied, with some horror, back issues of his magazine. Before reading Maclaren-Ross, though, with his detailed account of *Poetry London*'s shambolic editorial procedures, I hadn't realized how close I was to becoming a Tambi of the 1960s. Dreadful thought. After all, in literary terms, I knew myself to be an enemy of everything that Tambi represented. He was all for slackness and spirituality; my thing was austerity and formal discipline. Where then was the affinity?

Clearly something was wrong but there seemed to be no chance that I would put it right, or want to. Sohoitis had replaced provincialitis and this time there seemed to be no cure. 'Why shouldn't a good poem be written in a noisy pub?' I'd even hear myself enquire, too loudly. Just the kind of thing that Dylan Thomas used to say, and he was another of my literary bugbears. For the sake of literary-critical standards, perhaps I should be heading back to Paddington or Oxford.

I didn't, though. Instead, I began making forays across Oxford Street into Fitzrovia, scene of Tambimuttu's most triumphant failures. In my mid-twenties, I wanted to know more about what not to be. I wanted to know more as well about Maclaren-Ross, who seemed— from his elegant prose memoirs—to have had a properly aloof involvement in the Tambi scene. Maybe it was possible to dabble in Bohemia without trading in one's brains. I already knew something of Maclaren-Ross from superior wartime magazines like *Penguin New Writing* and *Horizon*. A story of his, called 'A Bit of a Smash in Madras', had been much admired, and all the more so when it was discovered that the author had never been to India. He had also written well about Alun Lewis, a selection of whose writings I had put together a year earlier.

Getting to know more about Maclaren-Ross turned out to be something of an error. It transpired that, far from having been a detached and sceptical observer of Fitzrovia, he was one of its key denizens: a champion pub-bore and scrounger. Even Tambimuttu, I discovered, thought twice about drinking with Maclaren-Ross. No revelation could have been more damning. Tambi, after all, was nothing if not unparticular—both as pubman and as editor.

During the war years, Tambimuttu was a reassuring fixture on the English poetry scene. If he could not always pay for the next round, he was invariably in need of verses to fill out the next issue of his magazine. Without him, there would have been no wartime poetry scene to speak of. Some critics wish there hadn't been, but figures of the day, especially the poets, were inclined to think that, on balance, Tambi served a useful purpose.

Tambimuttu had arrived in London from Ceylon in 1938, aged twenty-three, and had immediately made tracks for Russell Square, home of Faber and Faber and, of course, T. S. Eliot. Tambi, it seems, had a letter of introduction. Eliot took a shine to him and gave him an anthology to edit. 'T. S. Eliot,' said Tambi, 'says I'm going to be a great poet. I could have cried when he said that. He's so kind.' A year later, *Poetry London* was founded. The first issue carried a message from Tambimuttu announcing that 'Every man has poetry within him. Poetry is the awareness of the mind to the universe. It embraces everything in the world.' 'No man is small enough,' another message ran, 'to be neglected as a poet. Every healthy man is a full vessel.' Over the ensuing half a dozen years, quite a few vessels were filled and emptied in the cause of Art. 'I love ecstasy,' said Tambi, as he downed another pint. 'I am not a man. I am a spirit. I am everyone. I am everywhere.'

By 'everywhere' he meant, specifically, a dozen or so pubs and clubs stretching northwards from Old Compton Street to Fitzroy Square (or—on a heavy night—say, Goodge Street). And pubs usually meant beer. Wine and spirits were difficult to come by, and horribly expensive. Few people could afford to drink at home, or in restaurants. And Tambi, in any case, hardly ever seemed to eat. His own modest living quarters, used for sleeping in and storing manuscripts, were in Whitfield Street, close to Pollock's Toy Museum and only a few apprehensive steps away from the Marie Stopes clinic. From Whitfield Street, he had set out to colonize the surrounding terrain: Charlotte Street, Rathbone Street, Scala Street, Rathbone Place, Percy Street.

Tambi named his kingdom 'Fitzrovia'—in deference, perhaps, to the Fitzroy Tavern, the pub on the corner of Windmill Street and Charlotte Street where Orwell and Dylan Thomas used to hang out in the 1930s. The name 'Fitzrovia' had, of course, been used before to describe the territory between Fitzroy Square and Oxford Street ('the northern extension of Soho', as the guidebooks call it) and the

Ian Hamilton

area had literary connections long before Tambimuttu set up shop there. At the beginning of the century, the magazine *Blast* had been plotted in the Tour d'Eiffel (later the White Tower) and during the 1930s drinkers from the BBC had often drifted to Charlotte Street when they grew tired of their own customary haunts near Portland Place: the George or the M.L. (or Marie Lloyd). By the time Tambimuttu raised his standard, so to speak, Fitzrovia already had one or two established cultural-eccentrics: most notably Augustus John and Nina Hamnett ('Modi [Modigliani] said I had the best breasts in Europe. You feel them; they're as good as new'). Still, Tambi somehow made the area his own. Back in Ceylon, he sometimes claimed, he'd been a prince. He knew a thing or two about assembling a court. He knew too how to affect the regal manner: 'The critic is not our concern,' he'd tell his followers. 'Let him get squashed under his microscope. As Shakespeare did. We'll give the public what they want and to hell with the critics.' The editorial posture of *Poetry London* was vehemently anti-intellectual, anti-Auden and—as a corollary—anti-*New Verse*, Geoffrey Grigson's Auden-worshipping small magazine which had held sway in the 1930s. For Tambi, the curse of Auden had been to eliminate from English poetry all traces of the mystic and the mantric. Tambi, by way of his magazine and by way also of his own voluminous verse writings, would resuscitate these vital elements: 'Give us back the robe of splendid sap,' he wrote, 'Lap us in the gold, the power and ooze/Of rounded hours in the melon's belly/Singing gills of the sunfilled juice.'

This was the kind of thing he wanted for *Poetry London*: high-sounding, vatic, vapid. Now and then he would forget himself and print poems by people like Keith Douglas and even by Julian Symons, his Audenesque arch-foe. On the whole, though, people knew where Tambi stood: a yard or two above the ground—unless of course he'd fallen over, which he sometimes had. Absurd figure though he was, there can be no doubt that, for a time during the miserable war years, he turned his Fitzrovia into a kind of haven for aesthetic vagrants. The theatres were closed, the National Gallery was empty, the BBC was churning out propaganda, the concert halls were silent. If you were a poet-soldier on forty-eight-hour leave from a training camp or war zone and looking for bookish company, you would head straight for Tambimuttu. So too if you were a poet-deserter, a poet-conchie, a poet-radio-producer, a poet-film-maker working out of Wardour Street. Not only would you find company in Fitzrovia; there was also a good chance that you'd offload some of your verses.

Your verses might not actually get printed but acceptance was better than nothing—and worth at least the pint or two that Tambi and his pards would gratefully accept as their reward. The story goes that Tambimuttu, at the end of a long Fitzrovian pub-crawl, would dump the day's accepted manuscripts into his chamber pot at Whitfield Street. And there some of them remained, throughout the war. When *Poetry London* eventually folded, in 1944, Tambi collected together, in one bumper, book-length issue, all the poems that he'd accepted but not used (apart from those which still mouldered in the chamber pot, presumably). He then held, on publication day, a big party for contributors which he paid for with their fees. Afterwards, each of the party-goers was asked to get hold of a receipt so that Tambi could claim back the overall tab from his backers—the soon-to-go-bust Nicholson and Watson.

The magazine itself was truly dreadful but nobody seemed to care. In an epoch of snatched pleasures, of casualty lists, bomb-alerts and blackouts, Tambi's Fitzrovia represented freedom and delinquency, the unregimented life of the imagination. In a precarious world, one thing to be sure of was Tambi's whereabouts at five-thirty on a weekday.

His typical evening would begin at the Swiss Pub in Soho's Old Compton Street. From there, after an hour or so, he and his followers would set off across Oxford Street to Rathbone Place. First stop in Rathbone Place was the Black Horse and, after that, they all went to the Wheatsheaf, which became known as Fitzrovia's nerve centre. Around the corner from the Wheatsheaf, in Gresse Street, was the Bricklayer's Arms, known also as the Burglar's Rest because some thieves had broken into it one night and quaffed the stock. The Burglar's Rest was where you sneaked off to for some peace and quiet if you'd picked up a girl, say, in the Wheatsheaf, or if you wanted some fellow-poet to really concentrate on the new mantra you had just composed.

This, then, was the regular Fitzrovian drink-route. And when closing time descended, at ten-thirty, Tambi and his crew would track back towards Soho, where the Highlander in Dean Street used to stay open for an extra half an hour. Eating, if it happened, was attended to after the pubs had shut—unless, by chance, someone was feeling rich, in which event the Poetry Londoners would give the Highlander a miss and try to sneak into L'Etoile or the White Tower before eleven p.m., when even the posh restaurants' drink licences expired. If funds happened to be short, the revellers would lurch from Dean Street to some late-night caff, or they would seek out an illicit drinking club, of which there were a few, if you knew where to look: the Harem, off Rathbone Place; the Gargoyle, in Meard Street; the Caribbean, in Denman Street, and so on.

In my *Review* days, when I quite often used to wander across to Fitzrovia from Soho, many of Tambi's landmarks were still standing. There had been just one destructive air-raid during the war, but none of the pubs was damaged. Tambi would put this down to magic, and without doubt the war for him was magical—the high point of a literary career which afterwards went steadily downhill. I met him once, in 1968 or thereabouts, when he was trying to raise money for a new publishing adventure. He had, he said, developed important connections with the Beatles' Apple Corporation, and the Beatles were going through their Maharishi phase. Asiatic spirituality, he reckoned, was ready for a comeback. Tambi died in 1983, of a heart attack. He'd had a fall, it was reported, in his 'office'. And this office was, it seems, the headquarters of another latest project: to promote the idea of a London-based Indian Arts Council. I'm not sure of the address but it must surely have been Charlotte Street—home now, I note, of an Indian YMCA.

A couple of weeks ago, I found myself in Greek Street once again. *The Review*'s hovel was now someone else's real-life office and the strip club had become a restaurant. But then everything in Soho seems to be a restaurant these days—apart from the restaurants I used to go to. All of these have either disappeared, or been renamed, or made over into singlet bars for gays. Not that there's anything wrong with that, as Jerry Seinfeld likes to say. But even so, after an hour or so's bemused investigation, my instinct was to head off for Fitzrovia. Here surely I would find a whiff of datedness, of how things used to be. Not so. Bertorelli's, one of my own *Review* haunts, is now tarted up to look like an airport hotel; the White Tower is a Cigar Club, whatever that may be. And all the pubs are full of foreign students, wall to wall—apart from the Wheatsheaf, which is full of postmen (from the Rathbone Place sorting office just along the street). All changed, changed utterly. But what was I doing here—again? What did I hope to find?

And this takes me back to the beginning: to Better Books, to Paddington, to Greek Street, to those two-tones on the stairs, those smelly drains. It takes me back to Tambimuttu and his pubs and finds me, yet again, admiring them more than I should. I mean, where would you go nowadays to run a little magazine? Where is today's Wheatsheaf? The Groucho, Blacks, the Union? Well, hardly—for one thing, those places cost a fortune. Also, they're full of servants of the Zeitgeist. Bohemias are ways of life you both sink to and aspire to. You live like *this* because you actively don't want to live like *that*. And can't afford to even if you do.

And Bohemias are personal: they age and die. Try taking a drink nowadays in the 'legendary' Fitzroy Tavern. It too is packed with students but downstairs it has a Writers and Artists Bar—supposedly to commemorate the Tavern's arty past. On the walls of this dark and dingy basement are framed snapshots of Dylan Thomas's grave and of George Orwell setting off for Spain. And there are one or two portraits of Augustus John. It's all immensely shoddy and half-hearted and none of the pub staff knows why it's there. Give me the Groucho any day—except, that is, on Thursdays, when the Writers and Artists Bar offers poetic entertainment by something or somebodies called The Cunning Linguists. On Thursdays at the Fitzroy, according to a poster, you can meet 'saucy poet Michelle Taylor and Shamanic poets Tim Gabaski and Vladimir Yeremenko Tolstoy'. And at the top of the bill you'll find one Jaspre Bark: 'he's wet and wild...a veritable golden shower of per-*verse*-ity.' Is this then today's *Poetry London*? Or today's *Review*? Is this, for someone, a Bohemia to flee to? I guess it is—but if it is, I think I'll stick with mine, what's left of it. □

A LONDON VIEW/Doris Lessing

This room is a converted roof space at the very top of the house and it looks
south-east. I have my bed along the French window, which fills the wall, so
that I can lie in it and look at the sky where the sun gets up in a variety of
dusky, pinkstreaked, red-flaring or plain skies, and travels past all day, and
then the moon follows soon after in all its many sizes, colours and shapes.
The moon is sometimes high, sometimes low down, and may disappear for
a while into the branches of the great ash tree at the bottom of the garden,
which is a long London garden the width of the house.

From the balcony outside the French window I look down at gardens
stretching the length of the street, some neglected, a bird-inhabited confusion,
some designed and formal, some the crammed delicious tangle amateurs like
me may achieve, roses, irises, lilies, clematis, all out together, but then a kind
of jungle, because I am too busy to keep it tamed. In these gardens wander
cats of all kinds, designer cats and moggies, and the trees are noisy with birds.
I and others feed them. Last week a woodpecker and two jays visited my
lower veranda to find nuts that might have been rolled into spaces between
pots, overlooked by squirrels and pigeons.

A big birch tree is as tall as the roof and the ash behind it is gigantic.
There are cherries, apples, pears, a blackthorn, planes, and around a great
green space the size of a small airfield are trees and bushes. This green field
is a reservoir—the Victorians put their water under lids of earth. Across it,
if it is fine, you see over roofs to the Houses of Parliament, and down to
Canary Wharf, and, looking left up a hill it is Hampstead, and if you didn't
know, you'd think it was a hill of trees with an occasional roof dotted about.

From my high window I might as well be in the country. It is quiet up
here in the day and at night silent, not a sound.

Down on the pavement you could think this was a London street with
houses packed up behind it. Beyond the other face of houses are playing fields
and an old cemetery, so in fact this conventional city street runs between
green fields and trees. No one driving along it could possibly guess the truth.

It is not on the top of a hill, but almost: the reservoir is the top. The
street running up to ours is so steep that when there is snow the cars slip
and slide, so it is better to drive around another way. Not long ago this was
a wild green hill that people might ascend going north-west, then, after
resting on a flattish place, start climbing again to the heights of Hampstead.
This knot of streets was built in 1890, all at once, as one of the first
commuter suburbs. In the area below the reservoir, to the south, until the
First World War were fields, cows, little streams. I knew an old woman who

used to take a penny bus ride on Sundays from Marble Arch to where the mill was that gave Mill Lane its name—soon to be replaced by boring flats—so she could put her feet into the streams and watch cows.

As I write leaves are spinning off the trees and the gardens seem drowned in gold and orange and green, and the grass on the reservoir is emerald green in watery sunlight.

A LONDON VIEW/Penelope Lively

Last thing, I watch the night mail go out. The back windows of my house gaze down into the yard of Islington's main post office—a great block of Edwardian red brick, its façade an uncompromising array of windows, its only architectural flight of fancy the peculiar stunted campanile at each end of the building. A wrought-iron plaque on my garden wall, boundary with the post office yard, reminds me that the wall is the property of the Postmaster General, 1909. At night, the yard and the row of back gardens glow in the light of the post office's orange sodium lamps—best in rain when the glow turns to gilt, sharply gilded foliage and glittering lakes on the tarmac of the yard. Then, the ceremony of the night mail begins—the line of stationary Royal Mail vans in the alley just behind the wall, waiting their turn to swing out into the covered yard and back up to the building's entrances. The sodium lights turn the red vans khaki brown; they sit there with engines idling, shadowy figures at the wheel thumbing a newspaper, flicking a fag end through the window. The choreography is perfect. Four vans move forward simultaneously—advance, swing right, reverse, line up flank to flank—and at once the loading starts, the flat thud and wallop of mailbags. They are going to the airports and the stations. The night mail: 'Letters of thanks, letters from banks… The typed and the printed and the spelt all wrong.' And the post office becomes suddenly of global significance, a node in an invisible web of communication, launching a million messages. The last four vans line up…thud, wallop…the brief gleam of red departing lights. Silence. A cat walks across the empty tarmac of the yard. The place is once more local and domestic.

GRANTA

A SMALL BENGAL, NW3

Amit Chaudhuri

A bout five or six years after the war ended, and soon after India's independence and the beginning of the end of the British Empire, Belsize Park in the borough of Camden became home to a number of Indian, mainly Bengali, students. They lived in neighbouring houses, and were often neighbours in the same house; they talked with, and jostled, and cooked for, each other, and had small rivalries and sympathies between themselves; but they knew they were a transient lot, because they were here to pass exams, and very few intended to stay, to get swallowed by the London that had become their temporary home. Time went by quickly, although, in retrospect, the procession of years would sometimes seem long.

Strangely enough, while Kilburn came to be known as a black and Irish area, and Golders Green a Jewish one, Belsize Park was never identified with its Bengali student population. Perhaps this was so because it was made up of itinerants rather than emigrants; most had left by the mid-Sixties—if not England, then at least Belsize Park. They were mainly young men and, now and again, women, in their late twenties or their thirties, diligent and intelligent on the whole, who had come to study for professional examinations whose names seemed to have been invented to enhance their job prospects: Chartered Accountancy, Cost Accountancy, MRCP, FRCP, FRCS. For these Bengalis, at least, there was a romance about degrees that had the words 'Chartered' or 'Royal' in them which will now probably seem absurd. The few who stayed on in England were often the ones who hadn't been able to get the degree they'd come here to acquire; they couldn't face their mothers and fathers without it; thus they drifted into the civic life of London, became railway clerks or council officials, or moved elsewhere, and eventually bought a house in Wimbledon or Sussex or Hampshire; at any rate, they left Belsize Park. Those who stayed on had their reasons—'staying on': those words had possibly as much resonance for them, though for entirely different reasons, as they did for the last Anglo-Indians—and none of those reasons, it is safe to suppose, had anything to do with an overwhelming attachment to England.

But most studied, and left; and, in Belsize Park, the emphasis was on exams and recreation. They'd brought Bengal with them though Bengal itself had become a state of mind, partitioned into two, half of it in India and half of it East Pakistan. They fell into a routine of buying 'wet fish', shopping at Finchley Road, going to work, listening to Tagore songs, in between bouts of memorizing the pulmonary functions of the heart or the intricacies of taxation law.

Some of the students had wives, and were newly married. The wife, like Draupadi in the *Mahabharat*, who married five brothers at once, not only played wife to her husband but often to all her husband's friends, making food for them, being indulgent to them when they were depressed, exhorting them to study hard, and generally lightening the air with her feminine presence. Later, the men would always remember these surrogate wives, the Mrs Mukherjis and Mrs Basus and Mrs Senguptas. In India, the new wife comes to her new home and is greeted by her husband's family and a way of life both pre-arranged and untested; every couple must, in the end, make what they will of their own lives. Here, in Belsize Park, the making of that life was both more naked and more secret; the new bride would be received not by her in-laws, but Cost Accountants-to-be and would-be surgeons and physicians. She would come not to her husband's house but to a bedsit with wallpaper and cooking hobs which was now to be her own, and which cost three pounds and ten shillings a week.

Among the tenants was a young man who was supposed to be studying Chartered Accountancy but was actually doing everything but study. He was thinner than normal; his mother had died when he was seven years old. When he had left India in 1949, he had been twenty-seven years old; he had lost his homeland with Partition; and he had got engaged to his best friend's younger sister. In 1955, she travelled to London with her younger brother to marry the young man. They, my parents, were among the people who lived in Belsize Park in the Fifties.

In a photograph taken at the time, my mother leans over my father, who is reading a newspaper; she hides her hands behind her back because she has been kneading dough. In another picture, apparently taken soon after the wedding, my parents have just arrived in Shepherd's Bush and are standing on the steps of a house, seeming slightly unfamiliar with each other though in fact they have known each other from childhood, my father dressed in the bridegroom's white dhoti and kurta, my mother's sari draped over her head. They have recently walked round the holy fire in a town hall near Euston Square. Now they would be reacquainted with each other as husband and wife; my father would rediscover his lost mother's affection in the woman he had married; they would travel in Europe; they would make friends among their neighbours; my mother's singing voice would acquire a new fame in Bengali circles; her reputation as a cook would be established.

Both, in the first years of their marriage, went out to work in the morning, and had their daily meeting-places outside work hours; during break-time, my mother would hurry to Jermyn Street, where my father worked for a few years in the Accounts Office of India House, and they would go for lunch or tea to the Lyons restaurant nearby. Once a week, they would have a Chinese dinner at the Cathay restaurant; watching, through a window, Piccadilly outside. Nearer the exams, my father would study at home while my mother went out to work as a clerk.

Without a harmonium or any other accompanying instrument, my mother would keep practising the Tagore songs that she had learned as a child, in Sylhet, which had become part of East Pakistan. Her singing was full-throated; her voice would carry in the silent afternoons; once, the spinster landlady, Miss Fox, came down to complain.

Then, in 1961, a year before I was born, my parents left for Bombay; my father had, after passing his exams, got a job that paid for his and my mother's fares back; the ship would take two weeks to reach India. As the ship sailed forth, my mother (so she tells me) stared at the cliffs of Dover to imprint them on her memory. In a year, she had conceived, and, at the age of thirty-seven, she gave birth to her first and only child in Calcutta.

This is what they left behind. Haverstock Hill leading on one side to Hampstead, and Belsize Avenue sloping downward to Swiss Cottage and Finchley Road on the other. Other lives begin; other stories; and the human capacity to create is at least as strong as the capacity to forget. □

GRANTA

THE PRINCE AND I
Ferdinand Dennis

The Albert Memorial, 'Africa'

The Prince and I

My long and ambivalent relationship with the Albert Memorial started soon after I was brought as a child to London from Kingston, Jamaica. I was old enough to possess fragments of memory from another place, young enough to be wide open to the influences of my new city. We lived in Paddington in the north-west corner of the borough of Westminster and London's many monuments, museums and art galleries were only a short bus or tube journey away. My primary school (called Wilberforce, perhaps after the abolitionist of slavery, though he never formed part of our lessons) organized class outings, and it was on one of these trips, as we walked through Kensington Gardens, that I first saw the grateful nation's tribute to Queen Victoria's dead husband, the Prince Consort. The Albert Memorial: designed by George Gilbert Scott, erected at the peak of British power in 1872, 175 feet high, and decorated with sculpture, mosaics and bas-reliefs dedicated to all kinds of human achievement (AGRICULTURE, RHETORIC, COMMERCE) and human achievers (HOMER, SHAKESPEARE, MICHELANGELO), as well as of ideals (CHARITY, PRUDENCE, HUMILITY) and, larger than all of these, seated and holding a copy of the catalogue to the Great Exhibition of 1851, a statue of the prince himself.

Of course, I knew nothing of these things then, and, much as I would like to, can't remember how I felt when I first saw Albert and his memorial. I imagine the mixture of awe and reverence that big things elicit from small innocents. My impressions of my second visit, a few years later, are more distinct. I was then in the first year of my secondary school, Rutherford Comprehensive, which was only fifteen minutes' walk away from Marble Arch and the start of the West End. Trips to London's historic and cultural sights happened at least once every term and so I found myself again on the steps of the memorial, listening to one of our teachers, Mr Hallam (or was it Mr Stein?), as he spoke lyrically about the Prince Consort's dedication to the arts and sciences and the importance of those pursuits.

There was, for me, something inspirational about this and other early visits to the memorial (it was a favourite destination for temporary teachers who had been put in charge of classrooms full of bored and inattentive pupils). This is your legacy, those alfresco lessons seemed to say. Choose your area, commerce, agriculture, manufacturing, science. You too can walk in the footsteps of the great. You too can reach the glory symbolized by the holy cross at the memorial's pinnacle. Years later, when I could no longer pass the memorial without thinking of the fiction it perpetuates, it could still manage somehow to stir within me a childish belief in the possibility of glory, even of immortality.

I can't say how many, if any, of my fellow pupils at Rutherford were similarly affected. Rutherford was hardly the sort of establishment that nurtured scientific and artistic pioneers. It stood near Paddington Green, newly built on the site of a previous school which had taught the children of the poor and disreputable—prostitution was once a feature of the area—since the last century. Its pupils came from the surrounding council estates and the narrow terraces which held immigrant families like my own. Footballers, pop stars and local criminals were the heroes—not dead poets—and the school during my time there became a battleground between these different expectations. Its four 'houses'—Lords, Dickens, Faraday and Browning—were, presumably, modelled after English public schools, and their influence was echoed by the headmaster's long black gown, severe demeanour and firm belief in discipline.

His name was Mr George and he led the charge for higher values and aspirations. Everything about him—his upright bearing, his cloak, his hair plastered tight with Brylcreem—inspired confidence in parents who came from the former colonies. They always took the opportunity on parents' day to renew their permission for him to punish their children as he saw fit. Nodding and smiling, Mr George would thank them and repeat his commitment to make young gentlemen out of his pupils, to instil courtesy, obedience and purpose. To those of us with some experience of schooling in the Caribbean, Mr George's severity and readiness to resort to corporal punishment were familiar. One of my memories from Jamaica, where I had spent two years in a Catholic primary school, was of a nun forcing a boy caught swearing to wash his mouth out with soap and water. School and painful punishment were, in my mind, inseparable.

Despite Mr George's strenuous and unrelenting efforts, the native pupils remained recalcitrant. As these white boys reached their teens, the football culture seized them. On Monday mornings they would exchange stories of Saturday's fights with the supporters of visiting teams to the West London clubs: Chelsea, Fulham and Queen's Park Rangers. They spoke about the sharpened coins, which had been spun into the visitors' section, how they'd filed the tips of umbrellas, the punch-ups lost and won.

We, the boys from the Caribbean or with Caribbean parents, had fewer outlets for our adolescent energy. We were assimilated but not integrated. By that I mean we bore British names, attended Christian churches, collected conkers in early autumn, let off bangers on bonfire night. We had travelled part of the journey into Britishness. But the football stadium, perhaps the most important arena for celebrating and reaffirming working-class belonging, was a no-go area for us. At football grounds, we knew, they likened us to monkeys and drew on an astonishingly rich vocabulary of offensive racial terms. The passion of football was also the passion of whiteness.

Consequently, much of our energy was directed towards the pupils from Sarah Siddons, the girls' school on the other side of Paddington Green. Then, one Easter, a group of boys went beyond the boundary of exploratory sexual playfulness and into the region of sexual assault. Parents of some girls complained that their daughters had been molested in the emergency stairwell of Edgware Road underground station. Mr George delivered one of his famous fire-and-brimstone speeches to the school assembly. He spoke of the recent 'black spots' that had begun to appear in the school, 'black spots' that he would not tolerate, 'black spots' that threatened to ruin the school's good reputation, 'black spots' that he would expel. It was, perhaps, merely an unfortunate choice of metaphor, for the culprits were known to everybody and all were black. I wasn't one of them, but the headmaster's words stung me. I felt as if he was talking directly to me, and, though I was blameless, I was flushed with feelings of shame and guilt.

Why? Perhaps because I had been in London for five years by then and at some point lost my island identity. That I was a Jamaican had become secondary to the supposed colour of my skin. Even now, in my early middle-age, the fragments of memories from those early years in Jamaica reveal companionable schoolmates with a variety of shades, from different races, who did not insult each other. They are, of course, a child's memories, frozen by time and distance, polished to a consolingly dazzling finish. For Jamaica would, before my youth had ended, reach into the capital of the former mother country with its own racial response to freedom from Empire.

Some weeks after Mr George's 'black spots' speech, one of our regular teachers was absent and we got a supply teacher in his place. Unimaginatively, he took my class for yet another visit to the Albert Memorial. I walked around the monument as usual, looking at the sculptures grouped at each corner which represent the four continents of Europe, Asia, Africa and America. And now a feature of the memorial struck me as somehow wrong. Both Africa and America lie at the back of the memorial, facing away from the road and the Albert Hall.

In the north-east corner,

AFRICA: an Egyptian princess sitting on a camel, with a half-naked sub-Saharan African figure, a 'noble savage', resting on a bow and gazing at a European female.

In the north-west corner,

AMERICA: a Liberty-like figure sitting on a buffalo surrounded by two other Europeans and a Red Indian.

Where among these groups was I and the people like me? In Africa. But where were the islands of the Caribbean? Surely close to America. It puzzled me that nobody like me could be found in the American corner. The supply teacher, a young bearded Welshman, said something to the effect that art was neither history nor geography, but art. I was left to solve the puzzle for myself.

My father provided something of an answer, at least to the African part of the question. His reply was characteristically terse: 'Because that's where our ancestors came from. Africa.' But then the Europeans, with their ancestry in Europe, were represented in America as well as where they came from while we were not. Yet the black musicians we saw on *Top of the Pops*, Cassius Clay, the athletes who had given Black Power salutes at the last Olympics— these were living proof of that presence. My father didn't answer me, but gave me a strange glance which, as a parent myself, I now recognize expressed a mixture of surprise that I could conceive the question and an inability to answer it. Perhaps I do my father a disservice here, wrongly attributing to him ignorance rather than the wish to protect me from knowledge best left concealed.

I think there was also in my father's silence the security of a man who knew exactly where he came from—rural Jamaica—and why he had moved—to work. Africans, regardless of their physical similarities, were strangers, more foreign than white Britons, even. He was a carpenter and a landlord and he carried himself with the proud bearing of a skilled artisan. He did not encourage familiarity with the neighbours, who all addressed him as Mr Dennis, and his few friends who visited the house were without exception Jamaicans from his birthplace, Port Antonio. He considered himself superior to the bus conductors, railway guards and factory workers among the other West Indians in the neighbourhood. This sense of superiority transcended race to include the poor whites, many of whom were Irish rather than English.

He might almost have been a figure on the memorial himself. His values were those of the ambitious Victorian artisan: frugality, temperance and hard work. While many other Caribbean men went to betting shops, he invested in stock market shares and monitored their performance by reading the *Daily Telegraph*. Otherwise unemotional, he displayed a deep passion for buildings. On Sunday afternoons—and over Christmas—when the city was empty, we often drove east down Marylebone Road and past the Angel to the original City of London, stopping at the Thames, because, of course, South London is another country. My father had worked on many buildings in the City and he would point them out with tremendous pride, as though he had erected them single-handed.

He had a home in London; he loved London's buildings; but he had no ambition to settle in London for the rest of his life. Typical of many Caribbean immigrants, he wanted to go back eventually to the West Indies. One of the most common phrases I heard from the tenants in my father's house was: 'Back home'. When a wooden crate appeared in someone's front garden, passers-by would stop and gaze at it as if it were a public monument, and would exchange the remark that somebody living in that house was going 'back home'. On most Friday evenings, a Dominican who lived on the top floor bought black pudding and *sous*—spicy pig's trotters boiled to a gelatinous state—from one of her compatriots who walked the neighbourhood selling her wares from a pail. Mrs Lavinier, the tenant, always described her purchase as tasting like 'back home'. My father was not a great drinker, and the little he did was done at home, never in a pub. Occasionally he would share a bottle of rum with a visiting friend and their conversation would be littered with the phrase 'back home'. Throughout the neighbourhood on Saturday nights, record players would play lively and melancholy music that sometimes went on until the early hours of Sunday morning. Men who had drunk too much from the cup nostalgia would stagger down the street.

For many, 'back home' remained a dream. I remember one of my father's tenants was a Mr Johnson, a lonely drunk who had fought with a white colleague at work and been dismissed. On some nights, in the gaps between the rumble of the freight trains, we could hear Mr Johnson crying in his room. Even sadder was the mild-mannered Jamaican, Mr Ramsey, who left my father's house for home in a great fanfare, only to return three months later, having been stripped of his possessions by rapacious relatives who refused to be contented with the few cheap presents he had brought back for them. He came back to our neighbourhood, though not our house, nursing the permanent loss of his back-home dream.

My generation, the children of these homesick immigrants, could not share it. Though many of us were born in the West Indies, we could not continue with an identity which had been forged by the British Empire. We were becoming British, not as members of some far-flung tropical colony, nor as Britons of the so-called mother race. In a new way. Terms such as 'West Indian', 'coloured' and 'negro' were abandoned in favour of the more assertive 'black', no matter the pejorative connotation of Mr George's speech. It infused the word with a positive meaning, one that perfectly reflected the state of conflict in which this new identity was being made. We bandied around phrases. 'I am black and I am proud' and 'Black is beautiful'.

Most of my friends left school around this time to take up jobs in garages and print shops. Those of us who stayed on were concerned only with passing exams. I missed my friends terribly. When the powerful but unfocused feeling of race stirred inside me, prompted by a derogatory remark on the streets or some 'comedy' on the television, I could turn to nobody for comfort or answers. My father was of little help, though he recognized that something was wrong. On several occasions, reacting to some allusion I had made to race, he said that he was sorry that I had not spent more years in Jamaica and come at a later age, when I would have been properly rooted. By that I suppose he meant that the racial slights would have had less effect. The nostalgia of the adult immigrant on the one hand; the discomfort of racial awakening in a white country on the other. They, it seemed, were my only choices.

Then in the summer of 1974 I struck up a friendship with an engaging young man who, like me, was working as a porter in the Harrods food hall. Dean Baptiste was thin, tall and extremely dark, with eyes sunk deep. He came from St Lucia. It turned out that he lived near me, across the 'A-penny steps', a cast-iron footbridge across the Grand Union canal. He was two years older than me and about to go to university. We often rode home together on the number 52 bus.

One fine evening we decided to walk home through Hyde Park and Kensington Gardens. We stopped at the Albert Memorial. Dean too had been taken there to see it as a schoolboy, but while it puzzled me it enraged him. That evening he described it as a monstrous lie, a typical piece of European falsehood. He explained that the statues at the corners of the base represented areas in the former British Empire—and that the African gazing at the European in the African corner was intended to represent the civilizing influence of Britain on us 'Africans'. He pointed out the chain on the African's feet— barely visible then, even less so today—and mentioned slavery. Dean was probably the first person I heard describing 'us' as Africans and uttering the word 'slavery' in the same sentence. My only contribution to this conversation was to recall how the absence of an African in the American corner had once puzzled me. Dean gave me a look of incredulity, as if he could not believe my ignorance. Then he impatiently reeled off a list of books and writers I should read: C. L. R. James, Eric Williams, Stokely Carmichael, Eldridge Cleaver. A book by Julius Lester was called *Look out Whitey Black Power's Gonna Get your Momma*.

At the end of the summer Dean went off to university, and I

resumed my A-level studies, along with reading some of the books he had recommended. I bought them from a little shop called 'Grassroots' in Ladbroke Grove, and they became important to me. They expanded statements such as 'Black and beautiful' and 'I am black and proud' into entire arguments. By Christmas, I could explain why the Albert Memorial had Europeanized the features of the Egyptian female and why an African figure was absent from the American corner. I had at times an almost intoxicated feeling, as if I were discovering some secret about myself, Britain and London; as if I were stealing forbidden knowledge in the warm privacy of my father's house. And as I read, I listened. Jamaican reggae music was making its mark on me. An early classic by a band portentously known as 'Count Ossie and the Mystic Revelation of Rastafari' had the lyrics: 'In 1568, Queen Elizabeth the First granted John Hawkins a licence to carry 450 slaves from Africa to the Caribbean. Carried us beyond our borders.' In sweaty clubs suffused with the scent of ganja, many members of my generation experienced what amounted to a religious conversion. When they emerged into the cold morning air, they had a whole new language to express the disaffection born of growing up black in Britain. Rastafarianism had arrived. Its ideas, disseminated through the infectious beat of reggae, became an inescapable part of our coming of age in 1970s London.

Rastafarianism made a religion of themes from black history—enslavement and exile from Africa, repatriation, cultural heritage. For a time it satisfied a profound hunger for a cultural tradition with its own language, rituals, myths, heroes and God. The music of its protestation was extremely seductive, and its terminology soon became a part of our everyday conversation. On cold winter days 'this Babylon'—meaning Britain—was a phrase that was bound to trigger warming laughter among us. I never became a convert, though I did come close to conversion during my first year at Leicester University, where I felt isolated and depressed. At the end of that academic year I came home to London wondering whether I would continue with my degree. My father, unwittingly, steadied me. He was not a man with whom to discuss ideas. But a house and its drains, roof, walls, floors, pipes, wires, paint—all these things he understood. 'These old Victorian houses,' he often said with relish, 'always need working on.' When I got back to London, he was about to start building an extension at the back of the house and persuaded me to help. It was hard physical work, complicated by many frustrating hitches. By the time we finished, my father's exemplary patience made me see the importance of completing a job once started. I knew I would probably return to university in the autumn.

My remaining doubts were dispelled when I met Dean Baptiste again. He was skinnier, his eyes more deeply sunken, his face bonier (though that might have been an effect of the red, green and yellow woollen hat he wore, with strands of dreadlocks peeking through its sides). Dean had found faith in Rastafarianism and dropped out of university early in his second year. Now he lived in a liberally-run youth hostel with several other Rastas. I spent a lot of that summer, the hot summer of 1976, in their company.

Dean was the leader of these young men, none of whom shared his education or strength of conviction. We often talked late into the night over cans of lager and, when we could afford them, joints of ganja, or what Dean called the 'holy herb'. During one of our talks, he reminded me of the day we stopped at the Albert Memorial. He did so as a prelude to explaining why he had taken to stealing rare library books on African history, or, as he put it, liberating knowledge of the African past from the clutches of 'Babylon'. Then, in mid-July, he commissioned an artist friend to draw some charcoal sketches in the style of a then popular Jamaican artist, Ras Daniel Heartman, intending to sell them as prints at the Notting Hill Carnival, which the previous year had attracted many thousands of people to Ladbroke Grove. The carnival in 1976 turned out to be even larger. The prints quickly sold out, vindicating Dean's view that black people were hungry for images of themselves. But on the second day of the carnival clashes broke out between the police and dreadlocked young men dressed in green battle-fatigues. In the shadow of the Westway flyover, with the powerful sound systems blasting out lyrics calling for Babylon to be burned down, the crowd hurled bottles and bricks. I noticed that my friend, Dean Baptiste, was prominent among the rioters.

Some anger, deep and ancient, was given expression that summer. But it was a volatile thing, as likely to be turned inward as outward.

In the week after the carnival, Dean's zealotry sometimes looked close to madness. He spoke of armed attacks against the police and raids on the British Museum to capture stolen African treasures. Sometimes he wanted to start a 'black house' which would exhibit the recovered treasure in London, and sometimes he wanted to return the treasure to Africa. He tolerated no dissent from the youths around him. Autumn came and I went back to university. I saw Dean about a year later. He was dressed in a multi-coloured robe and standing outside a record shop on Portobello Road, shouting: 'They stole our history, now they want to steal our songs.' I have not seen Dean since. Some years later a mutual friend told me that he had been 'sectioned'—put away—in a home for the mentally unstable.

The carnival riots presaged the much greater disturbances of the early 1980s: the riots in Brixton and Tottenham in London, in Birmingham and Liverpool. The rioters took their inspiration from Rastafarianism. The response to the riots was a plethora of social and cultural programmes which acknowledged that Caribbean immigrants and their British-born children were part of the British nation. Sometimes in the many public debates that followed, debates about returning artefacts looted in the colonial years, or the appropriate term for people of African descent, I have heard echoes of Dean Baptiste's anger. His generation changed Britain, and London especially. The Notting Hill Carnival is now Europe's largest street festival; whites now outnumber blacks among the crowds; dreadlocks are worn by white youths as well as black. A less visible legacy is the restoration of Africa to the cultural consciousness of the children of Caribbean immigrants. Black-owned shops and organisations bear African names: Yemanja, Kush, Ashante, Kuumba. Colleges and evening classes offer courses in Swahili, Yoruba, Ibo. I could, if I wanted to, even enrol for an introductory course in Hieroglyphs. We are centuries removed from the continent, but rightly or wrongly we claim it all.

My father's own longing for return—though not to Africa—eventually got the better of his admiration for London's architecture and he returned to that other island a dozen years ago. I left our old house in Westminster for other parts of London. Hyde Park, Kensington Gardens, the Albert Memorial—these places belonged to my youth and I rarely went near them. I read that the memorial was being restored. Sometimes I caught a glimpse of it covered in plastic sheets and scaffolding. Then, in the autumn of last year, the Queen unveiled the restoration with a lot of pomp and media coverage. No expense had been spared. The statue of the prince himself, which I remembered as a dull grey object, had been re-gilded. The prince was golden and glowed in the television lights like some fabulous being from Greek mythology.

Towards the end of October I took my ten-year-old daughter to see the memorial in its new splendour. I wanted to know what she would make of it. I knew that she already possessed a sense of race. A few years before she'd described herself as black, and I'd said that was debatable; that a person was not colour, that it would be more accurate to describe her skin as brown, that she'd been born in England, which made her an English girl of Jamaican parentage. I was, you understand, trying to fulfil my parental duty by speaking of the ideal—an identity based on place rather than questionable notions of race.

Now we stood before the memorial and, as I pointed out the great writers, musicians and poets on its frieze, I was struck by the uncomfortable thought that it had indeed supplied part of the ambition that turned me into a writer. I asked my daughter what she thought. 'There's too much going on, it should be simpler,' she said with her implacable, modern taste for the minimal.

I laughed and decided that this was not the time to interpret Albert's memorial or the features which had once puzzled me. One day, on its steps, I would like to talk to her about the glory of creativity, artistic and scientific. But I know that, though her London is different from the one I grew up in, we will first have to pass, in the north-west corner, the African figure who seems to have spent much of the twentieth century calling out that neither his nobility nor his savagery were any greater or lesser than those of the men who froze him in stone. □

A LONDON VIEW/Jenny Uglow

My favourite view is just a sudden vertical glimpse. It's the drear end of November and I've walked across the old meat market of Smithfield, past the great façade of St Bartholomew's Hospital, past new flowers for William Wallace (blame *Braveheart*) and wilting carnations for the Protestant martyrs. Healing and death. I turn down Little Britain and under the ugly concrete arch with peeling posters and frowning notices—SAVE BARTS!, OCCUPY!, PLEASE DO NOT PADLOCK YOUR BICYCLE TO THESE RAILINGS—into St Bartholomew's Close.

Today the church is masked by 1960s concrete and shivering medics mutter into mobiles by the parking meters. This is where William Hogarth was born—that fierce visionary who caught London's eighteenth-century crowd with such ironic, knowing force. His house stood where the Department of Psychological Medicine now stares across at the complacent Butcher's Hall. Amused, but cold, I turn south, a few paces, close to the wall and look up—and there, between the red-brick school of nursing and an old warehouse with blacked-out windows, soars the dome of St Paul's. A swelling curve among the angles, a gilded cross over the street lamps, a classical pediment above the buses. Two steps and it's gone. I imagine Hogarth as a child, born in the year St Paul's was opened, running through narrow streets and seeing it, suddenly, day after day—the biggest edifice in London, vast, new, looming, shining, making his city seem the centre of the world. This view is still like being hit across the eyes. It's like a Hogarth print, where all the buildings crush together, and all London's history, change, and hope amid squalor are caught in a monochrome flash.

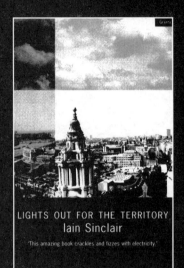
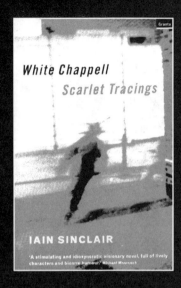
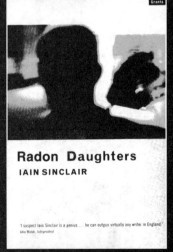

GRANTA

CHURCHILL'S CIGAR
Ian Buruma

Jewish children arriving at Liverpool Street station in 1939   HULTON GETTY PICTURE COLLECTION

It was in 1960, or possibly 1961, at any rate before the first Beatles LP, that I went shopping for cheroots with my grandfather. He was over in The Hague on a visit from England. I was about ten. I was born in The Hague. My father was Dutch and my mother English. To me a visit to Holland by my grandparents felt like the arrival of messengers from a wider and more glamorous world.

My grandfather, who had served as an army doctor in India during the war, liked Burmese cheroots. These were hard to come by in Holland; but, if there was one shop in The Hague that was likely to stock them, it was a tobacconist's named de Graaff.

G. de Graaff was an old-fashioned family firm. A portrait of the founder, a man with elaborate whiskers and a stiff white collar, hung on the wall behind the counter. We were served by the founder's grandson, a small, dapper man in a three-piece suit, with the slightly fussy manners of an old-fashioned maître d'. He opened some boxes of cigars for my grandfather to sample. One or two specimens were taken out, to be pinched and sniffed. A purchase was made. I don't know whether they were Burmese cheroots. But I can remember vividly the look on the tobacconist's face, when he realized my grandfather was an Englishman.

De Graaff said he had something special to show. He smiled in anticipation of my grandfather's pleasure. 'Please,' he said, and pointed at the wall, where Cuban cigars were stacked. And there, in an open space, between pungent boxes of Coronas and Ideales, hung a framed glass case, containing two long, cinnamon-coloured cigars, dry as old turds; one had been partly smoked, the other was untouched. The case had been sealed with red wax. At the bottom was a copper plate, bearing the simple inscription: 1946, SIR WINSTON CHURCHILL'S CIGAR.

I found out more about the famous cigar on my second visit to the shop, almost forty years later. The old de Graaff was dead. His son, a tall man with a somewhat ostentatious grey moustache, showed me the glass case, the two cigars and a letter from Queen Wilhelmina's court marshal, in which de Graaff was thanked for his supply of fine cigars. They had been presented at the Queen's lunch for Winston Churchill. One of the cigars had been lit by Churchill himself, wetted by his very own lips. The other came from the same box. The partly smoked cigar had been put away, because lunch was served, and the Queen couldn't abide smoking in her presence. However, the two precious relics were saved for posterity by Churchill's butler, who passed them on to one of the Queen's footmen, who presented them to de Graaff, who then had his solicitor draw up the document to vouch for their authenticity.

My grandfather would have been amused and, being a patriot, probably touched by this gesture. Then again, in those days he might have been accustomed to such small tributes being paid to the British. Through the late 1940s and 1950s, and even in the 1960s, the British were considered a superior breed in places like The Hague. For the British, together with the Americans and the Canadians, had won the war. So had the Soviet Union, but the Red Army was never anywhere near The Hague; and, besides, the Red Army was, after all, the Red Army.

The British are no longer regarded as a superior breed, even in The Hague. The image of Britain as the land of war heroes is disappearing. Now, when the British return to wage war in Europe, they come as soccer hooligans: history repeating itself as a beer-flecked horror show. But I still grew up with the image of British superiority, which gave me vicarious pleasure as well as the kind of slight resentment one might feel towards a very grand parent. It was an image that owed a great deal to snobbery, but to something else too, something more political in origin: a particular idea of freedom.

My grandfather, Bernard Schlesinger, was the son of a German-Jewish immigrant, which explains, perhaps, his particular brand of patriotism. I would watch him as a child, during the summer holidays, as he worked in his Berkshire garden, picking vegetables or pruning the fruit trees, dressed in corduroys and tweeds. Even though he earned his money as a paediatrician in London, he seemed to belong to the landscape: the fields, smelling of hay, the villages, smelling of horse dung and smoke, and the large Victorian vicarage which my grandparents bought after the war, smelling of candlewax and polished oak. This was his home. He would talk to me about the importance of loving one's country and of how he loved England. I did not understand the depth or the nature of his love. I was never unhappy in Holland, but from quite an early age it was a place I always thought of leaving. The world seemed more promising elsewhere (a state of mind which, once entered, will never leave you in peace). But to my grandfather England was not only the country he was born and raised in; after Hitler, it was, in his mind, the country that saved him and his family from almost certain death.

To be *saved*. Can the feeling of liberation ever be transmitted to those who have always been free?

In the final scene of *The Scarlet Pimpernel*, made in 1934, Sir Percy Blakeney, played with English gentlemanly panache by Leslie Howard, returns from France. He has just saved dozens of French aristocrats from Robespierre's Terror by smuggling them to England, the island of Liberty. On the boat, gazing at the cliffs of Dover as though witness to a revelation, Leslie Howard speaks the last words of the film to his French wife, played by Merle Oberon: 'Look, Marguerite,' he says. Then a pregnant pause, and then, with deep emotion: 'England!'

This last line was thought up by the producer of the movie, Alexander Korda. He reckoned it was sure to get applause. He was right. The picture was a great hit for his company, London Film Productions. Korda was being calculating, but only up to a point. Leslie Howard's words are a statement of pure Anglophilia. Korda was still a Hungarian (he naturalized later). He had always admired the dashing English hero whose courage and guile were disguised by the foppish mannerisms of an aristocratic dandy. The original story of the Scarlet Pimpernel was written by Baroness Orczy, another Hungarian. The script was written by yet another Hungarian, Lajos Biro, together with two Americans. And Leslie Howard, that most typical of slim, blond, blue-eyed English gentleman heroes? His real name was Steiner, and his parents were immigrants too.

The film was made one year after Hitler came to power, too soon for the horror of Nazism to have sunk in. But Korda, the Jewish showman with his Savile Row suits, his chauffeur-driven Rolls and his suites at the Dorchester Hotel, knew what he was doing. He once said that 'all Hungarians love the English. It is their snobbism, and I am a snob.' But that is not all there was to it. He had lived in Berlin. He understood the threat of Hitler's regime, not least to himself (he

Ian Buruma

was on the Gestapo hit list). And he admired the British 'way of life', by which he meant that old combination of deference to privilege and respect for civil liberties. Like Theodor Herzl, he saw the British Empire as an example of gentlemanly administration. A year after *The Scarlet Pimpernel*, Korda made *Sanders of the River*, in praise of that 'handful of white men' whose governance of the Empire 'is an unsung saga of courage and efficiency'. These are the opening titles of the movie, which no doubt were greeted with much applause, at least in Britain. But Korda sincerely believed in the idea of England as a safe haven from European tyranny—for good reasons. And this made him the ideal propagandist for the Allied war effort. It was in that role that he was happiest. As he put it: 'I felt, during those terrible days, that I "belonged".'

I have a relative, now in his seventies, who could not be more British, in manner, dress, habits and speech. His name is Ashley, as in Ashley Wilkes, Leslie Howard's most famous role. If one were to draw a caricature of the perfect English gentleman, he would come out looking like Ashley. He came to England from his native Germany some time between *Sanders of the River* and Dunkirk. He was a teenager then, who decided to shed his German skin and become an Englishman. He succeeded—and without overacting, without the exaggerated drawl and the splashy tweeds that often mark the immigrant. Ashley's remarkable effort to reinvent himself as an Englishman cannot be regarded simply as an act of conformism. To understand Ashley's generation of Anglicized Europeans, one must understand where they came from.

I had always been aware of refugees in my family. Dick came to England as a child in 1939, and lived with my mother's family during the war. He was still called Hans then, a name which was later dropped—too German. Hans expressed his obvious distress about being forced to flee into the arms of strangers by being a secretive, difficult boy. I first met Dick before he moved to the United States, where he became a distinguished scientist. I have seen him several times since, a small, dark, animated man whose accent became increasingly American over the years. Dick is an American now, whose Anglophilia was always tempered by memories of bullying at his school in a small English town. He had escaped from almost certain death in the Third Reich, but to his British classmates he remained a bloody foreigner or, worse, a German spy.

Then there were the 'hostel children'. The hostel was a large Victorian house in Highgate, rented by my grandfather to shelter twelve Jewish children rescued from Germany at the last minute on the so-called 'children transports'. The British government did not exactly welcome refugees at that time. The 1905 Aliens Act had been generous enough: persecuted persons would not be refused entry just because they lacked the means to support themselves. But this was changed when it really mattered, in the 1930s. To find refuge in Britain you had to have either a job lined up or a British guarantor prepared to support you. Otherwise you were trapped. After the ghastly events on *Kristallnacht* in 1938, when Jewish shops were ransacked, Jewish men arrested and killed and synagogues set on fire, an exception was made. Ten thousand Jewish children would be allowed to come to Britain, as long as they came without their parents, a condition of dubious magnanimity which traumatized many children for life. But, still, they lived. My grandparents took in twelve.

My grandmother sometimes mentioned the names of former hostel children to me: Steffie Birnbaum, Lore Feig, Ilse Salomon, Michael Maybaum... She had kept in touch with them, and their children, wherever they were, in England, the United States or Israel. Birthdays were never forgotten, help was offered with careers and personal matters, and—a typical Anglo-German touch—Christmas cards were always sent. But I never quite realized how much my grandparents, Bernard and Win Schlesinger, meant to the hostel children. I had never before met people whose eyes filled with tears at the mere mention of their names.

Then, in 1997, six years after I came to live in London for the third time, I met Walter. He lived not far from me in a comfortable two-storey house in Highgate. The furnishing was mid-twentieth-century modern, the international style I grew up with in Holland, a wooden sofa, glass tables, a floor lamp with a long conical shade. Walter's wife Linda came in with coffee and cakes and protested that I was not eating enough of them.

Walter placed a dark-grey box on the table in front of me. It was the size of a portable typewriter and was marked, in ballpoint pen, 'Hostel'. He opened the box. Inside was a stack of large brown envelopes. Walter smiled, tapped the brown envelopes and said with only a trace of a German accent, 'You could write a whole book about these files.' One of them had an address typed on it, which I recognized with a sense of excitement: St Mary Woodlands House, Nr. Newbury, Berks. My grandparents' old house, the one with the huge garden, my childhood Arcadia. The handwriting on the envelopes looked familiar too. It was my grandfather's. One envelope was marked 'Admin'. Another said 'Letters prior to opening of hostel'. Yet another: 'Details of all 12 children'. And 'Re: trunks, lists of clothes'.

The documents inside the brown envelopes were, at first sight, mundane: questionnaires, lists of one sort or another, vaccination papers and letters of recommendation from schoolteachers and welfare organizations. But they weren't mundane; they were bureaucratic lifeboats. These pieces of paper, now somewhat brittle to the touch, kept twelve children from being murdered.

From the beginning, the German destruction of the Jews was a matter of selection, of numbers and lists. The first and often cruellest choice began at home: which child should be put up for selection, to be removed to Britain, out of danger, but also out of sight, quite likely for ever? Tens of thousands of panic-stricken parents tried to get their children on the lists. The twelve hostel children, whose personal details were preserved in the grey box-file, were selected by a small Jewish committee in Berlin on behalf of Bloomsbury House, a Jewish refugee organization in London. The Schlesingers wanted the children to be not older than twelve, in good health, well educated and from liberal Jewish families: no kosher food would be provided at the hostel. One boy, Michael Maybaum, son of Rabbi Ignaz Maybaum, almost didn't make it on to the list, because the Schlesingers were worried that he might be too Orthodox and thus not 'fit in'. When nine-year-old Michael was finally selected, he wrote a letter from Berlin, asking whether he could bring his electric train. He signed the letter, dated 12 January 1939, 'Meikel', which sounded more English to him than Michael.

The information contained in the questionnaires prepared in

Germany for the Schlesingers was necessarily brief. The escalating persecution since 1933—the racial laws, the loss of jobs, the violence of *Kristallnacht*—are referred to as 'present circumstances' or simply 'events'. The discretion is painful to read. One mother, writing to the Schlesingers in perfect English on beautifully embossed letter paper, apologized that, due to events, she was a little 'preoccupied'.

Here is Ilse Salomon, aged ten, from Uhlandstrasse 15, Berlin, her circumstances described in bureaucratic shorthand.

FATHER: Richard Salomon.

PROFESSION: Formerly solicitor, now nervous disease, no income—savings are being used up.

ARE PARENTS OR RELATIVES RESPECTIVELY IN A POSITION TO SUPPORT AN IMPECUNIOUS CHILD IN GERMANY?: No.

GIVE A DETAILED REPORT OF THE FAMILY LIFE: Father ill, has been in a sanatorium for nearly 2 years, as a result of the events since 1933. Parents are very cultured people—now very sad conditions.

Ilse is in good health, testified to by Dr Werner Solmitz. A star of David is stamped in blue under his signature. Next to the star: *'Zur ärztlichen Behandlung ausschliesslich von Juden berechtigt'* (Permitted to give medical treatment to Jews only).

Inside the file is a letter, written in English, from Mrs Salomon to my grandmother:

Dear Mrs Schlesinger,
Only some days ago I received your address and I beg to thank you and your husband very heartily for my daughter's invitation. As you can think I am very sorry to be compelled to separate from my daughter, but otherwise I am very thankful that my girl will find at your's a new peaceful and happy home...

There is also a note by Ilse herself, written in German, in the first issue of the 'Hostel Newspaper' at Highgate:

I am an only child and always have wanted a little sister or brother... When you are alone, you have everything to yourself and are neither favoured nor disadvantaged. But you are always alone and friends are never as good as sisters. Now that I'm away from home, I realize how much I belong with my parents.

Ilse's mother finally got out of Germany alive. She was granted a visa to work as a 'domestic' in England. Ilse never said goodbye to her father. The doctors thought it would put too much strain on his nerves. He was murdered in 1944.

Attached to another file is a drawing of a train pulling out of a station. It is a third-class carriage with the words 'Berlin–London' written on the side. Children peer through the windows at two adults waving handkerchiefs. The train and the children are in black pencil. The adults are in colour, their faces smudged with bright-red lips. The drawing is by Marianne Mamlok. Her photograph is clipped to her birth certificate, stamped with the Prussian eagle of the Berlin registry office: a smiling girl with long pigtails. Her teacher, Alice Pach, recommends her highly: 'M. loves walks and open-air games. M. is sociable and companionable. Her companions love and respect her for her team spirit, helpfulness and gay disposition. The atmosphere of her home has favoured the development of her personal gifts and social feelings.' The questionnaire tells the story of how that same home had become a trap. Her father, a solicitor, 'is soon going to lose his profession. No prospect of earning a living in Germany. Owing to his physical state, it will be difficult for him to emigrate.'

It is almost impossible to imagine the anguish of parents who could hope to save their children only by losing them. They would call the selection committee every day, sometimes several times a day, to ask whether their children were on the lists. Most of them had only the haziest idea about English life, gleaned from the cinema and books. Some spent their last savings on 'English-style' outfits for their sons, so that they would fit in. Boys would arrive off the boat at Harwich looking like fancy-dress versions of Sherlock Holmes, with name tags hung around their necks.

Walter was the eldest boy in his group. Aged twelve and a half, he had a pretty good idea what was going on. He knew why he was being persecuted, unlike some of the younger children, who were utterly bewildered. Walter can remember *Kristallnacht*, when his father stayed away from home and his uncles disappeared. One of them came back months later, from a concentration camp, broken and emaciated, and silent about what had been done to him. Walter also remembers how one day he was patted on the head by a friendly SA man. Because he had fair hair, he was praised for being a beautiful little Aryan boy.

It was early evening when Walter told me his story. He fiddled with the conical lamp which wouldn't stay on properly and flickered in the dusk. I felt that I was asking too many questions. There was much he simply couldn't remember. But he had vivid memories of his parents. He dabbed at his eyes as he spoke about them. His father lost his factory to a Nazi in 1935. His mother taught at the Theodor Herzl School in Berlin. 'My father and mother,' Walter said, 'thought of themselves as good Germans.' We both pondered this for a moment. 'They never expected to see us again. They didn't realize quite what was coming... Well, they did know really. They told me after *Kristallnacht* that they probably wouldn't make it, but they would make sure that we did...' His parents were killed at Auschwitz.

The second time I saw Walter visibly moved was when he described his arrival at Liverpool Street station. The slums of the East End, glimpsed through the window of the boat train from Harwich, had been a shock. And then there was pandemonium. Announcements came through loudspeakers in a language he barely understood; strangers craned their necks at the barrier; frightened children were lined up with tags around their necks, like dogs or prize vegetables. Some foster parents openly expressed disappointment when the children did not match the charm of their photographs. Others were unable to recognize their charges. There was shouting and crying. And there, in the midst of this crushing strangeness, was the small figure of my grandmother, welcoming Walter and the others to England in fluent German.

One year later, she herself would be faced with the question of whether to send her children to strangers, in Canada. My grandfather was in favour. She decided against it. She hadn't been able to bear the thought of losing them. God knows what she would have done if she had been a German, living in Germany.

Thinking of my very British grandmother put the horror of what happened to the very German Feigs, or Salomons, or Mamloks into even sharper focus. The idea of becoming a refugee was almost

unthinkable to her. It would have turned her world upside down. The
humiliation would have been intolerable. In a letter to her husband
Bernard in May 1940, when he was with the army at Narvik, she
told him she had had lunch with a close friend of theirs, a Scottish
doctor. He had reassured her: 'He said I might be dead, but I should
never be a refugee, & for that I was truly thankful.' It was a sign
that she still fitted in.

Her expressions of British patriotism, and even her occasional
comments on foreigners, are in the spirit of the time. Nevertheless,
reading her letters now, I am taken aback by the total absence of
irony. You would never know she was the daughter of German
immigrants. After Dunkirk, she wrote to Bernard: 'What a brilliant
retreat our [British] forces have made from the very jaws of death.
I keep thinking of the Charge of the Light Brigade. What terrific
reverses we always have in every century, & what undaunted courage
& tenacity is shown by our men in every generation. It makes you
prouder and prouder to be British.' And the foreigners? 'Even the
nicest of foreign bohunks,' she wrote, 'have a totally different point
of view, and are naturally more defeatist than the tough British.' But
her patriotism was not just sentimental. In May 1940, her 'beloved
England' was the one thing that shielded her and her children from
almost certain death.

Looking through the files of Walter's grey box, at the bills, the
requests for help placed in the *Jewish Chronicle* and the letters sent
to scoutmasters and organizers of summer camps, I found aspects of
my grandparents that I recognized, while others came as a surprise.
Their concern for education, manners and fresh air and exercise was
all in my grandfather's public-school spirit. The question of religion
was less familiar, perhaps because it never came up when I knew
them.

The Schlesingers made sure the children were given religious
instruction. It was the only continuity granted some of the children,
once they had left everything they knew behind. Synagogues were
frequented, rabbis approached. Yet I never saw any sign of religiosity
in my grandparents. Their own children never received a Jewish
education. They went to boarding schools and took part in Christian
services, not out of any religious conviction, but because that was the

done thing, the way to fit in. My earliest memories of my grandparents are associated with Christmas.

There are a few signs of religious feeling in their wartime correspondence. In April 1941, when war news was so bad that my grandmother could only hope for a miracle to 'save our beloved England', she also wrote: 'I just can't see by the light of cold reason how we can come out of this on top, and yet I know that we must, and that all this horror is meant in some way to serve the divine purpose. I feel a great longing lately for St John's Wood.' St John's Wood is the Liberal Jewish Synagogue they sometimes frequented. They would do so more often towards the end of their lives. But in my grandmother's case even attending services at St John's Wood was perhaps more a patriotic than a religious act. She was responding to the King's radio speech on 'the gravest and most dangerous' hours in British history. He urged all British people to go to church the next day and pray.

The hostel files contain instances of kindness shown by British gentiles. And Walter, in particular, likes to remember how 'marvellous' the English people were, despite the fact that he still had to report to the authorities on his sixteenth birthday as an 'enemy alien'. (This would have been at roughly the time his parents were about to be transported to Auschwitz.) But saving Jews from Germany was essentially a Jewish enterprise, a matter of taking care of 'one's own'.

And yet, despite the occasional yearning for 'St John's Wood', I don't think Jewish solidarity sufficiently explains my grandparents' rescue mission. They were generous people, and of course aware of family ties in Germany. But it was more than that. It has to do with the lack of irony in my grandmother's patriotic sentiments and with their idea of England. Not all immigrants or children of immigrants were helpful when others rapped on the doors. Some Jews, anxious not to lose their places in society, were (and still are) afraid that newcomers, especially poor ones, could mean trouble. But to the Schlesingers the idea of England as a place of refuge was not just propaganda. They believed in it, in the way patriots do who cannot take freedom from persecution for granted. To them, the self-regarding clichés about Britain—fairness, liberty, tolerance and so on—were not clichés. They cultivated them, in the way educated German Jews cultivated German music, philosophy and humanism, and more superficial Anglophiles cultivate flowery accents and loud tweeds.

Their most remarkable gesture did not, in fact, concern Jews. The war had finally ended, my grandfather had just returned from India, where he had served as an army doctor, and the family looked forward to their first Christmas in peacetime. After six years of horror, after the sickening details of the German attempt to kill every last Jew had come out, after almost all remaining relatives in Germany had perished, the Schlesingers went to a local prisoner-of-war camp in Berkshire and invited two German soldiers to spend Christmas with them. It cannot have been an easy occasion. My aunt remembers awkwardness, with long gaps in the conversation. But the soldiers never forgot. It was what my grandfather would have thought of as the gentlemanly thing to do.

There was an element of Colonel Blimp in his attitude. In the wartime movie *The Life and Death of Colonel Blimp*, Blimp's German friend, the aristocratic Theo Kretschmar-Schuldorff, is captured by the British during the First World War. After the war is over, Theo is in despair about his country. Before returning to Germany, he has dinner at Blimp's house with a gathering of British officers and gentlemen. They reassure him that all will be well and that all England wants is fair play and fair trade. Theo is baffled by these Englishmen. He tells his German comrades on the way back home that the British gentlemen are children: 'Boys! Playing cricket! They win the shirts off our backs and now they want to give them back, because the game is over!'

But my grandfather was not naive. He knew what the Nazis had done. And he knew he would not have survived in the country of his father. Unlike Blimp, he had to make sure he fitted in, in England, and if others didn't like it, that was their problem, not his. That is precisely what Blimpishness was about, and what impelled him to ask the two Germans over for Christmas. It was an attitude that rubbed off on at least some of the hostel children. Walter stayed in Highgate all his life. He feels British. He fits in. He says the British are marvellous. Others fitted in, more or less, elsewhere: Steffie Birnbaum in Israel, Ilse Salomon in the United States. Some never managed to fit in anywhere.

Being uprooted by force early in life can turn a person into a fearful xenophobe, clinging to the place of refuge like a drowning person to a raft, resentful of others who might wish to climb on too. It can also have the opposite effect. Lore Feig is one of the hostel children who stayed in London, where she lives with her husband Manek Vajifdar, a Parsee. They met in 1947 at a meeting of the International Friendship League, the kind of well-meaning internationalist organization that flourished then. My grandfather had advised her against the marriage, and I was not altogether surprised to hear it. That, too, was part of his Blimpishness. Tolerance, fair play, good manners, these were all to be encouraged, naturally. But marriage to an Indian would have been, well, unwise. His advice was ignored, and he came round eventually. Lore and Manek have two children, both educated at the French Lycée in London. One is married to a Frenchman and lives in Paris, the other lives in South Africa.

Lore and Manek Vajifdar's house is located in the perfect English suburb, with flowery gardens, red postboxes, tall trees and polite neighbours. Their house is filled with presents and mementoes from foreign students: a Japanese doll here, a Chinese picture there. Lore thinks of the students as a kind of extended international family. She and Manek have, as she puts it, 'adopted' them.

Lore is a smartly dressed woman with white hair and beautiful pale skin. She served a lunch of chilled summer soup, meat with rice, and an English pudding. I thought of the questionnaire I had read, describing her, in 1939, as the pampered daughter of cultivated parents ('a refined, cultured house, an affectionate family life, entirely carefree till a short time ago'). I knew the large, somewhat pompous houses and tree-lined streets of Grunewald, the expensive Berlin suburb which she grew up in and never wanted to see again. It is difficult to associate Grunewald with violence. It is even harder to associate Barnes, or Highgate, or Hampstead Garden Suburb, with violence. The London suburbs feel like a refuge inside a country of refuge. But, even there, bigotry lurks between the neatly tended flower beds. Lore told me why she sent her daughters to the French Lycée and not to an English school. When Lore went to school in Richmond, during the war, her religious education teachers found it necessary to remind their pupils that 'the Jews killed Our Lord'. And her fellow pupils thought Lore was a German spy who sneaked up Richmond Hill at night to send signals to Nazi bombers.

Listening to Lore, I wondered where I fitted in, the grandson of the British couple who had saved her life. Lore, born a German, and Manek, a Parsee from Gujarat, were British. I was not, even though my accent was more English than theirs. Lore did not come to England by choice. Nor did Manek. He got stuck during the war. I had chosen London as my home. But national identity is not entirely a matter of choice. It is not the same as citizenship, which can be acquired. And a secular Jewish identity, which, unlike religion, cannot be acquired, is impossible to pin down: a shared facility for fitting in, perhaps? National identity is in any case a matter not only of how we see ourselves, but also of how others choose to see us. Lore told me she still hears English people refer to her as a German. It annoys her. 'I am not a German,' she said. Then, after a moment's pause, she added: 'Then again, I'm not quite sure what I am.'

On my way home to north London, I thought about the terror that drove so many people to this country and was reminded of a story I once heard from my first publisher. The story was about himself. He came to England from Germany on the *Kindertransport*, like Lore, and was sent to an English boarding school. His housemaster, a kindly man, asked him to have a cup of tea in his study. They talked a bit, about this and that, and then the housemaster asked him what he would like to be when he grew up. And the boy answered, 'I want to be an English gentleman. I want to be just like Leslie Howard.' The housemaster pondered this for a moment and said, 'But my dear boy, he was an Hungarian.'

As a child, going back and forth between the Continent and Britain on ferry boats that often stank of vomit, disgorged by drunken British soldiers, I used to get a little sentimental at the sight of the Dover cliffs, looming up on cold winter mornings, or disappearing into foggy nights. Crossing the Channel was an adventure. The sea was like a moat between different worlds, where people wore different clothes, ate different food, abided by different rules, and weighed with different measures. We would leave the Continent from the coast of Belgium, where the land was industrial and flat, the streets were lit by sinister yellow lights, and the air smelled of sea water and frying fat. Britain just smelled of smoke, curling from countless Victorian chimneys. The roads were narrow and twisty. Children wore uniforms. Cars looked old. Double-decker buses gurgled and screeched. There were signs that read: KEEP ON THE LEFT. I noted these differences with a mounting sense of excitement. For I knew we were on our way to my grandparents' house.

My grandparents are no longer alive. And I no longer take the ferry. It is too inconvenient, the crossing too long. I take the tunnel instead, by train. You pass through Folkstone without seeing a cliff, and Calais without a glimpse of the sea, or a whiff of *frites*. An announcement is made in English, sometimes with a French accent, and French, sometimes with an English one. You open your *Herald Tribune*, take a sip of espresso coffee, wonder what it would be like to get stuck in a tunnel under the sea, halfway between Britain and the European Continent, marvel at the way the train speeds up as soon as it enters France, and before you know it you're there. □

Writerly lives

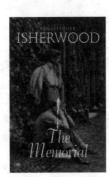

GRANTA

FISHING, WRITING AND TED
Graham Swift

AN APPRECIATION

Ted Hughes

I first encountered Ted Hughes as many of my age must have done, when I was a young teenager in the early Sixties being introduced in English lessons to those electric poems from *The Hawk in the Rain* and *Lupercal*. I still remember my English teacher reading out 'Pike'. At that age either you get smitten by the power of words or you don't, though I must admit that the force of that poem had something to do with my dabbling in a small-time way with hooks and floats and lines. Yet I nursed even then the secret dream of one day being a writer myself. I would never have dared tell my English teacher about it and scarcely whispered it to myself, so far-fetched and foolish did it seem.

As you get older the phrase 'If only I'd known then' gets ever more called upon. Sometimes it haunts you like a knell, sometimes it's the motto for unimagined privilege. Years later, in the 1980s, when I actually was a writer and had published books, I took up fishing again, after a long gap, or rather I was taught by a good and patient friend to fly-fish, something I had never done before. So I came to fish for, and sometimes catch, trout, salmon and sea trout.

That in turn led me, increasingly, to the beautiful, hidden River Torridge in Devon, where the fishing is a poor shadow now of the glory it was back in the early Sixties when I was a schoolboy and knew nothing about it, though that in a way is a blessing. It is an unmarauded river, and there are places where you can fish all day and never see a soul.

My visits there led me to meet some fishing friends of Ted and that in turn led to my meeting Ted—an introduction almost entirely non-literary and almost exclusively piscatorial. In subsequent years I got to see him now and then and even fish with him. I'm thinking of just a scattering of days and hours, so I can't pretend to have known him well or closely, but because those days and hours involved being by or near water, if not actually fishing, in places that Ted knew and loved, they went at once beyond the merely social and I got to know what good, keen, gentle company he was.

We mostly met in Ted's North Devon, though once I fished with him at almost the extreme opposite end of the country, on the wind-furrowed lochs of the Isle of Harris. As quite often happens when writers meet writers, especially off the literary tracks, we hardly ever talked about poetry or writing of any kind. Once, in a Devon pub, we got tentatively close, though our talk in fact was more about that additional, tricky work writers have to do simply to protect their writing time and space from all that, increasingly in a writer's career, can invade it. Ted was perhaps more besettingly involved in this work than others. He never appeared to me as anything other than calm and kind, sure of his inner ground. I think he had an admirably unwavering sense of what was properly private and what was properly public.

We mostly talked about fishing and rivers, local things, things before our eyes. I remember walking with him one afternoon down a stretch of the Torridge which was new to me, while he explained the intricacies and history of almost every pool, run, bend and lie. This was not Ted the poet but a Ted who, for all one knew, might have spent his years being a vigilant, devoted river keeper.

However they stand in his complete work, my favourite poems of Ted's will always be those in the collection *River*, not just because I have, in some cases, waded the very water, seen the boulders and eddies Ted must have had in mind, but because I have, at least occasionally, experienced that fisherman's state of special attunement, that becoming one with particularly charged, expectant conditions of water, weather and light, so I can attest to how hushingly close Ted gets to the feeling in words. 'Salmon-Taking Times' and 'Night Arrival of Sea-Trout' distil for me not just the essence of fishing for both species of fish but the whole seasonal, riverine harvest of associations each owns. While 'After Moonless Midnight', in which, turning everything around, it is the river that whispers of the angler, 'We've got him,' could hardly convey better the particular, almost dreading excitement of wading down a pool alone at night after sea trout.

Ted himself wrote, famously, about fishing and its similarities to the creative act of poetry. Analogies for how writing gets written can be stretched, but there is some basis in the piscatorial one, in that concentrated dealing with surface and depth, never knowing from one moment to the next what might, if anything, be there, sometimes having a guess, always a hope, sometimes an entirely irrational but palpable anticipation, and sometimes of course being taken totally by surprise.

With salmon and sea-trout fishing the analogy gets closer if only because it enters greater realms of mystery. Unlike the permanent residents, the migratory fish which move up a river only at certain times and in certain conditions do not feed, or hardly at all, so to fish for them lacks even the fragile logic of presenting the quarry with something imitating its food. No one *really* knows why salmon and sea trout take a fly at all, though they are more likely to be there and do so at some times rather than others, and a whole body of fishing lore has tried to reduce this to a precise science—or art—and failed.

It is the enigma of the 'take' rather than the general confrontation of mind and water which perhaps most parallels (without in the least explaining it) the creative process. And in salmon and sea-trout fishing it is the take not the capture which is the essential, heart-stopping thing. Sometimes it comes with a long, powerful, unmistakably connective pull, sometimes there is a boil and a white slash of spray, but when it happens it is always a sheer amazement. And it is not at all unlike how an 'idea'—that limp word we use for want of a better one—bursts, without recognizable correlation to design or desert, effort or receptivity, upon a writer's mind. In both cases, too, exultation can be immediately mixed with high anxiety as to whether fish and angler, idea and writer will part company.

Thanks to the generosity of a friend of his, I once fished with Ted another Devon river, the Exe, on a stretch where it briefly divides into some deep narrow streams. I have fished some pools on the Torridge *for years* without success but under the eye of Ted—which was not an 'eagle eye', it was a soft eye—I hooked within half an hour on a strange river a good-sized salmon, which in that narrow water put up a thrilling up-and-downstream fight. Then, when all was over and the beaten fish was being drawn in, the hook, as sometimes miserably happens, simply lost its hold and there was that awful, absolute separation.

Fishing is, if you think about it in a certain way, a fairly silly, childish activity, absurdly pursued by some till their dying day, a thing of no virtue or importance. This does not stop it offering up to fishermen moments of ineffable triumph that imprint every glitter of their glory permanently on the brain, or moments of abysmal disaster that will never, ever be forgotten or exorcised. Such dramatic highs and lows, life itself does not necessarily or so reliably or so intensely provide.

I have known real grief at losing fish—it usually comes mingled with bleak self-reproach, when you know you have done something wrong, lost your head, forgotten to check a knot. Hooking a salmon is, for me at least, such a rare event that any loss is grievous, but with that salmon on the Exe I think I honestly achieved that precarious angler's equanimity of relishing every second of an encounter I might never have had and of not mourning the loss since, as Walton severely puts it, you cannot lose what was never yours.

Fishing of course would be a truly poor thing if it were only about capture and loss, if it were only about fish. While fishing the Torridge I have seen things, known things—you have to use a tired phrase like 'getting close to nature'—which indeed have nothing directly to do with fishing but which I could not have seen or known, I think, if I had sought them deliberately in another way. Standing up to my waist in water I have watched an otter (which in England now is mostly a rare, never-glimpsed creature) occupy a stone barely a yard from me, as untroubled by my presence as a cat. I have watched a weasel do two things weasels are seldom seen to do, let alone in the space of the same minute: dive into water and come up again, then climb a good twenty feet up the nearest tree. I have watched a young deer trot along the bank till abreast of where I stood midstream, then decide to swim cross-river, so close to me that I had to lift my rod and trailing fly-line for it to pass beneath, like a guard of honour arching swords for a bride and groom. Such privileged moments have the magic of making you feel as a human being—it is a paradoxical privilege—secondary, if not superfluous to the general animal world. Ted's 'animal poems', far from being excursions from the relevant, have the salutary human effect of reminding us that we are just one component in a throng.

The same afternoon I lost that salmon something rather wonderful occurred. First, I hooked another salmon, a much smaller one, which Ted netted. Salmon fishing rarely gives you a consolation prize, even one that makes you churlishly wish fortune had been the other way round, but this is not the point. As the fish lay on the bank we both noticed something white and bony among the shingle. Ted picked it up and said I should keep it as a memento. It was the skull of a pike.

Well, I put it in a pocket and then maybe transferred it later to somewhere else, but at some point on that trip to Devon I lost it. Fishermen carry around with them masses of jumble, on their person, in their cars, and they are good at losing things, not just fish. And of course, it was only at the point of realizing I had lost it that the other realization came fully to me. That I had lost a pike's skull presented to me by Ted Hughes after the catching of a salmon, Ted Hughes the poet, whom I could never once have imagined meeting, but whom I had first known, like many who would never meet him, through that poem 'Pike'.

There is never a moment in life, perhaps, when we should underestimate the latent repercussions. All this was a few years ago when among the other things Ted was, or so it seemed, was indestructible, a big broad solid man. He died in October, the month after the fishing season ends on the Torridge. No more fishing there before the spring.

What a keepsake that pike's skull would have been, combining a set of chances and associations infinitely more amazing than even the take of a salmon, the loss of that fish that afternoon as nothing really to the loss of that skull. But then the loss of that skull is as nothing to the loss of Ted. He left in a blaze of poetic glory, *Birthday Letters*, the *Tales from Ovid*. The keepsake for us all, of course, is the poetry. Poets, above all mortals, are supposed to offer recompense for their decease by what they leave behind. But not, perhaps, if you have met them, spent time with them, even walked, waded into the very stuff of some of the poems. Then those trade-offs between life and art, nature and art, seem not so simply negotiable after all. □

NOTES ON CONTRIBUTORS

Anthony Bailey's biography of Turner, *Standing in the Sun*, is published by Chatto & Windus/HarperCollins. Julian Barnes's most recent novel *England, England* is published by Jonathan Cape in Britain and Knopf in the US. Ian Buruma's piece 'Churchill's Cigar' is taken from *Voltaire's Coconuts: Anglophiles and Anglophobes* which is published by Weidenfeld & Nicolson/Pantheon. Amit Chaudhuri's most recent book, *Freedom Song*, is published by Picador/Knopf. Ferdinand Dennis's most recent novel, *Duppy Conqueror*, is published by Flamingo. Ruth Gershon is a historian living in north-west London. Stephen Gill's pictures of the workers of John Brown's shipyard appeared in *Granta* 61. Ian Hamilton's 'Gazza Agonistes' appeared in *Granta* 45. His latest book is *A Gift Imprisoned: The Poetic Life of Matthew Arnold* (Bloomsbury/Basic Books). David Harrison is an artist. Philip Hensher's collection of short stories, *The Bedroom of the Mister's Wife*, will be published by Chatto & Windus. Howard Hodgkin's next exhibition will be at the Anthony D'Offay Gallery in London this autumn. Hanif Kureishi's most recent novel is *Intimacy* (Faber/Simon & Schuster). His play *Sleep with Me* premieres at the National Theatre in April. John Lanchester's novel, *Mr Phillips*, will be published by Faber/Henry Holt. His first novel, *A Debt to Pleasure*, won the Whitbread first-novel and Hawthornden prizes. Sergio Larrain's collection of photographs of 1950s London is published by Dewi Lewis. Doris Lessing's second volume of autobiography, *Walking in the Shade*, is published by HarperCollins. Her new novel is *Mara and Dann: An Adventure* (HarperCollins). Penelope Lively's most recent novel, *Spiderweb*, is published by Viking, and HarperCollins in the US. Andrew O'Hagan's first novel, *Our Fathers*, will be published this year by Faber/Harcourt Brace. Albino Ochero-Okello lives in Middlesex. He is a caseworker for the British Red Cross. Ian Parker is the television critic of the *Observer*. Dale Peck's most recent novel, *Now It's Time to Say Goodbye*, will be published in May by Vintage/Rob Weisbach. His new novel, *The Garden of Lost and Found*, will be published by Granta Books. Jay Rayner is a journalist with the *Observer*. His most recent novel, *Day of Atonement*, is published by Black Swan. Martin Rowson draws for several London magazines and newspapers. His graphic interpretation of Laurence Sterne's *The Life and Opinions of Tristram Shandy* is published by Picador/The Overlook Press. Will Self's most recent collection of short stories is *Tough, Tough Toys for Tough, Tough Boys* (Bloomsbury/Grove Atlantic). Helen Simpson's latest collection of short stories, *Dear George*, is published by Minerva. Iain Sinclair's forthcoming book with Rachel Lichtenstein, *Rodinsky's Room*, will be published by Granta Books. Lucretia Stewart's novel *Making Love* will be published by Chatto & Windus in May. Graham Swift's most recent novel is *Last Orders* (Picador/Vintage). It won the 1996 Booker Prize. David Sylvester has just completed a monograph of Francis Bacon. Jenny Uglow's most recent book is *Hogarth: A Life and a World* (Faber/Farrar Straus).